LEGAL RECOGNITION OF NON-CONJUGAL FAMILIES

The insufficient recognition of 'new families' is a legal problem that needs fixing in light of recent evolutions in family structures and norms. While Western jurisdictions retain marriage as the key referent for social policies, people increasingly form familiar bonds outside of marriage (such as non-conjugal unions, polyamorous relationships, and various religion-based families).

Part I of the book illustrates these evolutions, and the options lawmakers have to address the problem. Part II focuses on courtroom litigation on the basis that courts nowadays are central avenues of social change. It takes non-conjugal families as a case study and provides an analysis of the most compelling argumentative strategies that non-conjugal families can mobilise in Canada and the US, the EU and before the European Court of Human Rights.

Through its comparative, interdisciplinary and critical legal method, aiming at predicting the approach jurisdictions are set to take and the hindrances thereof to overcome, this book provides scholars, activists and policymakers with key conceptual tools to tackle the current invisibility of all new families.

Legal Recognition of Non-Conjugal Families

New Frontiers in Family Law in the US, Canada and Europe

Nausica Palazzo

•HART•
OXFORD • LONDON • NEW YORK • NEW DELHI • SYDNEY

HART PUBLISHING

Bloomsbury Publishing Plc

Kemp House, Chawley Park, Cumnor Hill, Oxford, OX2 9PH, UK

1385 Broadway, New York, NY 10018, USA

29 Earlsfort Terrace, Dublin 2, Ireland

First published in Great Britain 2021

A catalogue record for this book is available from the British Library.

Library of Congress Cataloging-in-Publication data

Names: Palazzo, Nausica, author.

Title: Legal recognition of non-conjugal families : new frontiers in family law in the US, Canada and Europe / Nausica Palazzo.

Description: Oxford, UK ; New York, NY : Hart Publishing, an imprint of Bloomsbury Publishing, 2021. | Based on author's thesis (doctoral - Università degli studi di Trento, 2019) issued under title: Marital status discrimination in the allocation of rights, obligations, and benefits : Legal paths to protect non-normative families. | Includes bibliographical references and index.

Identifiers: LCCN 2020053891 (print) | LCCN 2020053892 (ebook) | ISBN 9781509939954 (hardback) | ISBN 9781509947249 (paperback) | ISBN 9781509939978 (pdf) | ISBN 9781509939961 (Epub)

Subjects: LCSH: Domestic relations—United States. | Domestic relations—Canada. | Domestic relations—Europe. | Family policy—United States. | Family policy—Canada. | Family policy—Europe.

Classification: LCC K670 . P35 2021 (print) | LCC K670 (ebook) | DDC 346.01/6—dc23

LC record available at https://lccn.loc.gov/2020053891

LC ebook record available at https://lccn.loc.gov/2020053892

ISBN: HB: 978-1-50993-995-4
ePDF: 978-1-50993-997-8
ePub: 978-1-50993-996-1

Typeset by Compuscript Ltd, Shannon

PREFACE

Issues of care and intimacy found a new lease of life during the COVID-19 pandemic. For most people, reciprocal care meant survival, both physical and mental. Needless to say, a sense of overwhelming vulnerability blew over human populations across continents. This occurred to the dismay of many in the rich West, who had encountered that kind of structural, cross-sectional vulnerability much less often, compared to populations in other parts of the world. Neoliberalism only had concealed this inherent feature of human life under the carpet of an energising individualism.

The pandemic conjured up a second, strictly related issue: that of who is family to us. I spent my quarantine in Italy, the Western country where it hit first with incommensurable potency. I stared speechless at the most dramatic moments occurring in succession on TV and for weeks I had nothing to say, let alone write, in the face of all that suffering. In April, nearly one month after the national lockdown was declared, something unusual occurred. The Italian government announced the end of the harshest version of the lockdown and the beginning of what most countries tagged as 'phase 2'. Starting on 4 May 2020, we could exit our lairs to meet – at a one-metre distance – our family.

However, the initial definition of family was met with resistance, as it was entirely based on blood and legal ties. It covered persons as far away from us as uncles and cousins of one's husband/wife, while falling short of accounting for a plethora of relationships of the utmost significance to us. The ensuing debate only resulted in an extension of the relevant definition to cover the sexual partner in a durable relationship, a mythological relationship whose durability the police had no possibility whatsoever to ascertain due to privacy reasons. Yet, the category was there to convey the message that the stable sexual relationship is the only acceptable exception to an understanding of family based on blood or legal ties.

Then, the debate on national media outlets took an unexpected twist. Some voices ventured asking whether we should take 'family' to mean something else, such as an extended family of friends or a family of choice ('elective family').[1] Most people could only make it through one of the harshest lockdowns in the world – Italians could not take a walk further than 200 metres from their home – thanks

[1] A Camilli, 'E se ricominciassimo dall'iperfamiglia?' *Internazionale* (Rome, 29 April 2020), www.internazionale.it/opinione/annalisa-camilli/2020/04/29/congiunti-affetti-stabili-iperfamiglia; 'Fase 2: polemica sulla apertura ai soli "congiunti". Arcigay insorge' *Agenzia Nazionale Stampa Associata – ANSA* (Rome, 27 April 2020), www.ansa.it/sito/notizie/politica/2020/04/27/fase-2-polemica-sulla-apertura-ai-soli-congiunti.-arcigay-insorge_05f399c5-cfa4-48bd-9362-fd4bc3148266.

to the material and emotional support of some others, despite these persons not necessarily falling within the accepted meanings of 'family'. Also, if we were to put ourselves back on our feet, it was imperative to interact with those we cared for the most and who would most likely help us do that.

The lockdown easily became a metaphor for life, meaning that most of us only get to navigate our way through life by means of the support of persons positioning themselves outside state-sponsored family definitions. This applied to some of the most vulnerable categories in society – think of a transgender person repudiated by her parents who found support in a mutual aid group – but in a sense to all of us, regardless of whether we identify with any such category.

Crucially, the gamut of relationships we enter throughout life is infinite, without some of us even knowing that some networks we create are so central to us that they deserve the family tag. Therefore, before addressing lawyers, sociologists and scholars from all disciplines, this book addresses persons whose imagination 'could not imagine'. Its aim is to deepen understanding of the variety of ways in which we live family throughout life and of the possibility for expressions of choice to – even – gain legal recognition.

Trento,
6 June 2020

html (reporting the position of the largest Italian LGBTQ coalition, which is in favour of recognising so-called families of choice). I entered the fray myself through this interview: E Serafini, interview with N Palazzo, 'Non solo congiunti: "Ecco come lo Stato calpesta i diritti delle nuove famiglie"' *The Post Internazionale – TPI.it* (Rome, 28 April 2020), www.tpi.it/politica/coronavirus-congiunti-stato-calpesta-diritti-nuove-famiglie-20200428593826.

ACKNOWLEDGEMENTS

I have always had the feeling that I was exactly where I was supposed to be. This book is the result of intellectual encounters in all such places. The idea behind it comes from my doctoral dissertation, which I completed in Trento under the attentive, liberal and supportive supervision of Roberto Toniatti, to whom goes my deepest gratitude. Its focus has been refined over and over again through the invaluable support of colleagues and mentors at the universities where I have worked and studied. I especially wish to thank Giuseppe Franco Ferrari at Bocconi University for believing in this project, Luisa Antoniolli and Fulvio Cortese at the University of Trento, and Marco Ventura at Fondazione Bruno Kessler for patiently sharing their insights with me. Let me also thank Mathias Reimann and Robert Leckey: This book would simply not be the same without my stay in Montréal and Ann Arbor and these lucky encounters.

Looking back, I am impressed by the enthusiasm that surrounded this book project and the help that I have received, most of which was simply unexpected, like the most beautiful gifts are. I am aware that I should not take it for granted and that I am indebted to each and every one of you. Let me start paying off the debt by thanking Brian Bird, Thomas Casadei, Donna Greshner, Francesco Palermo, Angelo Schillaci and Masuma Shahid for their comments on parts of this work. I am also grateful to Richard Albert, Beatrice Gusmano and Wendy Schrama for their leads, and Jonathan Herring, whose generous comments on my dissertation were critical when I had the reckless idea to convert it into a monograph. Further, let me thank Thomas McMorrow, whose thoughtful, patient and encouraging advice came at a time in which I needed it most, and Mariano Croce, whose person and work is a true inspiration to me.

Ultimately, I wish to thank my family, which has been there in the harshest times where a broken leg and a pandemic seemed to stand in the way of the completion of this book. You are my favourite gift.

CONTENTS

TABLE OF CASES

Canada

European Union

France

Framework of the ECHR

Germany

Italy

The UK

The US

TABLE OF LEGISLATION

Cyprus

The EU

France

Germany

Greece

Hungary

International legal order

Ireland

Italy

Lithuania

Latvia

Norway

Portugal

Romania

Spain

The US

PART I

New Families and Law-Makers

1

New Families

1. What is the 'New' Family?

The level of care and commitment amongst individuals has not diminished, despite marriage rates falling in the West: people are investing in relationships outside of marriage and of the traditional model of family it embeds. Think of non-conjugal relationships of friends or relatives that lack a sexual component. Examples also include polyamorous relationships involving more than two persons, and various religion-based families such as polygamous unions. I should term these unions to be 'new families'. Such families are new not in an ontological sense. Some are truly a novel phenomenon, while others are more well known. Extended families, for instance, have always existed; indeed, they were legally paid reverence at some points in history. This occurred in the pre-industrialisation era in the US,[1] and in Eastern European societies constitutionalising the protection of extended families.[2] Non-traditional families are new in the sense that, epistemologically, we now have a growingly rich set of analytical tools to see them and especially to see them under a different light.

These formations challenge state-sponsored conceptions of family, that is what I term to be the 'traditional' or 'archetypical' (marital) family. Standard signifiers of the archetypical family include conjugality – ie, a sexual component – the dyadic, exclusive nature of the relationship, and a for-life commitment. However, consider two siblings who decide to emotionally and financially support each other on a long-term basis. They are not conjugal, in the sense that they are not in a sexual relationship.[3] Hence, they fall short of displaying arguably the most salient feature of the traditional marital couple: its sexual component. Nonetheless, they do care for each other deeply over the course of their lives. Should financial or other personal problems arise, they pledge to support each other.

According to this view, it is useful to think of family as a relationship marked by 'mutual care and concern, the expectation of some form of an enduring bond, sometimes a deep commitment, and a range of interdependencies – emotional and

[1] *Moore v E Cleveland*, 431 US 494 (1977).

[2] Ukraine, Moldova and Russia include a duty for adult children to support parents unable to work. *Slivenko and Slivenko v Latvia* (2004) 39 EHRR 24 (partly dissenting opinion of Kovler J).

[3] B Cossman and B Ryder, 'What is Marriage-Like Like? The Irrelevance of Conjugality' (2001) 18 *Canadian Journal of Family Law* 269, 294–300. See also Cambridge Dictionary, *conjugal* (2020), https://dictionary.cambridge.org/dictionary/english/conjugal (defining it as 'connected with marriage or the relationship between two married people, especially their sexual relationship').

economic – that arise from these features',[4] as a Canadian reform agency suggested doing in 2001. However, a caveat is required here. This definition is a good proxy for family. Yet, the variety of practices within constellations of family can be hardly captured by a monolithic definition. The most accurate definition is a 'queer' one, with 'queer' designating an inclusive project that encompasses more practices that can be identified and 'more spaces that can be mapped beyond a few reference points'.[5]

This conceptual impossibility to engaging in a comprehensive mapping exercise results in the ultimate rejection of status and a priori attributes. Queer theorists oppose the very idea that the family can be seen as an essentialised entity of its own with features that can be fruitfully mapped. 'Family' is built through discursive practices and does not exist outside of or prior to them. As with gender, family is also the result of performativity, which is understood as 'a set of repeated acts within a highly rigid regulatory frame that congeal over time to produce the appearance of substance, of a natural sort of being'.[6]

What is family then? Poststructuralist accounts might be scary. By persistently deconstructing and denaturalising seemingly natural objects, they might generate a *horror vacui*, that is, a fear of the empty spaces left by their deconstructionist fury. The resulting image is one of a non-essentialised notion of family which is free-floating from any normative anchor. Nonetheless, (one of) the logical outgrowth(s) of the theory is to see family as being linked not to an essence, but to a set of family functions, such as parenting or the formation of an economic unit between adults. Family is not something which 'is', but rather is something we 'do' in daily practices, with this 'doing' displaying characteristics which warrant the label 'family'.[7] These functions are familiar if we perceive them as such – that is, significant enough to deserve the label – and if a range of interdependencies arises therefrom. The second limb of the definition is necessary if one wants to preserve the specificity of family units from non-family units. This specificity would get lost should we be able to assign the tag 'family' regardless of whether some form of interdependency or commitment exists – ie, under a pure at-will model.[8]

In light of this introduction, one might expect states to have loosened their grip on the traditional family. This is not the case. The dominant understanding of family still adheres to a marital norm from a juridical and cultural perspective

[4] Law Commission of Canada, *Beyond Conjugality: Recognizing and Supporting Close Personal Adult Relationships* (2001) xxiv–xxv.

[5] L Berlant and M Warner, 'Sex in Public' (1998) 24 *Critical Theory* 457, 558.

[6] J Butler, *Gender Trouble: Feminism and the Subversion of Identity* (London, Routledge, 1990) 43–44.

[7] See, eg, D Chambers, *A Sociology of Family Life. Change and Diversity in Intimate Relations* (Cambridge, Polity Press, 2012); K Plummer, 'Intimate Citizenship in an Unjust World' in M Romero and E Margolis (eds), *The Blackwell Companion to Social Inequalities* (Malden, MA, Blackwell, 2005).

[8] M Thornton, 'Embodying the Citizen' in M Thornton (ed), *Public and Private: Feminist Legal Debates* (Oxford, Oxford University Press, 1995) 197; see also F Swennen, 'Un-coupling Family Law: The Legal Recognition and Protection of Adult Unions outside of Conjugal Coupledom' (2020) 28 Feminist Legal Studies 39.

in the West, by which term I pre-eminently refer to the Euro-American context.[9] In these societies, law has not yet abandoned its focus on a family that is nuclear, preferably heterosexual and exclusive. As a consequence, all who deliberately do not conform to the prevailing norm remain 'legal strangers' to one another, as well as social outcasts. A question arises as to why the commitment of new families is overlooked by the state. The reasons are complex and I will attempt to flag them up throughout this volume.

However, one tentative reason should be anticipated and lies in their subversive nature. All family unions outside of the dominant model expose the cracks of a seemingly coherent system of ordering. They are subversive to a pre-arranged and state-approved way of being family. Put in simpler terms, they are too queer to be accepted, let alone promoted. Queer knowledge is disruptive knowledge as it exposes the fissures and biases of a given system – be it political, social, economic or moral – through individual experience that deviates from 'traditional' steps. The state's insistence on 'proper' familyhood is in the end a means of ordering society and a form of subjugation of deviant experiences that need fixing.

Family law is central to this governmental project, which Foucault popularly labelled 'biopolitics'.[10] The term stands for the authoritative appropriation of lives and bodies by modern states and a concomitant covering them through technologies of regulation.[11] I will advance an argument that modern states' biopolitical aims are at the core of the so-called non-verbalised functions of family law. Such functions cannot be verbalized to the extent that they are reminiscent of an ancient attribute of sovereignty, *ius vitae ac necis*, whereby the state took control over life and death. While the juridical power associated with ancient sovereignty was tantamount to taking life or letting live,[12] contemporary biopower consists of 'foster[ing] life or disallow[ing] it to the point of death' by ostracising deviant experiences.[13]

A second perspective that I will adopt is a critical legal pluralist one. Integrating critical legal pluralism within queer theory offers the conceptual framework for the ambitious project of rethinking the approach to new families' recognition in the West. Legal pluralism reflects the view that in any given space, there is more than one legal system. Critical legal pluralists have especially contributed to debunking various false ideas attendant to law, amongst which is the law's centralism, monism and prescriptivism.[14] These terms respectively refer to a belief that law can only be

[9] M Strathern, *Kinship, Law and the Unexpected: Relatives are Always a Surprise* (Cambridge, Cambridge University Press, 2005).

[10] M Foucault, 'The Birth of Biopolitics' in P Rabinow (ed), *Michel Foucault: Ethics, Subjectivity, and Truth*, Vol. 1 (New York, The New Press, 1997) 78.

[11] ibid 73–79.

[12] M Foucault, *The Will to Knowledge: The History of Sexuality*, vol 1, trans R Hurley (New York, Pantheon Books, 1998) 136.

[13] ibid 138.

[14] See, eg, RA Macdonald and T McMorrow, 'Wedding a Critical Legal Pluralism to the Laws of Close Adult Relationships' (2007) 1 *European Journal of Legal Studies* 319, 321.

state law, that normative processes are unitary, and that law has nothing to do with human agency and with the aspirations of the addressees of legal norms. The chief merit of this approach is to promote the view that law is the byproduct of the desires, aspirations and motives of law users themselves. Law users, by means of such motives, desires and aspirations, are able to determine the direction law is to take.

Hence, on the one hand, the utility of queer theory is to reveal the cracks of this false success story of family and to expose the biases of a narrative that only seeks to promote a singular conception of family. On the other hand, the utility of a critical legal pluralist approach is its cogent deconstruction of the various mythologies associated with law, amongst which is the apparent expulsion of legal actors from normative processes. This integrated framework should enable us to reconceive current approaches to family regulation by radically rethinking both terms: family, which should no longer be seen as an essence but as a sum of familiar functions; and regulation, which should be synonymous with facilitating legal actors' own jurisgenerative processes through state-made law.[15]

While some approaches to legal recognition tend to fiercely run up against the key tenets of the proposed framework and promote a prescriptivist, monolithic, top-down understanding of law (from which a prescriptivist, monolithic, top-down understanding of family derives), other approaches do not. The task of this chapter is to outline the contours of the proposed theoretical framework, while that of the next chapter is to analyse how this theory is to put to work to reduce the lag between law and the sociological reality of families.

However, before doing that, we should address a preliminary question: why should a state recognise new families or families at all? Is there something special about families that sets them apart from mere individuals? A sociological functionalist would answer this question by looking at 'the empirical evidence of the effects of stable, longer-term relationships on the health, happiness and productivity of peoples' lives'.[16] Yet, this account is insufficient, as family networks might have different degrees of interdependence. Hence, utilising a fixed notion of interdependence – as the key marker of deserving families – would cut out other expressions and experiences.

I suggest placing emphasis on both the normative and empirical accounts outlined below as the most compelling reasons to reform family law. Empirically, if families have reached an astoundingly high degree of diversity and complexity, then law's continued focus on the traditional family creates a gap that is increasingly intolerable. The more families that deviate from the model, the larger the injustice that a traditional family-centred approach to family regulation works for all outside of the model. However, empirical data must be taken at face value. It is strategically effective to argue that in light of the rich landscape of modern families, law should follow suit and reduce the conceptual lag between the legal framework and such families. This is why I often resort to this argument. Yet, the relevant

[15] R Cover, 'Nomos and Narrative' (1983) 97 *Harvard Law Review* 4, 28.
[16] Macdonald and McMorrow (n 14) 325.

account should be supplemented with the normative conceptions outlined above. In particular, the account is deficient if it fails to consider the significance of self-authorship to the crafting of intimacy; that is, that to the extent one wishes to live family in a certain way, it is irrelevant whether that relationship is empirically relevant. Thus, Western states should recognise new families especially because self-authorship is the highest-ranked, most cherished value informing present-day conceptions of family.

The next two sections thus address the preliminary question of why a state should recognise new families. To this end, I first examine the ongoing changes in family patterns Western states are experiencing (section 1.I) and then look at normative conceptions of the family that gained traction in recent decades (section 1.II). In section 1.III, I endeavour to understand how we can move further forward by expounding the limits of current legal approaches to recognising families. Ultimately, in section 2, I illustrate the methodology that the book adopts. In particular, the book consists of two parts. Part I is mostly useful to policy-makers, and Part II to lawyers and advocates of new family recognition. Part I includes this introductory chapter, where I outline the theoretical framework and methodology, and Chapter 2, where I expound the abstract models to recognise new families. Part II focuses on the legal arguments that support the recognition of a subset of new family – the non-conjugal family – in four jurisdictions: the US (Chapter 3), Canada (Chapter 4), the framework of the European Convention on Human Rights (ECHR) (Chapter 5) and the European Union (EU) (Chapter 6). The aim of the methodological section in this chapter (section 2) is especially to clarify why Part II focuses on legal strategies, takes non-conjugal families as a case study and adopts a comparative method.

I. Evolution in Family Patterns

The relationship between law and family diversity can be seen as a chicken and egg problem. While there is general acceptance that 'law may affect the ways in which families behave or structure themselves, the changing nature of family relationships also has an impact on the law'.[17] Understanding the extent to which law is mould or mirror of family diversity requires grasping the magnitude of family diversity. This section endeavours to make a thus-framed inquiry.

Empirically, the category of family has been the object of startling attention in fields as varied as sociology, anthropology and law, to mention but a few. Empirical research sheds light on the manifold ways in which people nowadays arrange their personal relationships outside of traditional family models. From a sort of *koiné* of personal relationships, the marital family is now a category under strain throughout the West. In Europe, the 'Golden age of the family' – that is, the period in history experiencing the highest rates of marriage, birth at young ages and low

[17] *Canada (Attorney General) v Mossop* [1993] 1 SCR 554.

rates of divorce – started to wane in the 1960s. Likewise, a constant decline in marital rates is under way in both Canada and the US.[18] The trend has been linked, inter alia, to ongoing 'processes of individualization' which render personal relationships contingent on personal satisfaction and thus more unstable than ever before.[19]

A second reason for low marital rates is the increasing incidence of 'families we live with',[20] that is, the set of family units hardly reconcilable with the archetypical family. In particular, empirical queer sociology[21] has been the wellspring of a copious amount of scholarship on counter-heteronormative relationship forms that eschew the traditional model. Crucially, based on the (queer) definition of family provided above, one could infer that the most salient statistics are those we should yet conceive of.

The ways in which individuals resist dominant family norms are numerous. A family is thought of as nuclear, yet 'new generations' are less and less interested in forming a nuclear family. Recent research conducted by the Pew Research Center in the US looked at the rates of 'millennials' in a standard nuclear conjugal family (ie, living with a spouse, their own child or both). The research noticed that in 2019, only 55 per cent of millennials opted for this arrangement, compared to 66 per cent of the previous generation (the so-called Generation X) getting married in 2003, 69 per cent of 'Boomers' getting married in 1987 and 85 per cent of the 'Silent Generation' getting married in 1968.[22]

Traditionally, a family is conjugal, with the term 'conjugal' boiling down to the relationship having a sexual component. However, as the Chapter on Canada shows, there multi-generational families, a subset of non-conjugal families, are the fastest-growing household since 2001. This trend is common to European jurisdictions as well, with an increasing number of persons creating bonds of mutual support that lack a sexual component.[23]

A family is reflectively thought of as dyadic, with plural unions of more than two persons attracting criminal sanctions nearly everywhere in the West. Yet, polyamory is taking hold in Western jurisdictions as a viable arrangement of intimate relationships. A lack of comprehensive data prevents us from appreciating the breadth of the phenomenon. Nonetheless, lately, the Vanier Institute for the Family, the most renowned independent research institute on family diversity in

[18] See chs 3 and 4.

[19] S Budgeon and S Roseneil, 'Editors' Introduction: Beyond the Conventional Family' (2004) 52 *Current Sociology* 127.

[20] A Diduck, 'Introduction' in A Diduck (ed), *Marriage and Cohabitation: Regulating Intimacy, Affection and Care* (Aldershot, Ashgate, 2008) xiii–xvi.

[21] S Seidman, *Queer Theory/Sociology* (Oxford, Blackwell, 1996).

[22] Pew Research Center, 'As Millennials Near 40, They're Approaching Family Life Differently Than Previous Generations' (May 2020)' https://www.pewsocialtrends.org/wp-content/uploads/sites/3/2020/05/PDST_05.27.20_millennial.families_fullreport.pdf.

[23] C Smart, *Personal Life: New Directions in Sociological Thinking* (Cambridge, Polity Press, 2007).

Canada, conducted an online survey that called attention to how the phenomenon is garnering popularity. Almost two-thirds of respondents in its survey were in a self-proclaimed polyamorous relationship, and 40 per cent of the remaining respondents alleged that they had somehow been involved in a polyamorous relationship in the last five years.[24]

Likewise, a salient site of investigation is voluntary kin groups developed outside blood and legal ties. There is a flourishing field of research concerning so-called neo-tribes and friendship-based 'quasi-communes'.[25] The bearing of such phenomena rises at the same pace at which occasions of shared domesticity in young adulthood rise and marriage rates – especially at a young age – decrease. Empirical research has also homed in on the importance of 'friendship' for non-heterosexuals, with friendship existing on a scale that goes from mere acquaintance to persons belonging to an intimate circle.[26] However, recent research suggests that shared domesticity rather than friendship is the principal connecting factor for these networks.[27]

Traditionally, cohabitation under the same roof is commonly seen as quintessential. Yet, people living apart together (LATs) are drawing more and more attention as an object of empirical study. LATs are persons in an intimate relationship who decide or are compelled to live apart for a variety of reasons. In the early 2000s, in European countries such as the UK, Belgium, Norway, Sweden, Germany and the Netherlands, LATs accounted for 10 per cent of adult relationships.[28] Empirical research thus rips apart the 'hearth' myth, with hearth – a term tellingly synonymous with family – designating the inevitability of shared domesticity.

Further, 'perpetuity' is seen as important and commitment has always been 'till death do us part'. Yet, the case of the US powerfully demythologises this signifier of family. Empirical research demonstrates that the fluidity of families has skyrocketed, with many people divorcing, remarrying, recoupling in cohabitation arrangements etc.[29] Also, there seems to be a general social acceptance of these phenomena, with the Pew Research Center reporting generally positive attitudes towards such (re-)arrangements.[30]

[24] J-P Boyd, 'Polyamory in Canada: Research on an Emerging Family Structure' Vanier Institute of the Family (2017) 3, www.vanierinstitute.ca/polyamory-in-canada-research-on-an-emerging-family-structure.

[25] S Heath, 'Peer-Shared Households, Quasi-communes and Neo-tribes' (2004) 52 *Current Sociology* 161.

[26] J Weeks, B Heaphy and C Donovan, *Same Sex Intimacies: Families of Choice and Other Life Experiments* (London, Routledge, 2001) vii–viii.

[27] Swennen (n 8) 46.

[28] I Levin, 'Living Apart Together: A New Family Form' (2004) 52 *Current Sociology* 223.

[29] Pew Research Center, 'Parenting in America: Outlook, Worries, Aspirations are Strongly Linked to Financial Situation' (December 2015) 15–16, https://www.pewsocialtrends.org/2015/12/17/parenting-in-america.

[30] Pew Research Center, 'The Decline of Marriage and Rise of New Families' (November 2010) 1–3, www.pewresearch.org/pubs/1802/decline-marriage-rise-new-families (finding that 66 per cent of the public has either positive or neutral attitudes towards new family arrangements).

In practice, new families even escape binary classifications (eg, dyadic/non-dyadic, conjugal/non-conjugal), with many of them entering familial bonds characterised by 'suffusion and ambiguity'[31] and continuous overlaps. Consistent with the view that a queer world is a space of 'incommensurable geographies',[32] the complexity of modern family arrangements can be hardly captured by static classifications. The merit of the paired opposites provided above is chiefly that of unveiling the decreasing heuristic value of 'usual' signposts of family.

Ironically, the demise of the archetypical family raises the following question: is family a dead-and-still-alive 'zombie category', as sociologist Ulrich Beck had it,[33] or does it deserves keeping alive? In other words, should we use the term 'family' or is another term more suitable to designate the rich landscape of personal relationships? I argue in favour of keeping 'family'. This term continues to manifest itself as a central trope in Western culture and intellectual imaginaries. Its evocative character remains of the unobjectionable sort. When one uses the word 'family', such as when referring to a friend, one intends to signify the importance one attaches to the relationship. This is to say that the label of 'family' is a signal to third parties regarding the significance and salience of a given relationship. It is this evocative character that cognate terms such as 'household' would lack. In its being less evocative compared to 'family', an alternative lexicon would likely fail to live up to the mission of changing deeply rooted conceptions around the ways in which we build, live and frame our personal relationships. These reasons call for sticking with 'family' as the preferred term and conceptual category in the book.

II. Evolution in Normative Conceptions of Family

In discussing evolving normative conceptions around family, it is necessary to first draw a distinction between the vertical and horizontal axes of relationships. The term 'horizontal relationship' refers to the bond created by consenting adults (and hence an adult–adult relationship). By contrast, 'vertical relationship' refers to the bond between an adult and children or minors (and, as such, unable to be considered consenting adults).[34]

Why draw such a distinction? The normative conceptions of family that will be examined below, which include the growing influence of principles of autonomy, pluralism and equality on family law discourses, only concern the horizontal dimension of family–whereby two or more consenting adults decide how to organise their intimate life. By contrast, the vertical dimension is also affected by

[31] Swennen (n 8) 42–44; see also Chambers (n 7).

[32] Berlant and Warner (n 5) 558.

[33] U Beck and E Beck-Gernsheim, *Individualization: Institutionalized Individualism and its Social and Political Consequences* (London, Sage, 2002) 203.

[34] I include within the definition any situation in which there is a legal duty of support; for instance, parents who owe a duty of care to their children who have come of age cannot be considered parties in a horizontal relationship.

a normative shift, albeit contrary to the one outlined above, with law being more 'rigid', constrictive and less open to derogatory regimes when children are at stake. Children seem to warrant more and more intrusive scrutiny on the part of the state over the ways in which such relationships unfold. Therefore, we should be alert to the fact that raising children, under current laws, will attract more public intervention.

This is not to overlook the fact that parenting laws have their own contradictions and signifiers that also need rethinking. I was especially impressed by a Canadian court case concerning a non-conjugal couple of two friends and colleagues at the University of Ottawa. The non-biological parent was eventually legally recognised as a parent in light of the deep affection and contribution to the personal growth of Elaan, a disabled child with spastic quadriplegia.[35] I think the case powerfully attests to how parenting laws also have 'their own cracks' and should overcome traditional signifiers to account for the many ways in which we nowadays live parenthood. Yet, the subject matter would need an analysis of its own since the normative forces driving the development of parenting laws are distinctive. By way of illustration, I previously referred to some families challenging the view that commitment should be for-life. Such family will confront accredited views according to which children need a stable environment for their wellbeing and personal growth. Hence, and perhaps even reasonably so, they will not be able to dissolve their bond in the same way as childless 'temporary' families. Therefore, for the purposes of this book, only adult relationships are taken into account, with an awareness that children, if present, will most likely change the rules of the game.

With this premise in mind, I should like to analyse the normative forces that have driven the development of horizontal relationships in the last few decades. First, a shift in conceptions of intimate citizenship has undeniably contributed to conveying the idea that families outside the sacred precincts of marriage are no longer social outcasts. As to the trajectory that this shift has followed, nowadays relationships are informed by utilitarian ideals under which personal satisfaction is key. As Elizabeth Scott and Robert Scott persuasively put it:

> The transformation in social attitudes creates the possibility of a legal regime that fosters pluralism, allowing individuals to pursue their own vision of the good life in forming family relationships. On this view, fundamental notions of autonomy and fairness support the claim that the liberal state should offer individuals the freedom to undertake whatever family relationships maximize their utility and then should support those families equally.[36]

Under a pluralistic approach, everyone is thus allowed to pursue their own conception of the good life, and each and any conception deserves respect. According to

[35] N Bakht and L Collins, 'Are You My Mother? Co-parenting in a Non-conjugal Family' (2018) 31 *Canadian Journal of Family Law* 105.

[36] E Scott and R Scott, 'From Contract to Status: Collaboration and the Evolution of Novel Family Relationships' (2015) 115 *Columbia Law Review* 293, 297.

this view, autonomy and self-authorship are the normative centrepieces of family life. The latter particularly merits emphasis as it plays a non-fungible role in relationship regulation. The principle of self-authorship involves allowing individuals to maintain 'authorship' of their own life, including the possibility to create intimate relationships of choice, whichever these might be, and arrange them according to their own beliefs and convictions. In light of this principle, issues of intimacy and relationship regulation should in principle be left to parties themselves rather than be regulated through a top-down approach.

Historically, processes of individualisation went hand in hand with processes of detraditionalisation. Sociologist Giddens explained how utilitarian ideals made inroads in affective sexual bonds in conjunction with women's liberation movements.[37] As a consequence, conjugal relationships first gained symmetry and became characterised by a 'confluence of love', which he called the 'pure relationship' model. Second, they were affected by a concomitant shift occurring at the functional level, whereby sex became disentangled from reproductive needs, which he dubbed 'plastic sexuality'. Subsequently, LGBTQ movements – connoted by a liberationist stance in the 1970s – also strove to strip the most conservative aspects of the family away from it. In particular, the traditional moral drivers, amongst which were the socially constructed imperative of getting married, the necessity to raise children and to stay together 'till death do us part', gradually lost their tight grip. According to this view, the institution of family is now 'postmoralistic', to the extent that it pivots on a logic of personal blossoming and autonomy (rather than on such moral drivers).[38]

The 'most powerful current in modern society'[39] as it has been defined, the longing for personal satisfaction driven by individualism also produces contradictions. In particular, an augmented reflexive focus on expectations and personal aspirations creates a conundrum between indulging personal satisfaction and a never-fading desire for another person's love.[40] This conundrum is only solved through continuous negotiations taking place within relationships, with such relationships becoming ongoing processes rather than endpoints in themselves. It is interesting in that regard that the term 'settle down' is traditionally synonymous with getting married in southern Italy. This stands in sharp contrast with present-day conceptions of family that see family relationships as ongoing processes of (re) negotiation.

However, an important contribution to not overstating the perks of individualism comes from that body of literature on the so-called ethics of care. This string of literature casts autonomy and 'equality' as opposites.[41] Liberty-centred

[37] A Giddens, *The Transformation of Intimacy: Sexuality, Love and Eroticism in Modern Societies* (Cambridge, Polity Press, 1992) 2.

[38] B Bawin-Legros, 'Intimacy and the New Sentimental Order' (2004) 52 *Current Sociology* 241, 242.

[39] Beck and Beck-Gernsheim (n 33) 22.

[40] But see A Diduck, *Law's Families* (London, Butterworths, 2003) 27–28 (considering them irreconcilable).

[41] See especially M Fineman, 'The Vulnerable Subject and the Responsive State' (2010) 60 *Emory Law Journal* 251.

discourses depict individuals as self-sufficient, independent subjects who make rational decisions to pursue their best interests.[42] By contrast, this philosophical perspective calls attention to the ontological vulnerability every person experiences at repeated points in life. Mutual vulnerability and interdependency between individuals, so the theory argues, makes 'care a necessary, and rewarding, part of life'.[43] Since care itself generates vulnerability oppositions between a caregiver and those cared for become somewhat artificial.

The vulnerability care itself generates can, and does, factor into our most intimate decisions. However, it does not foreshadow per se the possibility to forge personal relationships according to one's most personal convictions, beliefs and aspirations, as some scholars seem to argue.[44] In other words, it is one thing to recognise the limits of the mythological self-interested autonomous subjects, a position with respect to which I fully sympathise, another is to see (a longing for) care as impeding the exercise of personal agency. Therefore, it is useful to supplement the first normative driver – autonomy – with the key tenets of ethics of care in order to gain a deeper understanding of the ways in which autonomy unfolds. By contrast, I do not share the view that vulnerability radically impedes autonomy.

Autonomy and pluralism are not the exclusive champions of the new normative order underpinning modern families. Equality (and nondiscrimination) is another one. US scholar William Eskridge convincingly argued that the processes triggered by utilitarianism – in particular, the transition from a set of mandatory family law rules to a choice-based system in family law – also carry an 'unprecedented baseline of nondiscrimination'.[45] In his view, the new baseline entails that the basis for allocating social goods cannot coincide with a bare promotion of marriage over other family unions. Hence, under a utilitarian approach, a state is still able to 'discriminate' amongst relationships. However, the distinction must be supported by a reasonable objective, which can no longer coincide with bare moral disapproval of some family forms. Courts in the West have embraced this view. Case law demonstrates that is becoming less and less acceptable to discriminate families on grounds such as tradition or morals.[46]

Recourse to equality talk is also strategically useful, in that it allows aspiring families to draw on the existing lexicon and imaginaries. This has been the strategy adopted by same-sex couples. In the courtroom, these families argued that they were capable of commitment, romantic love, fidelity, and forming a nurturing and child-friendly environment as much as heterosexual couples. Arguing for

[42] M Fineman, 'Feminism, Masculinities and Multiple Identities' (2013) 13 *Nevada Law Review* 619 (speaking of an 'adult liberal subject').

[43] J Herring, *Vulnerable Adults and the Law* (Oxford, Oxford University Press, 2016) 16.

[44] A Diduck, 'Autonomy and Vulnerability in Family Law: The Missing Link' in J Wallbank and J Herring (eds), *Vulnerabilities, Care and Family Law* (London, Routledge, 2013) 97.

[45] WN Eskridge, 'Family Law Pluralism: The Guided-Choice Regime of Menus, Default Rules, and Override Rules' (2012) 100 *Georgetown Law Journal* 1884, 1973.

[46] As chs 3 and 4 will illustrate, bare promotion of traditional marriage is no longer a valid state interest in North America. Europe deserves an analysis of its own due to the complexity of the legal landscape. Such an analysis is given in ch 5.

equality and sameness yields the strategically useful consequence of temporarily obfuscating the subversive nature of these family grids and increasing their social acceptance. At the same time, however, it has its limits. Notably, it obscures a root cause for which same-sex couples mobilised in the first place: pluralism (ie, the recognition of plural lifestyles, choices and ways of being).

III. Law's Friction with the 'New' Family

A legitimate scepticism could arise as to whether legal recognition is a suitable option. Wouldn't the manifold reality of modern families be inevitably sacrificed by legal recognition? Can legal recognition occur without a normalisation, assimilation and domestication of multiple expressions? The state's exercise of a normalising and civilising power when determining the conditions for entrance to and exit from a family regime is there for all to see.[47] If one wants to enter the scheme, one has to adhere to the dominant (usually marital) norm enshrined in it. Rights claims might thus mortify the transformative potential of new families. This is a classic critique levelled by queer voices at legal recognition.[48] Hence, an issue arises as to whether law is in its essence suitable to the task of accommodating this stunning diversity. I argue that it is. However, current approaches to relationship recognition are worth rethinking, for they are much more interested in constraining than in facilitating such expressions. I shall clarify the sense in which the current approach to relationship recognition 'constrains' families.

The starting point of the analysis is the observation that family status is a matter on which states keep a tight grip.[49] This phenomenon is fairly recent. It can be traced back to a time when law was eradicated from society and became a tool in the hands of the dominant elites – a time which in continental Europe is much more easily traceable, for it coincides with the French Revolution. This shift eventuated in a 'bulimia' of law, with bulimia designating pathologic, uncontrolled eating in large amounts. Former Italian Constitutional Court's Judge Paolo Grossi called the phenomenon legal absolutism ('assolutismo giuridico').[50] Legal absolutism was based on the assumption – perhaps presumption – that law was meant to cover every aspect of life, including those traditionally left to private regulation, chief amongst them family life.

[47] N Barker, 'Sex and the Civil Partnership Act: The Future of (Non) Conjugality?' (2006) 14 *Feminist Legal Studies* 241, 249.

[48] See, eg, JR Feinberg, 'Avoiding Marriage Tunnel Vision' (2013) 88 *Tulane Law Review* 259; M Bernstein Sycamore, *That's Revolting!: Queer Strategies for Resisting Assimilation*, revised edn (New York, Soft Skull Press, 2008).

[49] WG Friedman, 'Some Reflections on Status and Freedom' in RA Newman (ed), *Essays in Jurisprudence in Honour of Roscoe Pound* (Indianapolis, Bobbs-Merrill Co Inc, 1962); P Rescigno, 'Situazione e status nell'esperienza del diritto' (1973) *Rivista di Diritto Civile* 211; G Alpa, *Status e capacità. La costruzione giuridica delle differenze individuali* (Rome/Bari, Laterza, 1993) 29.

[50] P Grossi, *Società, Diritto, Stato. Un recupero per il diritto* (Milan, Giuffrè, 2006) 46–47.

This bulimia culminated in a state 'legal monopoly' over family law, which nowadays materialises in a plethora of legal rules policing access to, and exit from, marriage, the array of personal relationships worth protecting through legal benefits, and the choice of the forum to resolve family law disputes. Legal bulimia does not merely translate into a monopoly over the legal source that is set to govern the area – which is not problematic per se. It is its taking over of the *functions* that family law is set to achieve which is critical to social governance. A monopoly over the functions inevitably results in family law pursuing state-mandated goals as opposed to people's own objectives, aspirations and preferences. In this new light, the control exerted over the legal source is, less grandly and more subtly, instrumental to utilising family law as a device to pursue a predefined set of state objectives.

Identifying such objectives is not without its difficulties. I shall differentiate between what I would like to call verbalised and unverbalised functions. The distinguishing matrix is not merely whether these functions are spelled out, say, in a statute or court decision, but whether these they can be articulated in the first place. Much has been said concerning the verbalised functions of family law. A popular account is John Eekelaar's description of the three 'primary functions' of family law, namely adjustive, protective and supportive.[51] The adjustive function refers to the law granting economic protection following the breakdown of a relationship, based on an awareness that relationships are grids of interdependencies which inevitably create imbalances and vulnerabilities. The protective function consists of shielding family members from 'domestic' harm; ultimately, by supportive function, Eekelaar refers to a need to encourage the continual maintenance and flourishing of a relationship. But if one looks at the various 'branches' of family law, the list of (context-specific) functions is much longer. Illustrative examples are the aim of protecting offspring that attaches to family status and various social benefits or that of fostering legal certainty, an objective that is central to kinship-based succession laws.

Unverbalised functions are, by contrast, not spelled out because they cannot be spoken. Functions falling under the category are not spoken of for there is no need to – it is a common trait of law to direct attention to an object while in practice being concerned with the disposition of other objects.[52] But most importantly in my view, they are not speakable for they are reminiscent of an ancient attribute of sovereignty: that of exerting control over people's life and death (*ius vitae ac necis*).[53] This attribute was retrieved by Machiavelli from the Hellenic period to buttress his construction of the modern state. The modern state was cast as an

[51] J Herring, *Caring and the Law* (Oxford, Hart Publishing, 2013) 190, citing J Eekelaar, *Family Law and Social Policy* (London, Weidenfeld & Nicholson, 1984) 25.

[52] M Croce, *The Politics of Juridification* (Abingdon, Routledge, 2018) 1 (calling this property 'obliquity').

[53] Foucault (n 12) 135. Foucault cites Schmitt's decisionism theory; See C Schmitt, *Political Theology: Four Chapters on the Concept of Sovereignty*, trans George Schwab (Chicago, University of Chicago Press, 1985).

entity that shall secure peace at all costs, including by dispensing death – a means which Machiavelli framed not in terms of 'privilege', but 'duty'.

What does family law have to do with *ius vitae ac necis*? Chief amongst unverbalised objectives is the functionalisation of family law to pursuing 'biopolitical' ends. Biopolitics is a term popularly coined by Foucault, describing the state's taking hold of lives and bodies.[54] Foucault himself acknowledges the parallel with Machiavellian-style theories. However, a key difference exists: the juridical power associated with ancient sovereignty was synonymous to taking life or letting live.[55] It was a power which deduced – wealth, personal freedom and ultimately life – and either took away or left individuals alone: 'Its symbol after all was the sword.'[56]

Biopower – that is, the tool that puts to work biopolitics – is not deductive; it is a power 'to foster life or disallow it to the point of death'.[57] It is a power to administer life. Those living outside of the traditional model of family are not killed in public squares. Bodies are administered through a more subtle technique. Unlike mainstream feminist theories, the Foucauldian approach maintains that power is omnipresent, normalising and productive rather than hierarchical, repressive and prohibitory.[58] He thus outlines a decentralised non-juridical model of power where both institutional actors and non-institutional actors are endowed with the power of enforcing rules – through voluntary enforcement or pressure from third parties. Therefore, the fate of those who violate these norms (not rules) is to be left out of privileges and to conduct a life at the margins of society. It is the theoretical impossibility – in light of modern conceptions of sovereignty – to admit the state's disallowing certain lives 'to the point of death' that renders the function unspeakable in my view. It is this impossibility to admit that some lives are less worthy than others that renders this function unspeakable in the first place.

In somewhat similar terms, Schneider has offered a fine account of the ways in which family law fulfils that which he calls a 'channelling function'.[59] The channelling function is a second common unverbalised function. According to Schneider's account, signs are not wanting that family law channels the reproductive function into stable family units, taken as the fundamental unit of an orderly society.[60] Stable family units are supposed, inter alia, to regulate sexual conduct, reduce sexual conflict and perpetuate the species.[61] Clearly, in modern societies, this function cannot be spoken of either.

[54] Foucault (n 10) 73–79.

[55] Foucault (n 12) 136.

[56] ibid 136.

[57] ibid 138.

[58] WN Eskridge and ND Hunter, *Sexuality, Gender, and the Law*, 2nd edn (New York, Foundation Press, 2006) 489.

[59] CE Schneider, 'The Channeling Function in Family Law' (1992) 20 *Hofstra Law Review* 495.

[60] ibid 498 ('it is their very presence, the social currency they have, and the governmental support they receive which combine to make it seem reasonable and even natural for people to use them. Thus, people can be said to be channeled into them').

[61] KN Llewellyn, 'Behind the Law of Divorce: I' (1932) 32 *Columbia Law Review* 1281, 1288–95.

In the realm of family law, the balance between state-mandated (unverbalised) goals and law users' own goals is all tilted towards achieving the former. The famous trend towards contractualisation, whereby family unions recently gained more manoeuvrability through private ordering, does not affect this assertion: the state has yet to allow individuals to be in families of choice 'for real'. Think of the legal invisibility of polyamory or other subversive practices that are 'outlawed'; think of the bounded way in which a family regime comes up, without there being a possibility for users to disaggregate it into various tiles (parenthood, economic partnerships etc) and/or perform different family functions with different persons.

Hence, a question arises as to whether state law can be detached from state-mandated functions to mitigate the risk of normalisation ensuing from the state regulation of the family. In other words, can states make law that detects and accommodates law users' own objectives? I acknowledge, as others have, that it is possible. Notably, there are grounds to argue for a consensual divorce between family law and state-mandated functions. A few points merit consideration in this respect.

As a premise, it should be noted that the notion of 'law users' was coined by Laura Nader to criticise the law's drifting in the direction of the 'dominant user', that is, corporate entities, moulding US law through intense claimant activity. The notion is nonetheless useful, in that it refers to the law's capacity 'to be made and changed by the cumulative effects of its users'.[62] The concept was compellingly described by Mariano Croce as referring to how the 'direction of law largely depends on who is motivated to use the law and for what purposes. This is why, from a methodological standpoint, social agents are given equal sociological significance to all the players who partake in the legal process'.[63] Law is thus an organic process that moves in an evolutionary fashion; however, the direction this process takes is not the deliberate making of legal engineers, but – also – the result of the 'cumulative efforts of its users'.[64]

In similar terms, Canadian scholar Roderick A Macdonald upheld a theory of law as 'engagement, process, and aspiration'.[65] His position was especially taking aim at the orthodox litany that sees law as an artifact detached from the persons whose conduct it wishes to regulate. His reframing of law as process was conducive to redirecting attention onto legal actors, whose purposes the law is set to serve and whose behaviour is critical to discern what the legal regime governing their conduct is. Thus, both the law user of Nader and the legal actor of Macdonald engage in a jurisgenerative process whereby they contribute to creating and giving shape to the normativity of their own legal regime.

[62] L Nader, 'A User Theory of Law' (1984) 38 *Southwestern Law Journal* 951, 952.

[63] Croce (n 52) 4.

[64] Nader (n 62) 952.

[65] RA Macdonald, 'Here, There … and Everywhere – Theorizing Legal Pluralism; Theorizing Jacques Vanderlinden' in N Kasirer (ed), *Étudier et enseigner le droit: hier, aujourd'hui et demain – Études offertes à Jacques Vanderlinden* (Montréal, Éditions Yvon Blais, 2006) 393–94; Macdonald and McMorrow (n 14) 322.

It is this theoretical understanding of law that is especially useful to contemplating the possibility for law users/legal actors to actively participate in legal processes. This participation implies determining the direction of law, ie, the law's content and intendment, through self-produced normativity. Such theory is anti-prescriptivist to the extent that it rejects the belief that law can be effectively set apart from those whose conduct it is to govern. How this conception is put to work is a different issue that I will address in Chapter 2 by exploring which relationship-recognition mechanism most resembles the theory.

Returning to the issue of whether divorcing law and state-mandated goals is even possible, one can glean some insights by drawing from various contributions. The contributions I parse out, despite looking at the issue from very different angles, all converge in terms of unravelling some misconceptions underpinning current legal approaches to governing society. The two vantage points I offer are those of a staunch supporter of free market economics and of renowned critical legal pluralists rejecting the monism and centralism of law.[66]

As to the first, Hayek, a classical liberal intellectual, has laid out a popular distinction between *taxis* and *cosmos* that can assist us in tackling this issue. These two terms in classical Greek refer to an artificial order and a spontaneous order respectively. *Taxis* is based on the belief that orders can only be created through external forces, while *cosmos* is a self-generating order. Importantly, since *taxis* is someone's deliberate making, it cannot but be simple, concrete and 'serve a purpose of the maker'.[67] By contrast, *cosmos* can reach a degree of complexity which goes beyond human prediction. Further, since it is not the product of someone's deliberate making, it does not serve a specific (external) purpose.[68]

Crucially, *cosmos* is not incompatible with made rules. Its spontaneous character is preserved anytime 'its particular manifestation will … depend on many circumstances which the designer of these rules did not and could not know'.[69] Conceiving modern society as a spontaneous order, he concludes that '[t]o maintain that we must deliberately plan modern society because it has become so complex is therefore paradoxical'.[70] The most appropriate response to complexity is to improve and enforce the rules conducive to the creation of *cosmos*, with the limit being the impossibly to replace people's own knowledge and purposes for different ends.

From a radically different perspective, namely an original legal-pluralistic perspective, Paolo Grossi and Santi Romano argued that law should not be moulded by a political power which pursues its own plans. Grossi, a legal historian who was

[66] The two terms respectively refer to a belief in the unity of normative processes and a belief in law as being ultimately state law.

[67] FA Hayek, *Law, Legislation and Liberty*, vol 1 (London, Routledge, 1998 [1973]) 38.

[68] ibid 39 ('Since such an order has not been created by an outside agency, the order as such also can have no purpose, although its existence may be very serviceable to the individuals which move within such order').

[69] ibid 46.

[70] ibid 50.

nostalgic for medieval times, when law was much closer to society than it is nowadays, saw society as a 'living, growing body' which cannot stand any restrictions imposed from above. Its legal-pluralistic approach, which draws heavily from Santi Romano's theory of legal institutionalism,[71] leads him to level charges at the state's 'exhausting' all the law which is to be found in a given society.[72] By contrast, if one were to cut society, say, as a cake, one would glimpse different layers, with the most superficial layer being state law, an intermediate layer comprising customs and a deeper layer comprising private individuals' own rules.[73] These layers all form full-fledged legal orders. Santi Romano's theory has as its chief corollary legal pluralism as co-existence of multiple (state and non-state) legal orders, and the capability of the legal order to solve conflicts arising from competing normative orders. In similar terms, Grossi argued that law is a 'mirror',[74] which only helps society express its own complexity and salience. However, nowadays the peaceful co-existence of legal orders has faded away, with made law assuming 'authoritarian' traits rather than mirroring society.

Yet, all these thinkers diverge from our proposed theoretical framework (grounded in queer theory and critical legal pluralism) when they place emphasis on an order which is not (at least fully) ascribable to individual agency. This is especially visible in Hayek's work. According to him, as with organic compounds, we cannot create the desired outcome by merely placing atoms in a given position. A second way in which von Hayek parts from us is his application of the theory to the market, the *cosmos par excellence*. But their deconstructive part, debunking some present-day mythologies associated with law, preserves its full usefulness as a theory that sheds light on the present moment.

To conclude, the question raised above is astoundingly complex. Yet, two radically different perspectives – a classical liberal one and a legal-pluralist one – demonstrate how the disentanglement of law from its most constrictive traits – amongst which is replacing people's ends for its own ends – has been at the centre of important reflections in the past century. Articulated arguments have been made that law can be successfully disentangled from such traits, contrary to modern prescriptivist narratives based on the false assumption that law must cover the whole surface of life and pursue a predetermined set of functions. Intimacy and family matters are emblematic in this regard. They lay claim to space which is free from top-down regulation which sacrifices people's own aims. Chapter 2 will thus seek to understand how to put to work the proposed theory and achieve its ambitious goal.

With this key conceptual premise in mind, I move to outline the methodology which I adopt in the book. Notably, I clarify why the bulk of the book concerns strategic litigation. Further, I shall clarify why I take non-conjugal families as a case study. Ultimately, I reject contentions that family law is an area that is not

[71] See S Romano, L'ordinamento giuridico (Firenze, Nuova Biblioteca, 1977 [1918]).
[72] Grossi (n 50) 187.
[73] W Cesarini Sforza, *Il diritto dei privati* (Milan, Giuffrè, 1963 [1929]) 22–23.
[74] Grossi (n 50) xi.

amenable to comparison and clarify why the comparative method is critical to the objectives of this book.

2. Methodology

As argued above, this work has the ambition to present the current non-recognition of new families as a legal problem. The root causes of their invisibility are profound and likely need multiple synergetic actions to be unravelled. Realistically, both political and legal action is needed to overcome the myth of the traditional family. Yet, in an unceasing 'faith in law', the book zooms in on the strategies and legal arguments that can be advanced before judicial courts – and to a lesser extent in the political arena. It is especially devoted to exploring *legal* arguments that are helpful in making strides in the recognition of new families.

The book consists of two parts: Part I focuses on policy arguments, while Part II focuses on legal arguments presented in the courtroom. Part I includes this introductory chapter and Chapter 2, the latter of which offers arguments in favour and against each mode of recognition of new families. In interrogating which mode comes closest to the proposed bifurcated theoretical framework – a queer/legal pluralist – the analysis therein gathers some material to craft sound policy-based arguments.

However, legal strategies remain at core of this book. Part II offers an in-depth comparative analysis of four jurisdictions: the US, Canada and the two metanational systems of the ECHR and the EU. Aware that each family signifier deserves an analysis of its own, the focus of Part II is 'conjugality', which in the four jurisdictions under review is mostly taken to mean 'sexual component'. Furthermore, the comparative method is adopted as it seemed the most suitable approach to understanding how Western states regulate families and the hindrances to be overcome in order to further the recognition of new families. The fundamental methodological choices regarding Part II – legal strategies, non-conjugal families and the comparative method – are illustrated in further detail below.

I. Why Legal Strategies?

Often legal strategies are only one prong of a broader change initiative, which can consist of law reform projects, legislation or other forms of political participation (organising marches, assembling, forming advocacy groups etc). However, recourse to run-of-the-mill politics is becoming less central compared to legal strategies. This process is called the 'juridification' of society.[75] It is set to designate

[75] See, eg, A-M Magnussen and A Banasiak, 'Juridification: Disrupting the Relationship between Law and Politics?' (2013) 19 *European Law Journal* 325; LC Blichner and A Molander, 'Mapping Juridification' (2008) 14 *European Law Journal* 36.

a growing relevance of legal skills to innovation processes and a redistribution of authority from political actors to judicial courts. Locating this phenomenon within the broader shift occurring at the level of how individuals frame their identity, problems and responses to such problems – with respect to which legal discourse is nowadays critical – allows us to grasp its real stakes: the entrance to rather than banishment from courts of politics.[76]

This sweeping phenomenon, which Ran Hirschl calls 'judicialization of politics',[77] is taken to include at least three interrelated aspects. At a more abstract level, it points to the sway that legalistic jargon and processes have over decision-making. It also refers to a redistribution of authority to the judicial branch. This redistribution allows courts to make decisions relating to public policy through, inter alia, their rights jurisprudence. A third meaning is the involvement of courts in so-called mega-politics, ie, 'core political controversies that define (and often divide) whole polities'.[78] While family definitions are usually thought to fall within the purview of social policy, they are more aptly to locate at the crossroads of the second and third of Hirschl's meanings. This is especially so in jurisdictions, notably European ones,[79] that see family as a foundational institution of national identity, with extreme examples including Greece, which describes it in its constitution as 'the cornerstone of the preservation and the advancement of the Nation',[80] and Hungary, which sees it as 'the basis of the survival of the nation'.[81]

As to the intrinsic value of political avenues of change, their characteristics might render them less fertile a terrain of change compared to courts. Notably, power and political interest, the two energies which commonly animate politics, may result in both citizens and political representatives, each through their own majoritarian devices, taking decisions which might be at risk of 'bias, self-interest, myopia'.[82] When it comes to the delicate matters dealt with by this book this danger is magnified: there might be little if any political interest in debunking family stereotypes and taboos unless they attract the support of a large constituency. I think that both left-wing and right-wing political parties in the Euro-American space have no special interest in protecting, say, non-conjugal couples. In the absence of massive social movements furthering their cause, they see no short-term benefit in doing that. Further, rejecting the spectre of polygamy/polyamory often finds bipartisan consensus due to the reduced social acceptance of these phenomena. A backlash might even come from progressive constituencies should the recognition of polyamory or polygamy be included in the party platform.

[76] Croce (n 52) 7.

[77] R Hirschl, 'The Judicialization of Politics' in RE Goodin (ed), *The Oxford Handbook of Political Science* (Oxford, Oxford University Press, 2011) 254.

[78] ibid 256.

[79] See ch 5.

[80] Article 21 of the Greek Constitution of 8 December 1974.

[81] Article L, 1 ch 'Foundations' of the Constitution of Hungary of 18 April 2011.

[82] A Kavanagh, 'Participation and Judicial Review: A Reply to Jeremy Waldron' (2003) 22 *Law and Philosophy* 451, 472.

By contrast, scholars have noted that courts, unlike political actors, have no interests of their own to pursue and are in principle above the fray of politics.[83] Their being above the fray of politics is surely open to debate, but it is undisputable that some features render courtrooms more inviting an environment than political avenues. The first is what Bickel called 'leisure' and insulation from political noise. Such insulation allows courts to conduct the highly intellectual task of balancing competing interests, assessing the long-term impact of government policies and systematising such policies into a coherent whole through the language of law. Related to this aspect is the 'ethics of principled decision making' that they are bound to follow.[84] In addition to a duty to offer reasons for their decisions is the prohibition of *non liquet* which is the duty to answer judicial questions and claims. There is no comparable duty for elected majorities. All things considered, this amounts to saying that carefully drafted legal arguments with a sound legal basis have a much higher likelihood of success compared to the most compelling policy-based arguments made before policy-makers.

Judicial strategies might also have a positive impact on political strategies. Since law-makers are not bound to act, they might often need some 'motivation' to do so. Legal precedents serve this function. Policy-makers interested in capitalising on their attachment to the rule of law and human rights might want to demonstrate that their action is consistent with what the courts say. This is why it seems sensible to obtain legal precedents before approaching law-makers: the more pertinent and generalisable such precedents are, the greater the leverage in political 'negotiations'.

Yet, focusing attention on courts also has its pitfalls. Chief amongst them is the inevitability of selective inclusion, that is, of adopting a narrowly tailored strategy that focuses on a subset of new family. It is not realistic – not under current legal doctrines in the Euro-American context – to ask courts for a brand-new recognition scheme that is optimal for the recognition of new families. For instance, it is not realistic to demand the introduction of a flexible registration scheme allowing more than two persons to register and assign different benefits to different beneficiaries (ie, to break up the notion of family into multiple functions). This is not a random example. In the next chapter, I will illustrate the recognition models that are more aligned to the adopted bifurcated theoretical framework. Amongst them is a thus-framed registration scheme. My contention is that there is no legal basis for arguing that such scheme must be introduced as a matter of law in courts, at least not in the jurisdictions examined in Part II.

What is problematic about selective inclusion is the dangerous effects it might yield on both included and excluded categories. As to the latter, critics of the approach argued that each time a social group is included, other groups are worse off to the extent that this process of inclusion entrenches their exclusion.[85]

[83] ibid.
[84] V Ferreres Comella, *Constitutional Courts and Democratic Values: A European Perspective* (New Haven, Yale University Press, 2009) 33.
[85] M Warner, *The Trouble with Normal: Sex, Politics, and the Ethics of Queer Life* (Cambridge, MA, Harvard University Press, 1999) 82.

In other words, the recognition of a subset of new family results in an authoritative condemnation of all those families which have not yet gained legal recognition. Same-sex couples' litigation powerfully attests to this. Marriage equality litigation staged arguments that singled out the acceptable, monogamous, stable same-sex couple by neatly separating it from all which did not adhere to that standard marital norm – an argument with which judicial courts were highly sympathetic. As a consequence, one could argue that focusing only on non-conjugal couples, as I set out to do in Part II, is detrimental to all other family grids.

This is a critical objection. While there is some truth to it, there is a pragmatic concern that I would like to stress. Debunking stereotypes associated with family is an uphill battle, one that is likely going to outlive me and many other researchers in the field. As a consequence, it seems not only useful but also indispensable to garner some useful legal precedent in courtrooms to 'motivate' policy-makers. However, in light of how judicial claims can be structured – an issue that I explore at length in Part II – a claimant is usually bound to focus on single signifiers (conjugality, cohabitation etc) to place them under more cogent scrutiny. This narrower focus – and only this narrower focus – allows new families to demonstrate how, on closer examination, distinctions based on that specific signifier do not pass muster.

A second string of arguments maintain that selective inclusion might also yield negative effects on members within the category. Litigation might require 'ideal litigants' to be successful. In the case of a non-conjugal couple, for instance, ideal litigants are two individuals who perform mutual caregiving work, cohabit and are in a long-term commitment that lends itself to be proven in court. This aspect, acting in tandem with legal decisions often being 'narrow' – and thus not amenable to generalisation – might actually advise against pursuing this tack. Yet, inclusion, no matter how selective, has the potential to change things 'from within', as Butler – and Marxist philosopher Antonio Gramsci before her – believed.[86] Juridified identities might be successful in changing widespread perceptions of categories through performance by appropriating and embodying them. Their performance has the potential to give rise to a 'sort of inverse colonization of the mainstream system'.[87] Far from entrenching the exclusion of non-normative subgroups within the included category, personal experience can thus demonstrate the elasticity of the category itself and affect the ways in which it is framed.

II. Why Focus on Non-Conjugal Couples?

'New family' is a composite category that encompasses realities as varied as families without a sexual component, conjugal families of more than two persons, nomadic families and so on. Each subset of 'new family' would deserve an analysis

[86] Butler (n 6).

[87] V Venditti, 'Exponential Rerritorialization: Reduce, Refuse, Reuse? An Exploration of the Territories of Inclusive Legal Norms and Gender Binary' in P Agha, *Law, Politics and the Gender Binary* (Abingdon, Routledge, 2018) 28–29.

of its own. Each group's social acceptance is distinctive. The public interests cutting against or in favour of legal recognition are also distinctive. Each single subgroup challenges in different ways the current dominant paradigm of family. It is worth recalling that this paradigm is the (arche)typical family: a nuclear, conjugal, dyadic, romantic, domestic, for-life relationship.

Non-conjugal couples in particular challenge the idea that the relationship should have a sexual element in order to be deserving of legal benefits. Family policy is replete with implicit or explicit references to sexual ties. However, conjugality in family relationships has not been sufficiently interrogated by policy-makers, as if the requirement that the parties must have sex to deserve state recognition were self-evident. This is what Fineman refers to when speaking of the 'sexual family'.[88] The inclusion of the modifier 'sexual' is deliberate. It aims to spotlight a feature that is taken as a natural prerequisite around which Western jurisdictions have built social and legal expectations towards 'family'. Especially salient is the link that this marker establishes between family and reproduction: the implicit ramification of taking sex as the hallmark of modern families is rendering them subservient to the reproductive imperative.

Lately, however, courts and academic lawyers have begun putting this requirement under pressure. Scholars have compellingly argued that a sexual relationship is not germane to achieving the objectives of the near-totality of family benefits.[89] Think of a survivor's pension: if we consider that its likely objective is the alleviation of the economic distress that flows from losing an economically interdependent partner, does it really makes a difference whether the parties had sex?

Multi-party relationships, by contrast, challenge the dyadic requirement. Polyamorous families specifically dispute the idea that only two persons can enter into a conjugal relationship. The dyadic requirement is also challenged by non-conjugal families made up of more than two individuals, such as neo-tribes and quasi-communes of friends. Here, the extension of family benefits is often opposed on the grounds that the applicable legal regime would be too difficult to administer and too costly. By contrast, when multi-party relationships include a sexual component, as with polygamous and polyamorous unions, the objections put forward are chiefly moral in nature. For instance, in continental Europe, this set of objections falls under the 'ordre public' exception, preventing non-dyadic relationships validly entered into abroad from gaining domestic recognition under private international law.

The different ways in which each type of new family engages with traditional signifiers attracts a distinct reaction on the part of the public authorities. In the face of novel phenomena, state reaction can range from repression, tolerance and indifference to recognition, protection and promotion. When it comes to multi-party sexual relationships, social acceptance is at its lowest, arguably second only

[88] M Fineman, *The Neutered Mother, The Sexual Family and Other Twentieth Century Tragedies* (New York, Routledge, 1995).

[89] eg, Cossman and Ryder (n 3).

to incest – in Levi-Strauss' words, a universal taboo across human societies.[90] As a consequence, the grip of the state on policing these families is tighter. The prohibition of polygamy through criminal provisions testifies to the extent to which the state finds such relationships socially repugnant. Interestingly, in May 2020, Utah – ie, the state in the US with the largest Mormon population – decriminalised polygamy among consenting adults by rendering it a mere administrative infraction. However, one should not be deceived and think that this is a stepping-stone to its full legalisation. Utah has entrenched its animosity towards polygamy in its Constitution, which contains a perpetuity clause whereby plural marriage is 'forever prohibited'.[91]

By contrast, non-conjugal families of friends or relatives pose a lesser threat to the social order. When it comes to non-conjugal families, the worst-case scenario is one of non-hostile indifference. It is hardly one of repression or 'tolerance', since they fall short of disrupting current notions of proper sexuality. Their lacking a sexual component is useful to the extent that it avoids the 'destabilizing risk of infidelity',[92] and the public disapproval that non-conventional sexual bonds have always attracted. Consequently, it has been noted that the path to non-conjugal families' recognition might be 'smoother'[93] even compared to same-sex couples, which, comparatively, aroused more vehement ideological resistance.

Hence, a first compelling reason for focusing on non-conjugal families is the lower social resistance they encounter. Not only do these families attract less resistance by the general public, but their performing caring activities makes them look quite good in the eyes of society. Care is recognised as an essential feature of a well-functioning society,[94] despite law often falling short of acknowledging and rewarding care work. Non-conjugal families perform essential caregiving functions, which society considers praiseworthy. Thus, the social acceptance of, say, a multi-generational family, where a grandparent and a grandchild look after each other and prioritise the welfare of the other, is much higher compared to the social acceptance of polyamorous and polygamous families.

The state has an obvious interest in promoting the formation of networks of care. The performance of caregiving functions avoids individuals becoming public charges; familiar bonds satisfy the dependency needs of the most vulnerable members within the family by making sure that they make it through illness, disabilities or run-of-the-mill blues.[95] States have an indisputable interest, which judicial courts themselves recognise, in incentivising families to form 'unions of care', characterised by mutual long-term commitment. I will explore this interest and its variations at length in this book.[96] The ability of non-conjugal families to

[90] C Levi-Strauss, *The Elementary Structures of Kinship* (Boston, MA, Beacon Press, 1969).
[91] Article III of the Utah Constitution of 5 November 1895.
[92] Scott and Scott (n 36) 71.
[93] ibid 71.
[94] S Levy, 'The Relational Self and the Right to Give Care' (2006) 28 *New Political Science* 547, 548.
[95] See Fineman (n 88).
[96] See chs 3, 4 and 5.

satisfy dependency needs surely works in favour of rethinking the proper object of state recognition and support to include them.

Compelling lines of argument for recognising non-conjugal families can be found in the mentioned body of literature 'ethics of care'. Jonathan Herring suggests shifting the law's focus from sexual bonds to (the broader notion of) caregiving relationships, arguing from Eekelaar's three 'primary functions' – adjustive, protective and supportive.[97] He argues that sex is not necessary for any of these functions to be effectuated. In similar terms, Maxine Eichner contends that the state should recognise all long-term care-taking relationships, regardless of whether they are conjugal, multi-party etc.[98] In her view, these relationships should not only be recognised but also actively promoted, for they satisfy dependency needs in ways that other relationships do not. An orderly legal framework, in which such families can develop, in turn promotes health and wellbeing, not to mention what she calls the 'dignity' of family members, which is the sense of legitimacy and acceptance flowing from state authoritative recognition.

A further reason to take non-conjugal families as a case study is that legal research on the issue will not be conducted in a *vacuum*, that is, in an empty space where everything must be contemplated 'from scratch'. By that assertion I mean that, albeit incidentally and insufficiently, non-conjugal families are already legally recognised in some jurisdictions. This gives their legal arguments greater traction. It conveys the idea that they are not advancing an exotic claim. By 'incidental', I refer to the instances where a subset of non-conjugal family (comprising relatives) is visible in law because it is able to shoehorn its situation into an existing legal category. Think of succession laws in states reserving a portion of an estate to so-called mandatory heirs. In this area, two committed relatives might often be incidentally protected under the tag, since historically blood ties are the benchmark used to allot the deceased's estate. Yet, if they were committed friends – another type of non-conjugal family –, the surviving partner would get nothing. Also, in another area where the marital family is the benchmark, the two interdependent relatives would be invisible in the eyes of the law. By contrast, by 'insufficient' recognition, I refer to that handful of jurisdictions which have introduced legal schemes open to non-conjugal couples. These regimes usually offer a pared-down array of benefits. Examples in the Euro-American context include Alberta, Vermont, Hawaii, Colorado, the Netherlands and Belgium.[99]

A potential downside to this methodological choice is, by contrast, the awareness that non-conjugal families are not visible in the political arena. There is no empirical evidence of non-conjugal couples advancing a need for legal recognition.[100] For instance, while a vivid debate on recognising cohabiting adult

[97] Herring (n 51) 190.

[98] M Eichner, 'Principles of the Law of Relationships among Adults' (2007) 41 *Family Law Quarterly* 433, 438–39.

[99] See ch 2.

[100] R Graycar and J Millbank, 'From Functional Family to Spinster Sisters: Australia's Distinctive Path to Relationship Recognition' (2007) 24 *Washington University Journal of Law & Policy* 121, 153.

relatives took place when discussing the passage of civil partnerships in the UK, the absence of interest groups representing them was noted. Thus, the issue arises as to whether non-conjugal coupledom is an academic fetish. Does it make sense to focus on a group which does not mobilise socially or politically?

I argue that it does. Without entering into the chicken and egg debate on whether law shapes society or vice versa, it is undisputable that law might affect the process of identity construction. The absence of political salience – compared, say, to polyamory[101] – can be even an advantage. States might be more reluctant in welcoming into the pantheon of families those which are openly subversive. This is not to say that non-conjugal families are not subversive, but only that they are not yet aware of this – and nor is society. Thus, a seeming absence of political salience, acting in tandem with the apolitical motivation to reward socially praiseworthy care work, might actually streamline their legal recognition.

As to the number of parties to the relationship, this book will only focus attention on non-conjugal relationships comprising two persons. Chief examples are two adult relatives or two adult friends who usually live together and are financially and emotionally interdependent, while not engaging in sexual intimacy. Although I will also use the terms 'pair' and 'relationship' interchangeably, I also intend to employ the term 'couple' to promote the 'inverse colonisation' and resignification of the conceptual category. The term usually attaches to sexual affiliations. However, I employ it to provide a tangible example of how categories can be fruitfully detached from their own genetic imaginary.

The reasons why I focus on the non-conjugal couple are many. First and foremost, multi-party relationships pose more complex regulatory challenges. Their recognition is easily opposed by means of logistic arguments pointing to the necessity to put in place new administrative processes, rules and forms that at present are tailored towards dyadic families. Logistical concerns presented in the context of same-sex couples' litigation were easily dismissed, for the system required no modifications; all that administrators were asked to do was to stop considering the parties' gender for the purposes of determining eligibility. Hadar Aviram and Gwendolyn Leachman neatly noted that after the US Supreme Court recognised same-sex marriages for the purposes of allocating federal benefits,[102] same-sex spouses gained the marriage-based immigration status 'the very next day'.[103] This 'overnight' extension of benefits would not be possible in the case of multi-party relationships and would likely require massive amendments to the current laws and regulations.

Most crucially, the extension of costly benefits is opposed based on financial considerations. Part II demonstrates that the scarcity of public resources and the need to protect public resources seem to be the veritable constant across

[101] But see E Wilkinson, 'What's Queer about Non-monogamy Now?' in M Barker and D Langdridge (eds), *Understanding Non-monogamies* (New York, Routledge, 2010) 243–54 (arguing that the group has apolitical motivations at its basis).

[102] *United States v Windsor*, 570 US 744, 133 S Ct 2675 (2013).

[103] H Aviram and GM Leachman, 'The Future of Polyamorous Marriage' (2015) 38 *Harvard Journal of Law and Gender* 269, 318.

Euro-American legal systems. Financial interests also oppose the recognition of non-conjugal families (the more families are recognised, the more public money is spent by the state). Yet they are less compelling compared to multi-party relationships (since increasing the number of adults recognised within a single family is most assuredly more money for the state). Hence, only when explicitly referring to 'non-conjugal families of more than two persons' or 'extended families' will I mean a non-conjugal family of more than two persons.[104]

Crucially, the chosen focus on non-conjugal families is part and parcel of a broader strategy which seeks to place under scrutiny all the traditional markers of family. Rethinking the current prioritisation of conjugal couples offers powerful theoretical instruments to critically assess the whole fabric of family law and its use of relational concepts. Think of the emphasis that the claims of non-conjugal couples place on functional forms of recognition, practice and actual features of relationships. Think too of the emphasis they place on the need to find a connection between such features and the objectives a family regime sets out to achieve. This is useful, handy material that can be used, if appropriate, to critically assess other traditional markers. Conjugality is only the first of the many aspects that require critical contemplation. In this sense, the aspiration of this book is to create an interconnected web of critical reflections building on each other rather than hermetically sealed compartments looking at signifiers in isolation. This is also to say that this work is the beginning of a personal broader reflection on what it means to 'do' family.

III. The Comparative Method and Family Law

Is family law an area that lends itself to legal comparisons? A negative answer would render the whole of this book groundless. Luckily, nowadays there is little opposition to the contention that family law is suitable for comparisons.

Historically, family law has been depicted as an exceptional domain of law that does not lend itself to comparisons. There were three main proffered rationales. The first was that family law, unlike the market, governs relationships that are intimate and vulnerable in nature. The second was that it is less amenable to the changes that modernity and globalisation impose.[105] According to this view, family law is an expression of traditions, local *mores* and national peculiarities.[106] Third, exceptionalism emanates from the sacred rather than secular origins of this area of law.[107] Consistent with this view, Arturo Carlo Jemolo used a popular

[104] See, eg, ch 3, s 4.

[105] J Halley and K Rittich, 'Critical Directions in Comparative Family Law' (2010) 58 *American Journal of Comparative Law* 753, 754.

[106] MV Lee Badgett, 'Predicting Partnership Rights: Applying the European Experience in the United States' (2005) 17 *Yale Journal of Law and Feminism* 71, 85.

[107] Halley and Rittich (n 105) 754. This conception of the family as belonging to an inner circle which is sacred was popularly upheld by Benjamin Constant; see B Constant, 'De la liberté des Anciens comparée à celle des Modernes' in *Collection complète des ouvrages*, vol IV, pt 7 (Paris, Béchet Libraire, 1820) 253.

metaphor before the Italian Constituent Assembly, according to which family law is an 'island' that the waves of law can only lap upon ('lambire').

Friedrich Carl von Savigny played a crucial role in strengthening an exceptionalism narrative. He famously theorised the market/family dichotomy, contrasting family law with patrimonial law (which he calls 'potentialities law').[108] Notably, he sketched out famous paired opposites seeing family law as the domain of status and contract as the domain of will, family law as universal in the sense that its fundamentality is recognised everywhere and contract law as particular in the sense that each contract differs from other contracts, and, ultimately, family law as particular/local, in that it is an expression of *volksgeist*, and contract law as universal since it *can* be the same across states.[109] The theoretical justification for a special status was considering the addressees of family law rules as incomplete human beings. By contrast, under patrimonial law, the very same person was seen as an independent agent able to exercise their will.[110]

In the second half of the nineteenth century came the era of Classical Legal Thought (CLS).[111] CLS was a composite school of thought that, informed by legal positivism, placed trust in legal science to protect individual freedoms and property rights. It privileged commercial law over other fields of legal practice.[112] This school of thought promoted an additional dualism: the core/periphery divide, with contract law at the core of the legal science and family law (at best) at its periphery (as many saw it as an object of analysis for sociologists rather than lawyers). Marella provides a fine account of how this divide within private law percolated into comparative law, as a result of the reflections of Rodolfo Sacco and Alan Watson.[113] In the field of comparative law, the core/periphery divide optimistically associates patrimonial law with legal transplants from one system to another that can occur without interference from political or social conditions. By contrast, family law does not lend itself to transplants, for family reforms can hardly be detached from their socio-political context and from local *mores*. Family law is best understood as a domain circulating in functional terms[114] and under better law approaches. However, functionalism is depicted in a bad light, since the drive behind legal borrowings is the achievement of stereotypes such as progress

[108] FK von Savigny, *System of the Modern Roman Law*, trans W Holloway (Madras, J Higginbotham, 1867).

[109] ibid 757.

[110] D Kennedy, 'Savigny's Family/Patrimony Distinction and its Place in the Global Genealogy of Classical Legal Thought' (2010) 58 *American Journal of Comparative Law* 811, 814.

[111] D Kennedy, 'Three Globalizations of Law and Legal Thought: 1850–2000' in DM Trubek and A Santos (eds), *The New Law and Economic Development: A Critical Appraisal* (Cambridge, Cambridge University Press, 2006) 19–20.

[112] See Table 1 in Kennedy (n 111) 21.

[113] MR Marella, 'Critical Family Law' (2011) 19 *American University Journal of Gender, Social Policy and the Law* 721, 724.

[114] E Örücü, 'Developing Comparative Law' in E Örücü and D Nelken (eds), *Comparative Law: A Handbook* (Portland, Hart Publishing, 2007) 43–65; R Michaels, 'The Functional Method of Comparative Law' in M Reimann and R Zimmermann (eds), *The Oxford Handbook Of Comparative Law* (Oxford, Oxford University Press, 2008) 369.

and modernisation.[115] According to this view, transplants are mere political propaganda: a foreign model is only appealing as long as it enables the government to claim discontinuity with the past and the achievement of an allegedly more modern system.

Recent developments cast serious doubt on the claim that family law is intrinsically particular and local. Recently, a convergence of family laws across countries can be seen. Starting from the 1990s, comparative law projects seeking to pursue the harmonisation and convergence of Western legal systems thrived.[116] Family governance and human rights law played a critical role in furthering the view that convergence is not only possible but also necessary across the globe.[117] A telling example was the endeavour of the Commission on European Family Law (CEFL) to harmonise family law regimes in EU Member States. In order to achieve its objectives, the Commission had to collapse the market/family dichotomy and replace it with a more 'optimistic' view that exporting optimal solutions from other countries is possible in the domain of family law.[118]

A second motive behind convergence is its being an implement of neoliberal economic agendas. These agendas spread throughout the world spurred on by international financial institutions.[119] The undoubtable interest these institutions have in relation to sex, reproduction and the family, which are seen as fundamental components of the global legal order, triggered a renowned interest in family law.[120] The ability of families to supply human beings through reproduction and influence the economy through consumption renders the family contiguous to the market and hence a privileged focus of global governance.[121]

Critical Legal Studies then sounded the death knell for exceptionalism narratives by offering compelling arguments to collapse the market/family dichotomy. A fine contribution comes from Kennedy, who has further exposed the contradictions in the aforementioned paired opposites. By way of illustration, he showed that widespread legal conceptions about individualism and the technicalities-based nature of contract law are not accurate.[122] While ancient wisdom had it that altruism is only relevant to family law, he argued that contract law is informed by the two conflicting paradigms of individualism and altruism.[123]

[115] Marella (n 113) 729.

[116] F Nicola, 'Family Law Exceptionalism in Comparative Law' (2010) 58 *American Journal of Comparative Law* 777, 804.

[117] J Halley et al, 'From the International to the Local in Feminist Legal Responses to Rape, Prostitution/Sex Work and Sex Trafficking: Four Studies in Contemporary Governance Feminism' (2006) 29 *Harvard Journal of Law and Gender* 335.

[118] But see HD Krause, 'Comparative Family Law: Past Traditions Battle Future Trends-and Vice Versa' in Reimann and Zimmermann (n 114) 1110 (arguing that such a dichotomy has not disappeared, but is only reproduced in non-Western countries).

[119] Marella (n 113) 745.

[120] Halley and Rittich (n 105) 755.

[121] Marella provides the example of the World Bank, in whose work the contiguity of the family with the market was especially evident: Marella (n 113) 746.

[122] D Kennedy, 'The Political Stakes in the "Merely Technical" Issues of Contract Law' (2001) 1 *European Review of Private Law* 7, 13.

[123] Marella (n 113) 733.

To conclude, nowadays there is no serious opposition to the contention that family law is an area that lends itself to comparisons. Family law exceptionalism has been dismantled by recent transnational projects aiming at harmonising family law regimes and, for good or ill, under the impulse of neoliberal and human rights agendas. A more fruitful exercise is thus to ask whether the legal systems under examination are comparable rather than whether family law per se is comparable.

As a premise, it should be submitted that the book does not aim at harmonisation or convergence of solutions. The analysis is intensely context-specific: the legal arguments outlined in each chapter are conducive to introducing the remedies that I consider to be more appropriate in a given jurisdiction – namely, the US, Canada, the system of the ECHR or the EU. The context-specific nature of the inquiry is also necessitated by the type of selected jurisdictions. A path dependence leading a Western-educated researcher to focus on like-minded legal systems might lurk behind the decision to focus on such legal systems. Yet, I intend to reduce the hegemonic bias underlying this methodological choice by confining the scope of the research to the countries under examination rather than supplying universally applicable truths for legal systems around the world.

Turning to the issue of whether these systems are comparable in practice, there is an ever-present danger in comparing civil law countries and common law countries.[124] Such risks are only partially reduced by a decision to compare two common law countries with the two meta-national systems in Europe – namely the ECHR system and the EU. The increased compatibility of these two meta-national systems with common law countries derives from at least two key features. First, the system of the ECHR and the EU use argumentative and decisional techniques which are more akin to those of a common law system, despite the majority of Member States/Contracting Parties adopting a civil law system. The way in which the European Court of Human Rights identifies the relevant precedents is a good instantiation of how the common law method has influenced its approach.[125] Likewise, Michel Rosenfeld noted how the Court of Justice of the European Union (CJEU) is 'increasingly functioning more like a common law court'.[126] In his view, the Court's grappling with broad, value-laden concepts (eg, dignity) or principles (eg, non-discrimination) attests to this shift.

Second, these two meta-national systems are not immune from the fascination that some common law concepts and theories seem to yield worldwide. The example I offer in this regard is particularly relevant to the analysis as it relates to how equality is conceptualised. The majority of continental European jurisdictions

[124] See eg S Ferreri, *Falsi amici nelle corti. Leggere le sentenze di Common Law evitando le trappole linguistiche* (Turin, Giappichelli, 2019).

[125] V Zagrebelsky, 'Corte cost. n. 49/2015, giurisprudenza della Corte europea dei diritti umani, art. 117 Cost., obblighi derivanti dalla ratifica della Convenzione' (2015) *Osservatorio dell' Associazione italiana dei costituzionalisti (AIC)* 3.

[126] M Rosenfeld, 'Constitutional Adjudication in Europe and the United States: Paradoxes and Contrasts' (2004) 2 *International Journal of Constitutional Law* 655.

adopt an 'equality approach'.[127] They feature equality provisions under which citizens (and sometimes non-citizens) shall be treated as equals before the law[128] or under the law[129] (plus a host of provisions furthering substantive equality). In short, this is a conception of equality as rationality meaning that, save when an adequate justification is put forward, like cases must be treated alike and different cases must be treated reasonably differently. According to this view, equality acts as a 'self-standing principle of general application'.[130] This conception is so deeply rooted in European continental systems that often, even when the constitution includes an anti-discrimination provision whereby discrimination is prohibited based on certain grounds (race, sex etc), the prevailing conception is still one pivoting on equality as a principle of general application.[131]

By contrast, the approach adopted in Canada and the US is one based on anti-discrimination. This is to say that the duty of the state is mainly that of shielding the individual from invidious discriminations which occur because the person has or is perceived to have certain characteristics – with the very limited exception in the US of the (ultra-deferential) rational basis review. Unlike many of their Member States, the ECHR system and the EU adopt an anti-discrimination approach based on the grounds of discrimination. This approach to equality seems to have resulted from an import of the anti-discrimination model in force in North America which has subsequently been adjusted to and integrated into the distinct socio-cultural context in Europe.[132]

Thus, sound reasons ground the conclusion that neither family law nor unsurmountable differences between the selected jurisdictions render a comparative endeavour 'groundless'. As such, this book sets out to adopt a comparative methodology. This will first allow us to identify the most compelling lines of arguments to mobilise in these four jurisdictions to make strides in the recognition of new families. Second, it will enable us to trace similarities and dissimilarities in the approaches to their legal recognition each jurisdiction takes. Ultimately, the comparative overview allows us to understand the potential doctrinal or institutional hindrances that should be overcome in each system to further the recognition of new families, and whether these are distinctive or common to other Western jurisdictions as well.

[127] The equality approach is in force in several civil law countries, such as Italy and Germany. See C McCrudden and S Prechal, 'The Concepts of Equality and Non-discrimination in Europe: A Practical Approach' (European Commission, Directorate-General for Employment, Social Affairs and Equal Opportunities, Unit G.2, November 2009) 15.

[128] Examples include Bulgaria, Estonia, Cyprus, Finland, Germany and Italy.

[129] Examples include Belgium.

[130] McCrudden and S Prechal (n 127) 15.

[131] See, eg, M Barberis, 'Eguaglianza, ragionevolezza e diritti' (2013) *Rivista di filosofia del diritto* 191, 193–94 (noting that, after a handful of initial decisions embracing an anti-discrimination approach based on a closed list of grounds for discrimination, the Italian Constitutional Court soon moved to adopt a broader equality approach).

[132] L Giacomelli, *Ripensare l'eguaglianza. Gli effetti collaterali della tutela antidiscriminatoria* (Turin, Giappichelli, 2018).

2

Recognition Models

Introduction

This chapter provides a primer on the recognition models available for new families. The analysis offers tools to identify which model is more conducive to facilitating rather than constraining multiple expressions of family. More specifically, I endeavour here to identify which model – amongst those which positive law or legal scholarship offers – is more in line with an integrated theoretical framework that combines the insights of queer theory with those of critical legal pluralism, as outlined in Chapter 1. Based on a thus-formulated framework, 'family' has been reframed as referring to a set of family functions that one performs in interactions to which one attaches special meaning and from which a range of interdependencies arise. This makes it possible to eschew the dangerous, value-laden task of understanding what 'the family' is. Family law, as a consequence, is to acknowledge this postmodern shift and facilitate the performance of family functions. The anti-prescriptivist stance of critical legal pluralism is especially useful in this regard. It illuminates how legal actors participate in normative processes by determining through their own motives the law's direction and intention[1] rather than being passive recipients of a legal framework imposed from above.[2] This theoretical clarification opens up spaces for the increased participation of legal actors in the crafting of their own legal-regulatory regime.

In addition to outlining the different recognition models, this chapter has a twofold rationale. First, it offers the required background knowledge to navigate the next part of the book. The focus in Part II is on strategic litigation. Notably, each chapter in Part II homes in on a specific jurisdiction (the US, Canada, the ECHR system and the EU). For each jurisdiction, there is a section describing the 'Remedy' that is being sought in the courtroom in light of the current jurisprudence of the jurisdiction in question. The background knowledge necessary to grapple with such sections is pieced together in this chapter.

A second, perhaps more obvious rationale is to illustrate the gamut of opportunities available to policy-makers to align family law with our bifurcated theoretical

[1] M Croce, *The Politics of Juridification* (Abingdon, Routledge, 2018) 4.

[2] RA Macdonald and T McMorrow, 'Wedding a Critical Legal Pluralism to the Laws of Close Adult Relationships' (2007) 1 *European Journal of Legal Studies* 319; L Nader, 'A User Theory of Law' (1984) 38 *Southwestern Law Journal* 951.

framework. In illustrating these opportunities, the chapter gathers material suitable to feeding sound policy-based arguments. Compared with legal strategies in Part II, this chapter has one key advantage: arguments before policy-makers are not encumbered by the constraints that claimants routinely face in courts. Not only are claimants usually forced to convert their claims into juridical terms – a conversion process which is common to policy arguments as well – but they also need to come to terms with existing jurisprudence and its likely trajectories. Additional constraints have been outlined in the influential book by Gerald Rosenberg, *The Hollow Hope*.[3] These include constitutional rights being limited in their number and scope, law-makers' ability to override judicial statutory interpretations and a weak – perhaps non-existent – enforcement mechanism in the event of law-makers' non-compliance.[4] In this sense, there is more room for manoeuvre when approaching policy-makers compared to judicial actors. However, at the same time, any argument before policy-makers, no matter how persuasive, can simply be ignored or discarded without proffering any reason. If one were to condense the distinction between legal arguments before courts and policy arguments before policy-makers into a few words, these would be, respectively, 'less room for action/more bite' and 'more room for action/less bite'.

Before proceeding any further, I shall provide a roadmap. This chapter is divided into two sections. Section 1, entitled 'Discarded Remedy', argues that marriage must be dismissed as a potential instrument to recognise new families. Some scholars in LGBTQ research are tempted to discern whether legal arguments support the introduction of plural marriage.[5] As a result, they take somewhat for granted that marriage is a suitable instrument to recognise non-dyadic unions. However, section 1 advises against pursuing this route in light of structural hallmarks of new families and some inherent characteristics of marriage.

Section 2 is entitled 'Potential Remedies' and lists the recognition models that are suitable to recognise new families. These are ascription, the contractual model, registration, and hybrid models displaying various combinations of the other three approaches. This section can help see whether currently available models are up to the task of offering legal protection to new families without this involving a dangerous normalisation of practices. The adopted theoretical framework suggests mitigating this danger by allowing new families to participate in the crafting of their own legal-regulatory regime. Which model allows legal actors to participate in this jurisgenerative process is the key issue that I address below.

[3] GN Rosenberg, *The Hollow Hope: Can Courts Bring about Social Change?*, 2nd edn (Chicago, University of Chicago Press, 2008).

[4] ibid 13–21.

[5] See, eg, RC Den Otter (ed), *Beyond Same-Sex Marriage: Perspectives on Marital Possibilities* (Lanham, MD, Lexington Books, 2016); E Grande and L Pes, Più cuori e una capanna: Il poliamore come istituzione (Turin, Giappichelli, 2018).

1. Discarded Remedy

I. Marriage

Marriage is not an appropriate instrument to protect new families. The reasons for this are essentially twofold. First, in the West, it is too rigid an instrument as far as its personal scope is concerned. Marriage is the regime in family law that is most value-laden, embedding as it does not only a certain vision of family, but, more generally, of society – whether socially conservative or progressive, anchored in tradition or egalitarian values etc. As such, it garners a great deal of social 'attention', often finding itself at the centre of 'culture wars'.[6] This is not to overlook the fact that marriage has been an important tool in past reforms in term of enhancing the status of equality-seekers; it is merely to argue that marriage has become a repository of social and moral values which render its eligibility requirements less amenable to social change compared to other family regimes. Expanding the eligibility requirements of marriage is a daunting task that requires massive amounts of energy and economic resources, without this constituting a guarantee that the desired result will be reached. Part II contains an in-depth legal analysis illuminating the extent to which marriage is unresponsive to social change. By way of illustration, the promotion of a 'traditional' understanding of marriage is a state interest that courts uphold as valid, despite some partial attempts at eroding it.

Crucially, even if a reform of eligibility requirements could be obtained, marriage is not the ideal solution. We still attend weddings, but the view of marriage as a lifelong institution has eroded dramatically. There is an increasing awareness that the institution is too tarnished by a history of exclusion, discrimination and internal asymmetry.[7] This is why marriage is becoming, so to speak, passé. Heterosexual couples themselves are moving away from the institution in some Western countries precisely for such a reason. The UK Supreme Court recognised this shift in its *Steinfeld* judgment. The decision criticised the legislature for restricting its civil partnership scheme to same-sex couples although some opposite-sex couples object to marriage as a discriminatory institution marked by a 'historically patriarchal nature'.[8] Thus, both the 'rigidity' of marriage and its legacy of internal discrimination seem to cut against pursuing the marriage route.

[6] R Bradley Kar, 'Transformational Marriage' in R Fretwell Wilson (ed), *The Contested Place of Religion in Family Life* (Cambridge, Cambridge University Press, 2018) 375.

[7] See, eg, T Metz, *Untying the Knot: Marriage, the State, and the Case for Their Divorce* (Princeton, Princeton University Press, 2010); SB Goldberg, 'Why Marriage?' in M Garrison and ES Scott (eds), *Marriage at the Crossroads: The Brave New World of Twenty-First Century Families* (Cambridge, Cambridge University Press, 2012) 233–34.

[8] *R (on the Application of Steinfeld and Keidan) v Secretary of State for International Development* [2018] UKSC 32.

The most salient characteristics of new families also advise against pursuing this route. New families are by definition 'postmodern' and more interested in a pure relationship model imbued with ideals of personal satisfaction and egalitarianism – ideals that are better served by non-marital regimes. For instance, the French sociologist Wilfried Rault argued that the Pacte civil de solidarieté (Pacs) in France may be the future for marriage.[9] Pacs is a contractual scheme (which at present also confers a status) that provides a pared-down set of rights and obligations to *pacsés* couples. In addition to gaining increasing popularity – according to the latest statistics, in 2018 there were over 208,000 Pacs and 228,300 marriages in France[10] – Pacs attracts couples with distinct social and demographic characteristics compared to marriage. Notably, it is especially attractive to couples, both heterosexual and homosexual, who are disenchanted with the marital ideal. *Pacsés* couples are often more fluid, less 'obsessed with' exclusivity, only interested in the material rather than symbolic benefits of recognition,[11] and prone to tilting towards the 'pure relationship' model rather than the nuclear family with children.[12] In other words, a crucial rationale for rejecting marriage as a suitable option is that new families themselves (when eligible to marry) are moving away from the institution. The cases of France and the UK attest to how they might be more interested in alternative flexible family regimes to marriage, such as civil partnerships or a contractual model.

In addition, marriage does not seem to be an actual option for new families. Take the case of non-conjugal couples. Even if the eligibility requirements were amended so as to include them within the scope of marriage law, which I hardly think will occur, one still would not want to marry one's sibling in order to obtain family benefits.[13] This union would conjure up wrong images, amongst them the sexual nature of the relationship. Again, regardless of whether the eligibility requirements are amended, marriage will continue to convey the wrong message, thereby discouraging new families from formalising their relationship. Clearly, this danger is inherent not only to marriage, but to all schemes that are patterned after marriage – so-called marital-like regimes. Italian civil unions are illustrative in this regard. They were introduced in reaction to the European Court of Human Rights' judgment in *Oliari*[14] and to considerable social pressure stemming from Italy being the only Western European country in 2016 without a legal regime available for same-sex couples. This led the Italian government to introduce civil

[9] W Rault, 'Is the Civil Solidarity Pact the Future of Marriage? The Several Meanings of the French Civil Union' (2019) 33 *International Journal of Law, Policy and the Family* 139.

[10] Data available on the Statista website at: www.statista.com/statistics/460219/civil-partenerships-france and https://www.statista.com/statistics/464239/total-number-marriages-france.

[11] Rault (n 9) 142–43.

[12] A Giddens, *The Transformation of Intimacy: Sexuality, Love and Eroticism in Modern Societies* (Cambridge, Polity Press, 1992) 93.

[13] C Williams, 'Nova Scotia Sisters Who've Lived Together 38 Years Want Survivor Benefits' *CBC News* (Toronto, 28 October 2016), https://www.cbc.ca/news/canada/nova-scotia/nova-scotia-sisters-living-together-benefits-pension-access-1.3826095.

[14] *Oliari and Others v Italy* [2015] 65 EHRR 26.

unions as an alternative to marriage, ie, as a regime only open to same-sex couples. Despite the scheme dropping classic conjugal requirements such as 'fidelity', the law clarifies that, as a general matter, marriage law, including references to spouses in social statutes, apply to civil unions.[15] I know two women, one of whom is a lesbian and the other of whom is a heterosexual widow, who in their seventies decided to move in together and support each other permanently. Yet, as a non-conjugal couple, they found themselves in a Catch-22 situation whereby, on the one hand, they aspired to legal recognition and, on the other hand, they refused to enter into a civil union for its numerous references to conjugality, something that did not match their situation.

Based on these premises, I will advance an argument that marriage should be discarded *ex ante*, without even entering the cohort of models amongst which the most appropriate model should be chosen for the recognition of new families. Instead, we should redirect our gaze towards other legal-regulatory regimes. These regimes are discussed below.

2. Potential Remedies

The potential remedies available for new families are ascription, the contractual model, registration and various combinations of the three.

I. Ascription

The first model of recognition is ascription. As the term suggests, with ascription, parties are *ascribed* legal consequences regardless of whether they 'like' it – hence the wordplay 'conscription'.[16] This is a functional model of recognition to the extent that parties do not take formal steps to be recognised: legal consequences attach to their situation if the parties 'function' similarly to formally recognised families and typically marital couples.

A case in point is the institution of common law marriage. A cohabiting couple meeting certain conditions such as durability and holding out as a married couple can qualify for a host of private and public law benefits. Yet, states in the US are now moving towards a gradual phasing-out of these marriages and the UK has launched a campaign against the 'myth' of common law marriage in order to warn couples that only limited protections are applicable to these informal unions. By contrast, ascription is commonly employed in Canadian common law provinces. In Canada, in principle, cohabiting conjugal couples need not marry in order to

[15] Article 1, para 20 of Legge 20 maggio 2016, fn 76, 'Regolamentazione delle unioni civili tra persone dello stesso sesso e disciplina delle convivenze'.

[16] M Garrison, 'Reviving Marriage: Could We? Should We?' (2008) 10 *Journal of Law and Family Studies* 279, 296.

gain most marital defaults. The European equivalent is called informal cohabitation, a type of union that does not necessarily attract legal recognition, likely due to the influence of the civil law tradition.[17] At present, however, a number of states in Europe attach legal consequences to informal cohabitation.[18] Hence, it would be misleading to argue that the civil law tradition has prevented the legal recognition of informal cohabitants.

The means of implementing this model are twofold: pure ascription, which occurs when attachment of legal consequences is independent of the request of any of the parties; and partial ascription, which occurs when recognition comes at a partner's request (and, commonly, against the will of the other partner). In the former case, it is the government that initiates a procedure conducive to the attachment of the legal consequences. An example of this is the reduction of financial aid for university students in the US whenever the government ascertains that the student's parents are in a marital-like relationship. This system of recognition may result in economic injustice. Its consequences are severe when ascription results in what Erez Aloni calls 'deprivative recognition',[19] ie, the government's termination of public benefits. Think of a US resident woman who lives in a house with another person and receives the Temporary Assistance for Needy Families (TANF) – a federal welfare programme that supports needy families with children. This woman is in a relationship which she does not wish to formalise, for instance because it is unstable or abusive. Should the administration conclude that she and her cohabiting adult male are in a marital-like relationship, it will terminate TANF benefits. This will have major economic consequences for the indigent woman.

Furthermore, Aloni noted that deprivative recognition does not result in the simultaneous recognition of the privileges flowing from recognition, such as tax credits enjoyed by spouses. Put simply, it is often the case that ascription is only unidirectional: it only goes in the direction where it results in a deprivation of benefits.

Partial ascription, by contrast, is initiated by at least one party. A classic example is a claim for maintenance that a party brings following the breakdown of an informal partnership in jurisdictions granting this possibility to informal cohabitants. In any such case, the court will inquire into the nature and attributes of the relationship to see if the couple functions similarly to a married couple. Hence, this version of ascription is somewhat less problematic: the attribution of rights or duties might 'surprise' only one party instead of both. Yet, it does place a

[17] The different legal tradition likely weighed against offering legal protections to de facto couples in Québec, unlike what occurs in Canadian common law provinces, where parties to a common law marriage receive most marital entitlements. See *Québec (Attorney General) v A* [2013] 1 SCR 61.

[18] Examples of cohabitation laws include those of Sweden, Norway, France, Slovenia, Croatia, Hungary, Serbia, Ukraine, Belgium, Scotland and some regions in Spain. See W Schrama, 'Marriage and Alternative Status Relationships in the Netherlands' in J Eekelaar and R George (eds), *Routledge Handbook of Family Law and Policy* (New York, Routledge, 2014) 22, fn 62.

[19] E Aloni, 'Deprivative Recognition' (2014) 61 *UCLA Law Review* 1276, 1313.

significant burden on the party who does not want to commit, thereby potentially infringing on the value of personal autonomy. Likewise, partial ascription might create a barrier to the creation of new supportive networks: 'It often triggers an intrusive inquiry into partners' lifestyles and sexual and emotional intimacy … [and] [i]t could require people to define their relationship before they otherwise would wish to do so, and then effectively lock the parties into that definition.'[20]

In both cases – pure and partial ascription – the aim is to correct relationship imbalances and protect the vulnerable party from exploitation. Parties might not have yet articulated their set of expectations, as they often merely drift into cohabitation.[21] Ascription should correct this problem. However, this mode of recognition raises serious questions around the extent to which it is legitimate to sacrifice personal autonomy and freedom in crafting the legal regime of intimate relationships. The burden – both financial and non-financial – placed on those who do not wish to commit might be serious: the model might have a chilling effect on couples that are not ready to articulate their expectations in legal terms.

More specifically, I have argued elsewhere that this model is not suitable to the recognition of new families for two reasons: first, 'the category of new family is too heterogeneous to expect the state to make a great effort in categorizing or according the appropriate benefits to all of them';[22] and, second, '[b]y articulating their desires and expectations, new families also avoid the risk of assimilating into a hegemonic norm, as with state categorization.'[23] In other words, when employing ascription, there is an ever-present danger of functional reductionism.

This danger has materialised in Alberta, the only jurisdiction amongst those examined which thus far has adopted an ascriptive model to recognise non-conjugal couples.[24] In Alberta, any two persons can be recognised as 'adult interdependent partners' upon meeting a set of conditions, amongst which is their being in an economically and emotionally interdependent relationship. However, in defining the content of this clause, the legislature and then the courts have assessed all partners against a metric which echoes the typical functional attributes of married couples (conjugality, exclusivity etc). As such, in addition to the concerns outlined above, when it comes to regulating new families, one should be alert to the fact that a functional model of recognition can hardly be disentangled from marriage and its typical attributes. The marital ideal is too deeply ingrained in the thinking of legislatures and courts to believe that functional recognition (requiring an articulation of 'standard' attributes of families) could work.

[20] N Palazzo, 'The Strange Pairing: Building Alliances between Queer Activists and Conservative Groups to Recognize New Families' (2018) 25 *Michigan Journal of Gender and Law* 161, 186.

[21] W Holland, 'Intimate Relationships in the New Millennium: The Assimilation of Marriage and Cohabitation?' (2000) 17 *Canadian Journal of Family Law* 114, 151–67.

[22] Palazzo (n 20) 181.

[23] ibid.

[24] Adult Interdependent Relationships Act, Statutes of Alberta 2002, c A-4.5 (AIRA), on which see ch 4, s 1.

II. The Contractual Model

Individuals in a relationship can obtain some of the legal benefits attaching to family status through contracts and wills. Through private contractual law, they can design a legal-regulatory regime similar to that of marriage and take on marital-like obligations such as mutual support. Clearly, such individuals cannot design a regime identical to marriage. They can only make choices that bear upon matters that are at the free disposition of the parties. These typically include property, financial aspects of cohabitation, tenancy rights and usufruct, and duties relating to the household or children. By contrast, amongst the legal benefits that are not at the free disposition of the parties are public benefits, whose eligibility requirements are determined by the government: one could not freely assign the survivor's pension to a person of choice. Contracts are irrelevant to the social law apparatus of the state where the family resides.[25]

Therefore, if a contractual model is adopted, it is advisable to amend the current laws to expand the list of family-related matters which can be regulated through contractual law. An illustrative example in this regard is the Dutch cohabitation agreement *samenlevingsovereenkomst*.[26] The agreement can be entered into by two or more than two persons before a notary. In addition to covering areas at the free disposition of the parties, the law provides that when the contract includes a reciprocal duty of support – which is taken as a signifier of strong commitment – the parties automatically qualify for social security and welfare benefits, and for a significant inheritance tax exemption threshold. The Dutch cohabitation agreement provides a useful example of how a contractual model can overcome the irrelevance of the contracts to the social law apparatus of a state.

The principal advantage of a contractual model is its flexibility. Marriage and registered partnerships usually come with a fixed bundle of rights, obligations and benefits. This model, by contrast, allows for greater flexibility in crafting the content of the applicable legal regime. The 'tailor-made' nature of such regimes has a potential to enhance personal autonomy by seeing family members as actively involved in the process of relationship regulation rather than as passive recipients of a standard set of rights and obligations. This is consistent with present-day normative conceptions of the family, as outlined in Chapter 1, and notably to the values of autonomy and self-authorship which have taken centre stage in Western legal systems. As the Law Commission of Canada also put it, the possibility to 'forge one's own contractual regime and negotiate the terms of one's commitment [is] a valued tool in a free society'.[27]

[25] R Leckey, 'Families in the Eyes of the Law: Contemporary Challenges and the Grip of the Past' (2009) 15 *IRPP Choices* 1, 12.

[26] See ch 5, s 1.I.

[27] Law Commission of Canada, *Beyond Conjugality: Recognizing and Supporting Close Personal Adult Relationships* (2001) 115.

However, this model also has its shortcomings. As I have previously noted, it:

> [W]orks best when parties participate on equal footing with each other in the drafting of the agreement, share a relatively similar knowledge, and have balanced bargaining powers. When this is not the case, it is right to be concerned about the vulnerability of the weaker party … Additionally, private contractual law is cumbersome because it requires that parties invest a substantial amount of time and effort in reaching an agreement. The cost of agreement includes both direct costs – the legal fees required to enter into the contract – and indirect costs – spending time, effort, and energy entering into a mutually beneficial contract. Contracting also generates emotional costs for the parties. First, parties must articulate their expectations for the relationship. This could lead parties to develop an adversarial mentality that might result in negative feelings surrounding the negotiations. Agreements also suffer from an optimism bias. Any illusions about the likely length of the relationship or their own capacity to resolve future controversies will undermine parties' ability to accurately articulate their expectations.[28]

Two additional shortcomings highlighted by the Law Commission of Canada are a lack of certainty and a lack of official record. In terms of the former, while it is not clear what exactly the Commission refers to, it likely points to both legal uncertainty for public administrations (since contracts create non-uniform legal regimes that might be difficult to administer) and parties themselves (as it is unrealistic that parties have the wherewithal to anticipate all issues potentially arising in the long term and articulate their expectations through contracts).

The second shortcoming refers to the lack of a publicly held record, which is necessary to ensure an 'efficient administration of laws and programs where relationships could be relevant'.[29] It is worth noting that this is not an 'inherent' characteristic of the model. Recent socially conservative bills in US states attempting to replace marriage licences with private contracts or affidavits attest to this. Bills proposed in Oklahoma,[30] Alabama[31] and Missouri[32] were aimed at dispensing with state-sponsored marriage by leaving in its place, respectively, common law marriage affidavits, civil contracts and civil unions. While these bills are problematic from a liberal perspective in terms of their essentially seeking to prevent same-sex couples from marrying, the case of Alabama demonstrates that it is possible to institute a publicly held record whereby contracts are registered without additional administrative costs.

[28] Palazzo (n 20) 178–79. See also H Reece, 'Leaping without Looking' in R Leckey (ed), *After Legal Equality: Family, Sex, Kinship* (Abingdon, Routledge, 2015) 119.

[29] Law Commission of Canada (n 27) 114.

[30] HB 1125, 2015 Sess (Okla 2015), https://legiscan.com/OK/text/HB1125/2015.

[31] Section 13, 2018 Sess (Ala 2018), https://legiscan.com/AL/bill/SB13/2018; see also S.B. 20, 2017 Sess (Ala 2017), https://legiscan.com/AL/bill/SB20/2017 for the previous version of the bill.

[32] HB 1434, 2018 Sess (Mo 2018), https://legiscan.com/MO/bill/HB1434/2018; see also HB 62, 2017 Sess (Mo 2017), https://legiscan.com/MO/text/HB62/2017 for the first version of the bill.

III. Registration

Registration is a formal mechanism of recognition. By registering, parties gain a bundle of rights, obligations and benefits attendant to the scheme. Examples include civil partnerships, domestic partnerships, civil unions and designated or reciprocal beneficiary schemes.

Registration schemes run the gamut from schemes that are a functional equivalent to marriage (specifically created for same-sex couples) to registered partnerships which are an alternative to marriage and are open to both same-sex and opposite-sex partners. The former model is prevalent in Scandinavian countries, while the latter model is prevalent in Western Europe. Further, they might vary significantly in terms of their material scope. Regardless of the label used, registration schemes might provide nearly the same benefits as marriage or a pared-down list of benefits.[33] Civil unions tend to be an example of the former and are often referred to as marriage by another name, while French Pacs and reciprocal beneficiary schemes in Hawaii and Vermont are examples of the latter, with Vermont being the most extreme case as it only conferred health-related prerogatives – I use the past tense as the scheme was repealed in 2013.[34]

The advantages of registration are multiple. It saves time compared to a contractual model for it comes with an array of benefits packaged together 'by default'. A second advantage stems from registration being a formal mechanism of recognition, like the contractual model. In requiring parties to take affirmative steps to commit to each other, registration prizes the value of personal autonomy far more than a functional model of recognition which ascribes legal consequences regardless of the parties' will (ascription).

Yet, unlike a contractual model, registration displays less flexibility and more limited opportunities for families to craft their own legal-regulatory regime. Registration schemes usually come with a bundle of rights and fewer opportunities for parties to opt out of legal consequences that they do not wish to take on or opt into those they wish to include. However, a reply to this critique would acknowledge that a lack of flexibility is not inherent to the registration model. I argue that there are two forms of registration:

(i) registration by default, where a fixed set of benefits attach to the regime;
(ii) registration by design, where parties have a say in designating the beneficiary of their benefits and/or the type of benefits to confer.[35]

The former is the most common form of registration. Civil partnerships, civil unions and reciprocal beneficiary schemes all fall into the category, for registration

[33] E Aloni, 'Registering Relationships' (2013) 87 *Tulane Law Review* 573, 591–94.

[34] 15 Vt Stat Ann § 1301(b) (Westlaw, repealed 2013, Adj Sess No 164).

[35] Palazzo (n 20) 188. The chosen terminology conjures up the privacy-by-default/privacy-by-design dichotomy, coined by the Canadian Privacy Commissioner of Ontario in the 1990s, yet not the legal meaning acquired by these terms in the field of privacy.

comes with a 'legislatively established framework of rights and obligations that the parties to a relationship can take on'.[36]

More interesting for the purposes of this analysis is what I call registration by design. This variation is meant to respond to critiques rightly stressing that registration by default is too rigid. Registration by design parts from registration by default to the extent that it allows for parties' self-designation in some relevant aspects of their relationship recognition regime. Registration by design at its finest allows a party to freely choose the beneficiary or beneficiaries upon whom they want to confer benefits. Each benefit need not be conferred upon the same beneficiary.[37] Further, registered parties can choose which benefits to include and which to withhold. Hence, under a registration by design scheme, not only can parties customise the bundle of benefits that attach to the regime, but they can also customise the geography of intimacy, with different family functions being performed with different persons – and also, where applicable, at different times.

This system of recognition is especially useful to the cause of new families. It helps make more evident that people can perform multiple caregiving and other family functions over time. One of the seminal scholarly contributions regarding this aspect is Laura Rosenbury's article 'Friends with Benefits'.[38] Rosenbury argues that family law should introduce a mechanism whereby a person assigns some of the benefits traditionally attendant to marriage to individuals of their choice. In her view, one could decide that one's survivor's pension be assigned to a sibling, that family leave be shared with a grandmother and that hospital visitation rights be granted to a close friend.[39] Further, she requires that the distribution of the benefit(s) be done on a mutual basis in order to avoid those receiving caregiving benefits from simultaneously having to take on responsibilities.[40] Likewise, Erez Aloni has devised a registration by design scheme labelled 'registered contractual relationships' (RCRs).[41] In his view, future information technology will render multiple legal designations possible by increasing the government's ability to cross-check large amounts of data, including who has been designated and for what purpose (on the assumption that designating different persons for different functions will be possible).

I support Rosenbury's and Aloni's schemes as suitable to the recognition of new families. They are especially well suited to recognising family constellations of growing intricacy, which at present cannot find legal regimes able to mirror their complex design. Besides offering a better approximation of the complexity of these networks, in light of the dynamic interplay between legal categories and social facts, registration by design can also positively impact families' self-perception and

[36] Leckey (n 25) 12.
[37] Palazzo (n 20) 190.
[38] LA Rosenbury, 'Friends with Benefits' (2007) 106 *Michigan Law Review* 189, 231.
[39] ibid 230–31.
[40] ibid 232.
[41] Aloni (n 33) 608.

capability to arrange intimacy by providing them with more malleable concepts to frame their relationships.[42]

However, at present, some key questions are left unanswered. A workable proposal would need to address at least the following: 'How could someone designate different beneficiaries for different benefits? How could the government check which person has been designated as the beneficiary of a specific benefit? Should parties still be allowed to have multiple beneficiaries for the same benefit; if so, to what extent?'[43] Also, should there be a distinction between costly and non-costly programmes when deciding which programmes should be available for multiple designations?

The last example I should like to offer is a sophisticated recognition model named cont(r)actualisation, a system which addresses some of the previously raised questions. The model has been designed by Frederik Swennen and Mariano Croce as a way to eschew the entrenchment of the sexual family stemming from new families seeking legal recognition through existing legal labels.[44] The aim of their proposal is thus to dismiss other statuses (married, registered etc) and create an all-encompassing status that 'expands the symbol of family' by preliminarily enlarging the notion.[45] The grounding characteristic of their proposal is its disaggregating the 'monolithic' conception of family into modular components on the assumption that you can be family in your interactions. Hence, there is no such thing as an essence when it comes to family; there are merely familiar acts and performances to which law should turn its attention.

A first set of modules regards personal rights and obligations, and would comprise cohabitation, moral assistance and fidelity. A second set of modules broadly relates to economic interdependence and includes property, inheritance rights, division of labour relating to the rearing of children or the maintenance of the common household. While 'modules' already exist – with some jurisdictions allowing the ability to opt out of some of them but not others and in general limited opting in – what needs to be conveyed is the idea that one can perform different functions with different persons or just one function and still be deserving of the label 'family':

> The cont(r)actual model we are advocating would allow adults to divisibly and inclusively assemble modules themselves … When applied, for instance, to a polyamorous setting, it would imply that the same modules can simultaneously apply to more than one dyadic union and/or to a union comprising more than two parties or that all modules apply to amorous partners, and only some to metamorous partners … as in a *consortium partis vitae*. Dependent on the applicable modules, other branches of law or policy could also tie in.[46]

[42] F Swennen and M Croce, 'Family (Law) Assemblages: New Modes of Being (Legal)' (2017) 44 *Journal of Law and Society* 532, 548.

[43] Palazzo (n 20) 191.

[44] F Swennen and M Croce, 'Cont(r)actualisation: A Politics of Transformative Legal Recognition of Adult Unions' (2020) *Social and Legal Studies* 7 (forthcoming).

[45] ibid 13.

[46] ibid 14.

More tangibly, they recommend offering a template which contains a list of modules. This is obviously aimed at preventing critiques to the effect that ordinary persons might not be acquainted with modules. Asking persons to craft their own legal regime might in fact be time-consuming and impractical. In addition to the template, the two authors propose an opt-out system whereby all modules apply by default to registered parties and a possibility to opt out of single modules is simultaneously conferred. The sole exception to this robust opting-out system concerns maintenance obligations and a proportional contribution to common expenses. They call this the 'one, imperative, basic module'.[47] This exception aims to respond to concerns that unions should have a minimum degree of stability.

A less radical (as it were) version of registration by design would only allow parties to decide which benefits should be assigned to another person, without there being a possibility to choose multiple beneficiaries. A similar middle-ground option thus allows the parties to a relationship to customise the content of their legal regime. This version was implemented in the Designated Beneficiary Act (DBA) in Colorado.[48] The scheme does not allow the designation of multiple beneficiaries. Yet, it does permit any two persons to register and tailor the content of the regime by choosing which benefits to assign to the other beneficiary. This is precisely why it is called a 'designated' beneficiary scheme, unlike reciprocal beneficiary schemes that only offer a definite set of rights. Any two adults of sound mind (ie, who are legally competent to enter into a contract)[49] can become designated beneficiaries by filling out a single form that does not require the assistance of an attorney. On such a form, they 'check' the boxes next to the benefits they wish to assign.[50] Interestingly, unlike 'lighter' reciprocal beneficiary schemes in Hawaii and Vermont, the scheme in Colorado offers a larger set of benefits in relation to both private law and public law. These benefits range from health-related prerogatives to workers' compensation benefits, and from wrongful death compensation to health coverage for public employees.[51]

Thus, on the one hand, the scheme displays some important advantages, amongst which is the expansion of the notion of family to 'any' two persons, a wide package of benefits (including some public law benefits) and a possibility to customise the material scope of the regime. Yet, as shown above, the limit if you will of the DBA is the necessity of designating only one person.

IV. Hybrid Models

Some relationship recognition schemes are hybrid to the extent that they merge two general models into a new hybrid one.

[47] ibid 15.
[48] Colo Rev Stat § 15-22-105 (Westlaw 2d Reg Sess of 71st Gen Assemb).
[49] Palazzo (n 20) 201. See Colo Rev Stat Ann § 15-22-105(1).
[50] Palazzo (n 20) 202.
[51] ibid 203 and the accompanying text to fn 221.

A first example is a mix of registration and ascription. It was outlined in the influential book *Beyond (Straight and Gay) Marriage* by Nancy Polikoff and at present has not been implemented in the US.[52] According to her proposal, someone without a spouse or domestic partner should be given an opportunity to register and indicate a 'designated family member' to be the recipient of some family benefits. Based on her approach, called the 'valuing all families' approach, anyone should be entitled to assign such benefits to someone who is a dear friend, a relative, or a partner outside of marriage or a civil partnership.

In terms of what these family benefits are, Polikoff's registration scheme would not confer the whole panoply of marital benefits. She has in mind a 'light' scheme, packaging together only health-related prerogatives, abuse prevention and inheritance rights as if the person involved in the scheme were a spouse.[53] However, if a person dies without having designated a family member, an ascriptive system should apply to confer inheritance rights; in any such case, the government should investigate which beneficiary the person would have chosen had they foreseen the possibility of doing so.[54]

A second way through which ascription may correct the injustice associated with having not designated a beneficiary concerns wrongful death statutes. Polikoff argues that these statutes should compensate 'actual' dependants of the deceased worker rather than presumptive dependents such as spouses or civil partners. As a consequence, all who were dependent on the deceased worker should in principle be entitled to show dependency in courts and obtain compensation. Therefore, under her proposal, registration is complemented by transformative redistribution through ascription in order to correct unfair outcomes caused by a lack of self-designation through registration.

The system that gets somewhat closer to the one proposed by Polikoff is in force in Spanish territories such as Catalonia, Navarre and Aragon. These jurisdictions recognise informal cohabitation through a double-track system that requires either registration or the fulfilment of certain criteria (hence through ascription). For instance, in Catalonia, Article 234-1 of the Civil Code states that two persons who cohabit in a marital-like manner qualify as 'stable couples' if they cohabit continuously for more than two years, have a child or formalise the union through a notarial deed. A decree law in 2015 amended the applicable law on stable couples to create the Registry of stable couples, which is now a further avenue for recognition.[55] However, these Spanish systems, differ from Polikoff's proposal in their reference to the typical conjugal or marital-like couple. Further, while Polikoff sees ascription as necessary to correcting unjust outcomes caused by

[52] ND Polikoff, *Beyond (Straight and Gay) Marriage: Valuing All Families under The Law* (Boston, Beacon Press, 2009).

[53] ibid 134–35.

[54] ibid 135–36.

[55] Decreto-legge 24 gennaio 2015, n 3 recante modifiche alla legge 27 febbraio 2010, n 25.

a lack of registration, the Spanish territories see the two recognition mechanisms as parallel and alternative routes.

A second example of a hybrid model is a mix of a contractual and ascriptive model. This is best typified by the Alberta's Adult Interdependent Relationships Act (AIRA). In the Province of Alberta any two persons can become Adult Interdependent Partners (AIPs). The first way to become an AIP is by signing a written agreement (the contractual model), while the second is ascription.

Legal status is ascribed to two persons who have lived in a three year-long interdependent relationship or are in a relationship 'of some permanence' with children. In order to become AIPs, there must be a 'relationship of interdependence'. Under the law, for two parties to show interdependence, they must: '(i) share one another's lives, (ii) [be] emotionally committed to one another, and (iii) function as an economic and domestic unit'.[56] The latter condition is the most complex to ascertain. The condition has proven problematic in many respects, amongst which is the decision of the legislature to adopt the typical signifiers of marriage to detect when AIPs function as an economic and domestic unit. These signifiers include conjugality, exclusivity, their holding out as an economic and domestic unit (a condition borrowed from the semantics of common law marriage, where parties should hold out as a 'couple'), eating together etc.[57]

Persons related to each other by blood or adoption are not eligible for ascription; the only way for relatives to become AIPs is by signing an agreement. By contrast – and contrary to the recommendations of consulted experts – close friends and roommates meeting the eligibility criteria can have their status ascribed.[58] However, and interestingly, in the intention of the minister introducing the bill, 'non-conjugal' was synonymous with 'platonic' – ie, it was meant to mark out relationships with a romantic component that were not sexual.[59]

The debates surrounding the decision to carve out this exception for relatives demonstrate what seems to be the chief downside of ascription: its curbing of personal autonomy. Furthermore, the case of Alberta, with its repeated references to marriage-like requirements, typifies previously raised concerns that an ascriptive system might prove not only difficult to apply to new families, but also detrimental to them. Legislatures and courts can hardly do without typical markers of family when thinking about what are the standard functional attributes of families.

[56] AIRA, § 1(1)(f).
[57] ibid § 1(2).
[58] A Nijhawan, 'Alberta's New Adult Interdependent Relationships Act' (2003) 22 *Estates, Trusts and Pensions Journal* 157, 171.
[59] Alberta Hansard, Legislative Assembly of Alberta (col 1371, 19 November 2002) (arguing that only some 'special platonic relationships where [parties] clearly consider themselves to be a couple' would have the status ascribed).

Conclusion: A Better Model?

Registration by design is the abstract model that moves closer to the proposed theoretical framework. It injects self-created normativity into matters that have long been covered by the state's monopoly over family law. Under this model, self-produced normativity can give shape to both the geography of intimate connections (what these should be, what they should look like, how they should be distributed in time and space etc) and the content of the legal-regulatory regime governing these relationships.

The currently available contractual models also offer an increased opportunity for parties to participate in normative processes and create their own legal regime. However, they also present shortcomings unlike registration, the contractual model is more time-consuming, contingent on balanced bargaining powers and charged with the emotional costs that might result from negotiations. The model also requires knowledge of one's legal rights and an ability to assert them, unlike most registration schemes, which come with a default set of benefits or, in the case of suitable registration by design schemes, a template that can guide the normative activity of the parties. Furthermore, none of the currently available contractual models tackles head on the problem of the monolithic nature of the family and family functions. Of course, I can enter into a contract with A to do x and with B to do y, but these contracts will hardly have a bearing on conceptions of family unless this multiplicity is allowed within a uniform, single contractual regime (as the agreement the parties can enter in Alberta or in the Netherlands).

Registration by design is also preferable because it exposes how illusory and misleading the idea is that there is an 'essence' when it comes to family. When the model is put to work, there is no a priori requirement which can shed light on the actual meaning of family; one can merely choose which functions to perform and with whom to perform them. The resulting image of a non-essentialised, 'work-in-progress' family resembles notions that are free-floating from any normative anchor. What registration by design rightly does is thus the natural outgrowth of critical legal studies and queer theory: if family is not something which 'is' but rather something we do, then it becomes sensible to mark off different functions instead of 'ontological' characteristics.

Despite this, I have long been persuaded that there were no suitable registration by design schemes available. Many questions were left unanswered, with scholars tracing the right direction while at the same time stopping short of offering workable solutions – an example being Aloni and his acknowledgement that, at present, states lack the information technology required to permit multiple legal designations.[60] This aspect has persuaded me that a handy proposal to start upholding the idea that families should be creators rather than recipients of their relationship-recognition regime is the Colorado scheme (the DBA).

[60] Aloni (n 33) 608–09.

Again, this proposal has the benefit of being workable to the extent that it already exists and is actually 'working'. A second positive aspect is its contributing to a disaggregation of the monolithic conception of family. Through the scheme, one can include some benefits while excluding others. This prerogative conveys the message that there are no a priori functions that families should perform in order to merit the label. A further advantage of the DBA is its inclusion of public law benefits within its scope. This is a major advance, for a comparative overview of regimes open to new families shows that they often include only private law aspects, such as property, maintenance and division of labour within the household, plus healthcare prerogatives.[61] Public law benefits are – unsurprisingly – left outside the remit of most schemes open to new families because they are costly.

However, the Colorado law also has its pitfalls. One could legitimately wonder whether a scheme that only allows for self-produced normativity as regards the content yet not the parties to the relationship actually challenges a traditional conception of family. In the end, what designated beneficiaries can do is merely to choose which benefits to confer upon the other party and which to withhold. While there is some truth to this anticipated objection, I argue that the combination of a possibility to customise the legal regime plus the loose eligibility requirements under which any two persons can enter the scheme are a potent starting point to challenge the state-sponsored conception of family. Yet, they are merely a starting point.

In this sense, I find it imperative to work on a workable full-fledged registration by design mechanism that allows both multiple designations and a customisation of the legal regime (and not only the latter, as the DBA does). Swennen and Croce's proposal goes in the right direction. Unlike the DBA, it includes both dimensions. Importantly, instead of merely 'extending the protective function of family law to new assemblages', their proposal works at the level of symbolic signifiers to expand 'the symbol of family'.[62] Thereby, they challenge current monolithic conceptions of family in ways that other models do not – think of a pure contractual model. Further, unlike other registration by design schemes, they address some of the practical concerns raised above. It is especially useful the suggestion to create a template containing a list of modules and to provide for a robust opt-out system. Yet, the proposal does not specify how other branches of law (especially public law) could tie in. This omission is likely intentional to the extent that their work is premised on an awareness that the whole fabric of public law subsidies needs rethinking. States nowadays deploy the family to address a variety of social issues through public policy responses. Therefore, further analysis on this point is needed in the future.[63] In a polyamorous setting, does this proposal entail that each partner could become eligible to receiving a survivor's pension? This would

[61] Palazzo (n 20).
[62] Swennen and Croce (n 44) 13.
[63] Macdonald and McMorrow (n 2).

raise handy objections regarding the costly nature of the proposal. Or is perhaps the same amount of survivor's pension being distributed to surviving partners, with each partner thus getting a lower share?[64] These are pressing questions that need to be tackled in order for a registration by design scheme not to be subject to criticism.

However, I have little doubt that registration by design is the best way forward. It is the model that more intensely prizes personal autonomy while also offering the practical advantages of registration, amongst which is an increased possibility to know what one's legal regime might look like (without a necessity to be acquainted with legal hassles) and then to opt into preferred modules and out of aspects that one does not wish to include.

Most crucially, registration by design embeds a radical critique to current conceptions of family. In disaggregating family law into modules – ie, functions – and in devising a system that is multi-personal, intertemporal, and pluri-functional, it aligns with queer tenets and its related normative underpinnings, amongst which self-authorship is paramount. The increased possibility for law users to participate in moulding both the personal and material scope of the regime likewise comports with the key insights of critical legal pluralism, amongst which is a rejection of centralism, monism and prescriptivism. Ultimately, with its explicit and head-on rejection of a quest for 'the family', registration by design is the recognition model which presents the most radical, sweeping and robust critique of the state-sponsored family.

[64] This occurs, for instance, in Victoria when a deceased partner is survived by multiple partnership (eg a spouse and an unregistered domestic partner). See the website of the Victorian Law Reform Commission, 'Entitlements of the deceased person's partner or partners: Current law in Victoria', available at http://www.lawreform.vic.gov.au/content/current-law-victoria-0.

PART II

Non-Conjugal Families before the Courts

3

The United States

Introduction

The United States ('US') is a fascinating comparison. The municipalities and states it comprises have always been a site of social experimentation. Social innovation processes have also involved family law. To provide but two examples, innovative registration schemes open to relatives and friends have been enacted in some states, and, in July 2020, a municipality in Massachusetts recognised polyamory in its domestic partnership law.[1]

Likewise, academic settings in the US are particularly sensitive to the topic of new family recognition. The problem, framed in terms of – so to speak – 'marital privilege', has received a surprising amount of attention.[2] US scholarship has exposed the harms current legal systems inflict upon non-marital families. However, the issue of how to effectively align the legal framework with the landscape of modern families requires further attention. The literature outlining legal arguments to recognise new families other than same-sex couples in courts is scant.[3] This chapter fills this gap by crafting sophisticated arguments which support the recognition of a subset of new families: non-conjugal relationships.

The analysis engages with both constitutional litigation and family law litigation. The main takeaway is that constitutional litigation is not a promising avenue for non-conjugal family recognition. Current doctrinal developments counsel avoidance of this type of litigation, despite some legal precedents working to the advantage of such families. By contrast, family law courts seem to be a more receptive place for claims brought by non-conjugal families. More specifically, section 2 describes the two venues. Section 3 proceeds to expound the 'remedy' which, in light of the state-of-the-art jurisprudence, can be sought in the court. Section 4 then analyses the legal arguments which could be mobilised to expand the reach of family law to encompass non-conjugal families.

[1] E Barry, 'A Massachusetts City Decides to Recognise Polyamorous Relationships' *New York Times* (New York, 1 July 2020), https://www.nytimes.com/2020/07/01/us/somerville-polyamorous-domestic-partnership.html.

[2] See esp s 5 below.

[3] An article in which compelling constitutional arguments that could support the legal recognition of polyamorous relationships are crafted is H Aviram and GM Leachman, 'The Future of Polyamorous Marriage' (2015) 38 *Harvard Journal of Law and Gender* 269.

Before delving into the issue of which lines of argument are more suitable here, the chapter offers a primer on the recent evolutions in family structures and norms that the US is experiencing. The aim of this primer is to buttress arguments to the effect that family laws should be updated so as to align with such norms and structures.

1. The Changed Landscape of Family Structures and Family Law in the US

What does 'family' mean in the US? There is no single answer to this question, either empirically or legally.

Notions of 'family' are evolving at a fast pace in the country. Yet, the US government continues to see marriage as the fundamental family unit in society. Much to the dismay of many, marriage is the principal basis on which family benefits are allocated.[4] Clearly, the policy choice of privileging marital families over other familiar units is not unique to the US. However, there are country-specific reasons casting doubt on its soundness. This policy is based on shaky grounds if one considers the radical changes that family arrangements have undergone in the last few decades. The first trend is the proliferation of new family forms, including units eligible to marry, which – either consciously or unconsciously – are moving away from the marital model. The second trend is the 'crisis' that marriage as an institution is experiencing. A third trend concerns an aspect bearing on the marriage crisis: the introduction of non-marital regimes such as domestic partnerships or reciprocal beneficiary schemes. I shall briefly analyse each development in turn.

A first remarkable trend under way is the flourishing of diverse family arrangements. These include, but are not limited to, interdependent siblings, friends, relatives, unmarried conjugal couples, polyamorous relationships and various queer assemblies. More generally – and consistent with the definition of 'family' provided in Chapter 1 – the list includes all unions that we perceive as familiar in which parties are economically and emotionally interdependent, while not sharing the traditional hallmarks of the marital family.

The choice not to marry is becoming quite popular.[5] A few data sources can help us to understand the extent to which marriage is becoming less appealing as a form of intimate connection. In 2017, only 50 per cent of the US population above the age of 18 was married, compared to 58 per cent in 1990 and 72 per cent in 1960.[6] The number of children living in the marital family is also declining at

[4] See s 5.II below.

[5] US Census Bureau, *Historical Living Arrangements of Adults* (November 2019), www.census.gov/data/tables/time-series/demo/families/adults.html.

[6] Pew Research Center, 'As U.S. Marriage Rate Hovers at 50%, Education Gap in Marital Status Widens' (14 September 2017), www.pewresearch.org/fact-tank/2017/09/14/as-u-s-marriage-rate-hovers-at-50-education-gap-in-marital-status-widens.

the same pace as the number of children living with cohabiting partners or single parents is increasing.[7]

By contrast, a subset of non-conjugal families, multi-generational families, is markedly on the rise. In 2016, according to the Pew Research Center, '20% of the US population lived with multiple generations under one roof'.[8] The most common form of multi-generational family comprises two adult generations. This type of union is best typified by families with parents and their adult children (aged 25 and older), so-called 'boomerangs'. Other widespread forms of multi-generational family include three-generation and four-generation families.[9]

But, again, the most salient statistics are those we have not yet conceived of. Many contemporary family forms slip under the radar of census data because they are not yet seen as 'family'. Think about polyamorous relationships. There is no available data on these networks, despite socio-legal scholarship fabling about lively communities across the US (especially in the San Francisco Bay area and the State of California).[10] This is to say that census data only capture a tiny portion of this complex reality.

As might be expected, changes in family patterns are labelled as a 'breakdown' of the family. This label is manipulative in the sense that it purports to put a black mark on these developments and a scarlet letter on members of new families. However, empirical evidence shows that there is no longer any such thing as a dominant family structure in the US. Not only has family diversity skyrocketed, but so too has fluidity, with this trend translating in many people divorcing, remarrying, recoupling in cohabitation arrangements etc.[11]

A second remarkable development concerns marriage as a legal regime. Marriage is no longer the institution we once used to know. Once displaying a set of mandatory rules policing entry, exit and parties' behaviour, marriage now comprises a set of much more flexible default rules which prize autonomy and self-fulfilment.[12] With ebbs and flows, the trend is now clearly distinguishable. The decision to strike down distinctions based on legitimacy,[13] the recognition of abortion as a fundamental liberty protected under the Fourteenth Amendment,[14] the introduction of divorce, challenging the marriage-for-life ideal, the

[7] Pew Research Center, 'Parenting in America: Outlook, Worries, Aspirations are Strongly Linked to Financial Situation' (17 December 2015) 15–16, www.pewresearch.org/wp-content/uploads/sites/3/2015/12/2015-12-17_parenting-in-america_FINAL.pdf.

[8] Pew Research Center, 'A Record 64 million Americans Live in Multigenerational Households' (15 April 2018), www.pewresearch.org/fact-tank/2018/04/05/a-record-64-million-americans-live-in-multigenerational-households.

[9] Generations United, 'Multigenerational Households: A Record Number of Americans Live in Multigenerational Households Today' (2016), www.gu.org/explore-our-topics/multigenerational-households.

[10] Aviram and Leachman (n 3) 302–03.

[11] Pew Research Center (n 7) 16.

[12] B Stark, 'Marriage Proposals: From One-Size-Fits-All to Postmodern Marriage Law' (2001) 89 *California Law Review* 1479.

[13] *Stanley v Illinois*, 405 US 645 (1972) (striking down state laws conditioning recognition of parental status for fathers upon marriage).

[14] *Roe v Wade*, 410 US 113 (1973).

decriminalisation of 'ifornication' and adultery allowing sex outside of marriage are but a few of the ways in which the state has loosened its grip on the institution.

This shift at the legal-regulatory level is the byproduct of a shift that occurred at the normative level. The traditional vision of marriage founded on natural law has gradually been replaced by a utilitarian vision pivoting on pleasure and personal liberty. The rise of self-fulfilment as the normative centrepiece of adult relationship had profound implications on how we regulate the matter. William Eskridge tags this new normative framework as a choice-based approach to relationship regulation. The approach gives partners an opportunity to tailor the relationship to their needs and preferences by departing from legal baselines.[15] Developments in the field of contracts, such as the enforceability of pre-nuptial and post-nuptial agreements, epitomise this trend.[16] In the end, parties are free to customise and terminate the relationship at will, unless stated otherwise. A second normative shift is a corollary of utilitarian values taking centre stage in relationship regulation. Eskridge argues that the new normative framework carries an unprecedented 'baseline of nondiscrimination'.[17] The baseline requires allocating social goods based on grounds other than the bare promotion of marriage over other family unions. As a consequence, the promotion of tradition or protection of moral values become insufficient grounds on which to make distinctions in this area.

A third trend regards the introduction of new options on the menu of recognition regimes. The pluralisation of family regimes, known as 'family legal pluralism',[18] has played a role in the decentralisation of marriage within Western societies. Marriage is no longer the only option for families which want to gain legal protections in the US; nowadays, there is a variegated 'menu' which includes, alongside civil marriage, common law marriage, civil unions, domestic partnerships etc.[19]

Common law marriage is a form of marital-like cohabitation. The treatment that common law couples enjoy in the US is no longer one of complete invisibility.[20] However, the recognition of this form of cohabitation is on the decline. At present, it is only recognised in a minority of states.[21] In New Hampshire, it is valid for inheritance purposes only. Other states are gradually phasing it out by recognising only common law marriages executed before a certain date.[22]

[15] WN Eskridge, 'Family Law Pluralism: The Guided-Choice Regime of Menus, Default Rules, and Override Rules' (2012) 100 *Georgetown Law Journal* 1884.

[16] MM Ertman, 'Marital Contracting in the Post-Windsor World' (2015) 42 *Florida State University Law Review* 479.

[17] Eskridge (n 15) 1973.

[18] A Aloni, 'The Puzzle of Family Law Pluralism', (2016) 39 *Harvard Journal of Law and Gender* 317.

[19] J Halley, 'Behind the Law of Marriage (I): From Status/Contract to the Marriage System' (2010) 6 *Unbound* 1, 4.

[20] Eskridge (n 15) 1933–34. Traditionally, parties are considered to be in a common law marriage if four conditions are met: (i) they have the legal capacity to enter into a valid marriage; (ii) they made an agreement to marry *per verba de presenti*; (iii) they usually cohabit; and (iv) they hold themselves out as husband and wife.

[21] As of 2020, there are eight states that recognise common law marriage: Colorado, Iowa, Kansas, New Hampshire, Montana, South Carolina, Texas and Utah. An additional five states only allow marriages executed before a certain date.

[22] This is the case in Florida, Georgia, Indiana, Ohio and Pennsylvania.

Salient instantiations of family legal pluralism are the many registration schemes in force in the country. Domestic partnerships were first enacted at the municipal level and by private actors, such as corporations. Thus, at the outset, they did not constitute a proper alternative to marriage. The pared-down list of benefits accruing through them also attested to those unions not being comparable to marriage. By contrast, civil unions and state-wide domestic partnerships soon became valid alternatives. Civil unions came to be seen as marriage 'by another name'[23] and comprehensive state-wide domestic partnerships proved popular for they could confer all, or nearly all, marital rights and privileges.

Other non-marital regimes include designated beneficiary schemes and reciprocal beneficiary schemes. The difference between the two mainly consists of the former being 'tailor-made' – ie, giving the parties the opportunity to confer specific benefits upon each other – and the latter conferring a definite set of rights. In both cases, the number of entitlements is more limited compared to domestic partnerships and civil unions.[24]

Though less familiar to the general public and less popular amongst couples, these regimes hold promise for the recognition of new families, as argued in Chapter 2. Reciprocal/designated beneficiary schemes come in the form of a lighter and much more flexible regime. They can be usually entered into by completing a form that is easy to fill out (Colorado probably features the simplest scheme), without the assistance of an attorney. They range from schemes that only confer health-related prerogatives to laws that supply a vast array of benefits under both private and public family law.[25]

Ultimately, designated and reciprocal beneficiary schemes are characterised by looser eligibility requirements. Typically, they allow a wider range of families to register. Examples include unmarried conjugal partners and non-conjugal couples of friends and/or relatives. Some of these schemes are confined to people who are legally unable to marry, such as siblings, relatives and, at the time of the adoption, same-sex couples. This is the case in Vermont and Hawaii. However, in Colorado and Maryland, no such restriction applies. In Colorado, any two people of sound mind are allowed to formalise their relationship.[26] Likewise, in Maryland, 'two cohabiting individuals of any gender in a mutually caring relationship' can register.[27] Thus, in both cases, I could register with a committed friend, relative or sexual partner.

To conclude, this introduction has hinted at the remarkable changes that both family patterns and family law have undergone in the US over the past few decades.

[23] Eskridge (n 15) 1944–45.

[24] Colo Rev Stat § 15-22-105(1) (Westlaw 2d Reg Sess of 71st Gen Assemb); Hawaii Reciprocal Beneficiaries Act, 1997 Haw Sess Laws 383 (codified in part at Haw Rev Stat §572C (2008)); Md SB 785 (2009); Me Rev Stat tit 18-A (Westlaw through 2017); DC Code § 32-701 (Westlaw through 11 October 2018).

[25] N Palazzo, 'The Strange Pairing: Building Alliances between Queer Activists and Conservative Groups to Recognize New Families' (2018) 25 *Michigan Journal of Gender and Law* 161, fig 2 at 197.

[26] Colo Rev Stat § 15-22-105(1).

[27] Md Code Ann, Health § 6-101(a) (Westlaw through 2018 Reg Sess).

Taken together, the described developments illuminate the magnitude of the changes which are affecting family structures and norms. They lay the ground for the possibility for new families to engage in strategic litigation in order to further expand their legal recognition. The underlying assumption is that there is no way back from these concomitant shifts affecting the way in which persons live familyhood.

2. Venue

Taking a glance at past litigation makes it possible to conclude that the most interesting options for the recognition of non-conjugal families are twofold: constitutional litigation and family law litigation. This section glances over the differences between the two contexts.

I. Constitutional Litigation

Understanding where constitutional litigation occurs requires an analysis of judicial review. The US adopts a diffused model of judicial review, under which, all judicial courts can strike down laws or executive acts that are incompatible with the US Constitution. There is no specialised constitutional court entrusted with the power of invalidating unconstitutional acts, as is the case in continental Europe.[28] While in *Marbury v Madison*[29] the Supreme Court had to assert a power that could not be found in the text of the federal Constitution, nowadays it is uncontroversial that all judicial courts, are vested with such power. As a consequence, constitutional arguments can be submitted in ordinary courts.

However, the picture becomes a little more complicated if one considers that the US is a federal system. The ways in which federalism plays out at the constitutional level are numerous. First, this form of government prompts recollection of the existence of state constitutions alongside the federal one. As Justice Brennan observed: 'Prior to the adoption of the federal Constitution, each of the rights eventually recognized in the federal Bill of Rights had previously been protected in one or more state constitutions.'[30] However, the centrality of federal constitutional law is hardly disputable. When the US Constitution comes into play, both state and federal courts must ensure that the law complies with the prescriptions enshrined therein. State courts have a duty to interpret state law in a manner consistent with the federal Constitution and their decisions can be appealed before the

[28] For a discussion of its essential features, see V Ferreres Comella, 'The European Model of Constitutional Review of Legislation: Toward Decentralization' (2004) 2 *International Journal of Constitutional Law* 461.

[29] *Marbury v Madison*, 5 US 137 (1803).

[30] WJ Brennan Jr, 'State Constitutions and the Protection of Individual Rights' (1977) 90 *Harvard Law Review* 489, 501.

US Supreme Court. Most importantly, the authority of federal constitutional doctrine and choice made by state courts to apply such doctrine as their own caused state constitutional law to acquire less prestige compared to its federal counterpart.[31] Hence, it seems a wise methodological choice to assess current family laws against the federal Constitution.

II. Family Law Litigation

When it comes to family law litigation, the appropriate venue could be a specialised or ordinary court dealing with family law matters strictly speaking[32] – divorce, child custody, child support and adoption.

Yet, only a superficial reading would equate family law with the list of 'family law matters' as defined in US state codes – again, divorce, child custody, child support and adoption. On careful examination, family law turns out to be a complex web of rules conferring entitlements upon family members in a plethora of related fields. These fields range from welfare law to social benefits and from tax to inheritance. Taken together, this set of rules is known as 'family law 2 rules'.[33] Table 3.1 below contains a list of family benefits and the relevant venue to obtain them judicially.

Table 3.1 Benefits and applicable venue

	FL1	FL2	
	Private law benefits	**Private law benefits**	**Public law benefits**
List of benefits (main examples)	- Divorce/breakdown relationship - Child support - Child custody - Adoption	- Succession - Torts (eg, infliction of emotional distress)	- Pensions - Welfare - Health-related prerogatives - Workers' compensation - Tax
Venue	Civil/family court	Civil court	Administrative law judge and then civil court

[31] J Blocher, 'What State Constitutional Law Can Tell Us about the Federal Constitution' (2011) 115 *Penn State Law Review* 1035, 1037. But on the limits of federal courts to review or control state action see LH Tribe, *American Constitutional Law*, 3rd edn (New York, Foundation Press, 2002) 464–629, esp 567–73.

[32] States have jurisdiction in resolving family law disputes. The type of court dealing with such claims can vary across the states and can include state district/circuit courts with jurisdiction on domestic relations or a specialised family court or division. For a complete list, see the FindLaw website: https://family.findlaw.com/family-legal-help/state-family-courts.html.

[33] D Kennedy, 'Savigny's Family/Patrimony Distinction and its Place in the Global Genealogy of Classical Legal Thought' (2010) 58 *American Journal of Comparative Law* 811.

For torts, such as the wrongful death of a family member or the infliction of emotional distress for the loss of a family member, a (state) civil court is the court of competent jurisdiction.[34] For public law benefits, one should note that many of these benefits are granted by administrative agencies. They are then reviewed by administrative law judges (ALJs). An ALJ is an adjudicatory body within the administration which follows several court-like rules without being a judicial court. However, the decisions of ALJs can be appealed before civil courts. Therefore, when benefits administered by an agency are sought, I assume that strategic litigation occurs before civil courts, which, unlike ALJs, are judicial courts.

When it comes to non-conjugal families, it is much more likely for them to resort to courts dealing with 'family law matters' in this second broader sense (family law 2 rules). Less often, they will resort to family law courts. Occasions might include seeking a fair division of property upon the breakdown of the relationship – along the line of what cohabiting conjugal partners did in the 1970s[35] – or a declaration of parentage, as occurred in Canada.[36]

3. Remedy

The notion of remedy adopted here does not have a technical meaning. It does not refer to the type of judicial relief. For instance, in civil courts, judicial reliefs can be compensation for damages, or a declaration of the legal rights of the claimants. In constitutional litigation, the remedy is usually a legislative invalidation. By contrast, in this book by 'remedy', I refer more broadly to the ultimate goal a claimant is seeking to achieve in court. Typically, this would be specific benefits or access to a family regime, such as domestic partnerships, from which someone is excluded.

It is worth stipulating a distinction between comprehensive approach and area-specific approach. The former refers to an approach seeking to introduce a comprehensive recognition mechanism, such as a civil partnership, while the latter refers to an approach seeking to expand the eligibility requirements of specific legal benefits. In both constitutional and family law litigation, only an area-specific approach can be taken in light of current judicial doctrines, for the reasons I will illustrate below.

[34] *United States v Windsor*, 570 US 744 (2013), slip op, 16–17 ('regulation of domestic relations is an area that has long been regarded as a virtually exclusive province of the States … the Federal Government, through our history, has deferred to state-law policy decisions with respect to domestic relations').

[35] *Marvin v Marvin*, 557 P 2d 106 (1976).

[36] Reference is made to Lynda Collins, the best friend and colleague of Natasha Bakht, who succeeded in her claim to be recognised as a parent of Bakht's biological son, a profoundly disabled boy. See N Bakht and L Collins, 'Are You My Mother? Co-parenting in a Non-conjugal Family' (2018) 31 *Canadian Journal of Family Law* 105.

I. Constitutional Litigation: An Area-Specific Approach

Unlike in Canada and Europe, strategic litigation at the constitutional level has a low likelihood of success in the US. Both introducing legal protections through an area-specific approach and a comprehensive approach has obvious limits rooted in constitutional doctrine. Especially extrinsic to the US legal tradition is the idea that the Constitution requires the government to introduce socio-economic protections or that it upholds positive duties in general. As Judge Posner powerfully and succinctly put it, the US Constitution:

> [I]s a charter of negative rather than positive liberties … The men who wrote the Bill of Rights were not concerned that Government might do too little for the people but that it might do too much to them. The Fourteenth Amendment, adopted in 1868 at the height of laissez-faire thinking, sought to protect Americans from oppression by state government, not to secure them basic governmental services.[37]

Thus, the negative liberty-oriented constitutional doctrine is in principle opposed to granting claimants affirmative entitlements, requiring state intervention to be fulfilled. It is opposed both to granting new positive entitlements and to extending current entitlements to new beneficiaries.

The *Obergefell* decision, which legalised same-sex marriage under the equal protection and due process clause, operates a deviation from the doctrine. The practical implication of the decision was conferring a status upon new partners and the package of benefits linked to it as a result of this. Yet, on closer examination, there is no such thing as a negative freedom to marry (or to enter into another family regime).[38] When it comes to marriage, the state cannot merely refrain from a certain conduct. In line with this intuition, which is central to US constitutionalism, until recently, courts fell short of arguing that same-sex couples enjoy a right to marry. Their decision could nimbly rest on both textual and doctrinal grounds.[39] As is well known, 'there are three partners to every civil marriage: two willing spouses and an approving State'.[40] This triangular relationship requires the state to affirmatively step into the realm of relationships and design a scheme with defaults attendant to it. Unlike *Lawrence*,[41] a decision that decriminalised the private sexual conduct of homosexuals, where the state was merely to refrain from intruding in the same-sex couples' bedroom, with *Obergefell* states were called upon to open up their marital regimes. The decision in fact triggered massive amendments to laws and regulations confining the enjoyment of marital benefits to heterosexual spouses.

[37] *Jackson v City of Joliet*, 715 F 2d 1200, 1203 (7th Cir), cert denied, 465 US 1049 (1983).

[38] *Obergefell v Hodges*, 576 U.S. 644 (2015) (Roberts, J, dissenting), slip op, 17 ('Unlike criminal laws banning contraceptives and sodomy, the marriage laws at issue here involve no government intrusion. They create no crime and impose no punishment. Same-sex couples remain free to live together, to engage in intimate conduct, and to raise their families as they see fit').

[39] *Lewis v Harris*, 908 A 2d 196 (2006).

[40] *Goodridge v Department of Public Health*, 798 NE 2d 941, 954 (2003).

[41] *Lawrence v Texas*, 539 US 558 (2003).

The consequence of granting affirmative rights through *Obergefell* drew severe criticism from the dissenting justices. Justice Roberts raised objections based on the consolidated constitutional doctrine refusing to 'allow litigants to convert the shield provided by constitutional liberties into a sword to demand positive entitlements from the State'.[42] The distinction between negative and affirmative rights is of substance and is too well established to be overstated.[43] This suggests that the treatment of same-sex marriage must be seen as an exception rather than the norm in constitutional law. This deviation was only warranted in light of the existence of a fundamental right to marry and of the ability of same-sex couples to make a case for their inclusion in the regime (a route I suggest not pursuing in Chapter 2).

I argue that this doctrine is so rooted that it outweighs a positive aspect of US constitutional law: its reduced interest in the family. The US adopts a family privacy model.[44] This model protects family members from undue intrusions and state regulation of intimacy. Unlike the near-totality of European constitutions, the US Constitution does not mention the family or marriage; only later did a fundamental right to marry emerge through case law. However, until the *Obergefell* decision in 2016, the fundamental nature of the right was unsettled. This led prominent queer theorists such as Martha Nussbaum and libertarians such as Cass Sunstein to argue that there is no such thing as a fundamental right to marry in the US.[45] Crucially, the conclusion was instrumental to arguing that civil marriage could be abolished without abolition running contrary to the Constitution.

This seeing the family as a societal creation which deserves shielding from excessive state intrusion potentially profits new families. It virtually allows more autonomy in shaping one's intimate connections. However, the question of whether a new family can also gain official recognition attracts a negative answer. The above-mentioned constitutional doctrine adverse to claims for affirmative entitlements prevents new families from arguing that they deserve legal recognition as a matter of constitutional law.

For all these reasons, I argue that constitutional litigation has a low likelihood of success. As to whether a comprehensive or area-specific approach is more suitable, I counsel focusing on an area-specific approach. In addition to the aspects outlined above, two additional reasons suggest discarding a comprehensive approach, whereby a non-conjugal family seeks to introduce, say, a civil partnership.

First is the inapplicability of the *Obergefell* decision – ie, the only exception to the negative-liberty doctrine – to non-marital regimes. The fundamental

[42] *Obergefell* (n 38) 2620 (Roberts, CJ, dissenting) and also 2634 (Thomas, J, dissenting).

[43] *Deshaney v Winnebago City Department of Social Services*, 489 US 189, 196 (1989); *San Antonio Independent School District v Rodriguez*, 411 US 1, 35–37 (1973).

[44] JB D'Onorio, 'La protection constitutionnelle du mariage et de la famille en Europe' (1988) *Revue trimestrielle de droit civil* 1. The approach emerges in several leading judgments on reproductive rights, family relationships and childrearing, and sexual intimacy. See, eg, *Lawrence* (n 41).

[45] M Nussbaum, 'A Right to Marry?' (2010) 98 *California Law Review* 667; C Sunstein, 'The Right to Marry' (2004) 26 *Cardozo Law Review* 2081. See also N Tebbe and DA Widiss, 'Equal Access and the Right to Marry' (2010) 158 *University of Pennsylvania Law Review* 1375.

right to marry was inferred from the due process clause under the Fourteenth Amendment protecting the most fundamental liberties. However, the reasoning is hardly applicable to civil partnerships. There is no traceable fundamental right to enter into such unions under the clause. Nor can one argue that there should be such a right. When seeking to introduce a *new* non-marital regime, the due process prong would be unserviceable. The clause is not applicable to new statuses precisely because they are 'new', not if we accept an understanding of due process as summarised in the famous remarks from Justice Oliver Wendell Holmes: 'The law can ask no better justification than the deepest instincts of men.'[46] Namely, once you have enjoyed something for a long time, it takes root in your being and you cannot simply get rid of it. The aspiration to form a marital family, so the doctrine goes, pertains to such deepest instincts.

Second, non-marital regimes are seen as second-class regimes. Same-sex marriage advocates have successfully conveyed the idea that non-marital regimes are discriminatory regimes, and courts have upheld this view. Telling examples include the California Supreme Court decision *In Re Marriage Cases*,[47] which scrutinised the constitutionality of state domestic partnerships, and the Connecticut Supreme Court decision in *Kerrigan v Commissioner of Public Health*,[48] which assessed the constitutionality of state civil unions. In both cases, the two schemes were granting same-sex couples the same incidents of marriage. Nonetheless, the two apex courts reached the conclusion that excluding same-sex partners from marriage amounts to an impermissible violation of the partners' human dignity. Marriage and the non-marital regime, the Connecticut Supreme Court argued, are 'by no means equal … the former [marriage] is an institution of trascendent, historical, cultural and social significance, whereas the latter [civil union] most surely is not'.[49]

Dismissing non-marital regimes as discriminatory and contrary to the dignity of the claimants is problematic from our perspective. This overlooks the fact that, for some new families, non-marital regimes are the sole mechanisms for recognition. Further, as Chapter 2 has illustrated, marriage is not an actual option for new families; most of the time, they are not interested in marriage. They also display structural features that marriage seems unable to accommodate. Registration schemes are more suitable instead. Yet, marriage equality litigation demonstrates how LGBT(Q?) litigators made it much harder for new families to argue that non-marital regimes are ideal regimes.

By contrast, a number of judicial decisions corroborate the contention that non-conjugal families could successfully expand the eligibility requirements of specific family benefits (an area-specific approach). I adopt a broad notion of family benefit as encompassing all the benefits, privileges, rights and obligations

[46] OW Holmes Jr, 'The Path of the Law' (1897) 10 *Harvard Law Review* 457, 477.
[47] *In Re Marriage Cases*, 183 P 3d 384 (Cal 2008).
[48] *Kerrigan v Commissioner of Public Health*, 957 A 2d 407 (Conn 2008).
[49] ibid 412.

conferred by a public authority upon a family member. The adopted working definition has two consequences: first, entitlements conferred by private employers are excluded; and, second, the definition goes beyond public outlays or private law benefits to encompass all the entitlements and privileges a person receives for qualifying as a family member, such as evidentiary privileges and legal standing under wrongful death statutes.

Each benefit would likely deserve an analysis of its own. Benefits run the gamut from those that are easier to acquire to those that are much harder to obtain. An example of the former is compensation for wrongful death statutes. The benefit places the financial burden of compensating on 'guilty' third parties; thereby, it overcomes any objection that argues that public resources are scarce (and thus that public benefits should not be extended). It also wipes away the spectre of an unwarranted redistribution of private hard-earned resources (based on which private law benefits such as maintenance obligations are routinely opposed). Ultimately, This scenario is ideal for another reason: the loss of a loved one creates empathy and compassion. By contrast, a 'harder case' might concern wealth transfer taxation. Think of the marital deduction permitting spouses to transfer by means of inter vivos gifts or, upon death, assets free of any gift tax or estate tax.[50] In such cases, a non-conjugal couple would also argue that the family definition under the governing statute must be expanded to include them. However, any argument to this effect would need to overcome the described 'aversion' to claims seeking to extend public benefits to new beneficiaries.

Overall, the major hurdle is the doctrine that is hostile to granting affirmative entitlements. However, when an area-specific approach is pursued, non-conjugal families can benefit from a series of cases recognising that they fall under a larger conception of family protected by the Constitution. I will analyse these decisions in section 4.

II. Family Law Litigation: An Area-Specific Approach

In the context of family law litigation, the preferred approach is also an area-specific approach. The conclusion is somewhat necessitated by the type of arguments one can make in family law litigation. The typical scenario is one where the claimant argues that they are entitled to a family law benefit under a purposive and liberal interpretation of the law. A thus-framed claim would be along the lines of 'despite the current interpretation of "family" being limited to marital-like relationships, my relationship is no less deserving if one looks at the purpose of the benefit'. Such a claim would lay stress on the importance of looking at the reality of family patterns, instead of resorting to legal fictions (such as marital ties) to distribute benefits. In this sense, it resorts to a typical functionalist argument redirecting

[50] See 26 USCS §§ 2056(a), 2523(a) (Internal Revenue Code).

attention towards the actual features of a relationship that are relevant to pursuing the objective of the law. A non-conjugal family might thus be successful in arguing that conjugality is not relevant to the scheme and that other features, such as financial commitment and emotional support, are.

By contrast, it is unrealistic to imagine a claimant maintaining that they are entitled to access to a family regime (eg, civil partnerships) and to the full array of benefits therefrom. While one could readily find case law resulting in an extension of the eligibility requirements of specific benefits, there is no comparable case law extending family regimes wholesale to new families. The decision of whether to include other beneficiaries in civil partnerships, civil unions or designated/reciprocal beneficiary schemes is usually the exclusive province of the legislature (or, at most, of judges applying the constitution). It can hardly be seen as a form of interpretative judicial updating. Should a claimant make this argument (without contextually bringing a constitutional challenge to the law), it would be easily discarded as a form of undue judicial encroachment into legislative discretion.

4. Legal Arguments in Constitutional Litigation

Venue	Any court performing a judicial review of laws under the US Constitution
Remedy	Extension of specific family benefits
Legal arguments	1. Equal protection 2. Due process 3. Freedom of association

In constitutional litigation, an area-specific approach is more suitable. I previously contended that the likelihood of success of constitutional claims is generally not high. However, a case law analysis shows that there are pivotal decisions underpinning a larger conception of family, which could buttress claims aimed at accessing specific legal benefits.

The arguments I employ are based on the equal protection clause and the due process clause of the US Constitution. I ultimately outline a third argument based on freedom of association. Although some applicants and justices attempted to raise a thus-framed argument, I dismiss it as unable to compel the extension of positive entitlements.

I. Equal Protection

The equality clause enshrined in the US Constitution is known as 'equal protection clause'. Unlike equality guarantees providing for a unified standard – Canada is an example of this – the equal protection clause triggers differentiated standards depending on the identity of the claimant. There is a scale of protections associated with each ground, such as strict scrutiny with race and intermediate scrutiny with sex.

The rational basis test is a minimum rationality standard. It is triggered in the event that a ground cannot be invoked. It requires finding a mere rational connection between the allegedly discriminatory action and a legitimate aim.[51] This standard is highly deferential. A presumption of rationality operates in favour of state action. Thus, under a rational basis scrutiny, impugned laws are likely to be salvaged. Strict scrutiny, applying when the distinction is based on a sensitive ground such as race or national origins, is the most stringent standard.[52] In any such case, the aim must usually be a compelling one, and the law or policy must be narrowly tailored to achieve the aim and the least restrictive means to do so.[53] Ultimately, there is an intermediate scrutiny for discriminations against 'quasi-suspect classes', especially groups based on sex. Intermediate scrutiny applies a less demanding standard compared to strict scrutiny;[54] laws setting forth distinctions based on sex must be narrowly tailored to achieve a compelling government interest.

Non-conjugal families do not fall into any of the protected classes. They are neither a suspect nor a quasi-suspect class. They cannot be fruitfully linked to grounds of sex or sexual orientation. One could argue that the absence of the sexual component of the relationship engages sexual orientation as much as atheism engages freedom of religion, silence (or compelled speech) engages speech, and a refusal to associate engages freedom of association. However, this statement would be seriously misplaced. Non-conjugal families might well have one or more sexual partners, without these relationships amounting to family relationships in their view. Therefore, grounding their claim in sexual orientation discrimination would not be merely reductionist, but plainly wrong. It would conflate family relationships and sexual attitudes, and ultimately non-conjugal pairs with asexual pairs.

At the same time, this risks elevating to a political and identity dimension a component that the individual has decided to leave out of the limelight: sexual attitudes. I should like to offer an example here. A non-conjugal couple of two middle-aged women, one of whom is a renowned best-selling novelist, live in the

[51] The reasons triggering this less demanding standard are unclear. It seems that courts have ample leeway in terms of deciding whether to grant heightened scrutiny to certain groups. See, eg, *City of Cleburne v Cleburne Living Center*, 473 US 432, 445–46 (1985) ('if the large and amorphous class of the mentally retarded were deemed quasi-suspect … it would be difficult to find a principled way to distinguish a variety of other groups … One need mention in this respect only the aging, the disabled, the mentally ill, and the infirm').

[52] For a discussion of the factors considered in the decision whether strict scrutiny should be triggered, see, eg, R Randall Kelso, 'Standards of Review under the Equal Protection Clause and Related Constitutional Doctrines Protecting Individual Rights: The "Base Plus Six" Model and Modern Supreme Court Practice' (2002) 4 *Journal of Constitutional Law* 225, fn 20.

[53] SA Siegel, 'The Origin of the Compelling State Interest Test and Strict Scrutiny' (2006) 48 *American Journal of Legal History* 355.

[54] *Craig v Boren*, 429 US 190 (1976).

Italian countryside in the Umbria region.[55] The two women have lived together for over 10 years and have supported each other emotionally and materially throughout. They tag themselves as a 'same-sex couple', yet not gay: they do not call each other sexual partners nor do they hold out as a sexual couple, eschewing questions regarding whether they have sex. This is why they do not intend to enter a civil union in Italy, which was created to protect sexual relationships. Hence, registering for them was not an option as it would have distorted both their self-reflective framing of the relationship and the way in which they wished to convey it to the public.

Likewise, I argue that non-conjugal pairs cannot fruitfully invoke sex. Same-sex couples followed this route at the inception of their strategic litigation. Reference should be made here to the famous case *Baehr v Lewin*, where for the first time a top US court ruled that the exclusion of gay couples from marriage was unconstitutional[56] – namely, the Supreme Court of Hawaii reversed a lower court decision when finding that sex triggers strict scrutiny and that, as a consequence, Hawaii should have presented a compelling interest for the exclusion of gay couples from marriage. Most certainly, sex was used as a pretext to fill the void left by the lack of a prohibition to discriminate based on sexual orientation in the state Constitution. In principle, sex (nowadays broadly understood as gender) could be mobilised to remedy the absence of marital status as well. After all, persons in a non-conjugal couple happen to have a given sex/gender. However, with same-sex marriage or non-marital regimes being introduced in all US states, their sex would no longer bar access to a family regime. Therefore, sex is unserviceable.

Since no prohibited ground can be invoked, a deferential rational basis standard applies to claims brought by non-conjugal couples. In order to strike down a law under a rational basis test, the first step requires asking if the interest the state pursues is legitimate. If the interest is legitimate, the issue then becomes whether the measure adopted is not rationally connected to the stated interest.

i. *Is There a Valid State Interest?*

The first step under a rational basis test is to see if there is a valid state interest in excluding a non-conjugal family from a family benefit. Most programmes targeting married couples for preferential treatment do so for no other reason than to incentivise marriage. This interest can be framed in comparative terms as a bold interest in privileging marriage over other family forms. It could also be put in a more seemingly neutral way as an interest in maintaining 'a harmonious marital union' or 'a uniform definition of marriage'.[57]

Until recently, the validity of the interest in preserving marriage has been undeniable in both constitutional doctrine and subconstitutional doctrine. Courts

[55] R Scorranese, interview with S Tamaro, 'Sono madre senza figli: ecco la mia strana famiglia felice' *Corriere della Sera* (Milan, 19 July 2018).

[56] *Baehr v Lewin*, 852 P 2d 44 (Haw 1993).

[57] *Windsor* (n 34).

have been adamant in upholding such a state interest. This translated into courts consistently rejecting the extension of privileges to non-marital unions[58] and refusing to alter the definition of marriage.[59] Even in landmark judgments leading to increased legal protections for unmarried cohabiting couples, courts promptly clarified that the decision was without prejudice to the 'undisputed' state interest in preserving the institution of marriage.[60] A major example in this regard is *Marvin v Marvin*, which recognised the enforceability of post-breakdown agreements entered into by two cohabiting conjugal partners.

However, the liberty jurisprudence on the rights of same-sex couples casts doubt on the validity of a variation of this interest: the 'preservation of a traditional notion of marriage'. The two landmark judgments in the marriage equality saga reject the contention that preserving a traditional understanding of marriage is a valid state interest. In *Windsor*, the Supreme Court reasoned that appeals to tradition to justify discriminatory treatment were rejected in *Lawrence* and thus were no longer acceptable;[61] in *Obergefell*, it argued that upholding a traditional notion of marriage is not a valid interest, given that rights cannot be defined by who exercised them in the past.[62]

When the exclusion of non-conjugal families from legal protection is the result of moral views, the *Obergefell* decision will thus offer a solid basis for rejecting this ground as a valid state interest. In *Lawrence*, the Supreme Court started to doubt that a government can impose moral and ethical views.[63] This passage seemed to be included in an obiter dictum. But, then, it became integral to the holding in *Obergefell*. Now, there is little doubt that if state action is animated by a desire to force the state's own moral views on families, this interest would be rejected as unconstitutional.

Therefore, while the interest in preserving marriage is still alive in constitutional doctrine, the liberty jurisprudence started eroding it by crossing out a specific variation: the preservation of a traditional understanding of the institution. I should clarify in which sense the erosion of said interest is beneficial to non-conjugal families. The preservation of marriage is often proffered to reject new families' requests for family benefits. As a consequence, it becomes critical to de-emphasise it. The liberty jurisprudence offers conceptual and argumentative tools to argue that the interest in preserving marriage is undergoing a gradual erosion.

[58] *North Dakota Fair Housing Council, Inc v Peterson*, 625 NW 2d 551 (rejecting the contention that the North Dakota code prohibiting discrimination in housing applies to unmarried couples).

[59] *Brown v Buhman*, 947 F Supp 2d 1170, 1190, 1234 (D Utah 2013) (upholding the constitutionality of Utah's criminal ban on bigamy, while invalidating the cohabitation prong of the statute as being in violation of freedom of religion).

[60] *Marvin v Marvin* (n 35) 122 ('Lest we be misunderstood, however, we take this occasion to point out that the structure of society itself largely depends upon the institution of marriage, and nothing we have said in this opinion should be taken to derogate from that institution').

[61] *Lawrence* (n 41) 572.

[62] *Obergefell*, 576 US 2584, 2602 (quoting both *Loving* and *Lawrence* as precedents supporting this view).

[63] *Lawrence* (n 41).

However, *Belle Terre*,[64] a case decided in 1974, typifies the hurdles that might be encountered in advancing a thus-framed argument. The case concerned a zoning ordinance, restricting land use to 'one-family dwelling'. A 'one-family dwelling' was defined as a group of: (i) one or more related persons (by blood, adoption or marriage); or (ii) no more than two unrelated people living and cooking together. On that occasion, the Court used only a few lines to reject the equal protection claim brought by the landlord, whereby he asserted that roommates qualify as family. The Court applied a mere rational basis test and found no special hurdle in concluding that the law passed muster. When a rational basis test applies, the burden of proof lies with the party raising the constitutional challenge – here the landlord. The justices concluded that the landlord had not satisfied the burden. Interestingly, they recognised as legitimate the state interest in keeping the area as 'a sanctuary' informed by 'family values, youth values, and blessing of quiet seclusion and clean air'.[65]

I am not sure this purpose would withstand constitutional scrutiny nowadays. Regardless, I am confident that the peculiar factual circumstances weighed heavily in the rejection of the case. In *Belle Terre*, the petitioner was a landlord seeking to lease his apartment to six unrelated college students. Roommates usually do not perceive themselves as family. They are not necessarily mutually supportive. They do not necessarily eat together. They do not hold themselves out as family. The case was therefore not driven by a desire to protect family ties, but by a mere economic interest on the part of the landlord. It is thus important to 'distinguish' this case and contend that *Belle Terre* does not apply to non-conjugal families, but to non-interdependent roommates.

Thus, the state interest par excellence is incentivising marriage. Some corollaries, such as preserving the area as a sanctuary informed by family values or preserving a traditional understanding of marriage, while routinely upheld in the past, are now experiencing a slow erosion.

As to other community interests that are adverse to granting protections to non-conjugal families, each benefit would likely deserve an analysis of its own. At a minimum, one should draw a distinction between private and public law benefits. When private law benefits – placing obligations on one of the family members – are at stake, recognition encounters less resistance. Solid and undisputed reasons buttress the state interest in accommodating non-conjugal families in a mutually caring relationship to avoid such families becoming a public charge. This interest posits that private individuals, rather than the government through public subsidies, should take care of other family members.[66] Decisions such as *Marvin*, which

[64] *Village of Belle Terre v Boraas*, 416 US 1 (1974).

[65] ibid 9.

[66] There are countless examples in the state case law: *In Re Hein*, 253 P 3d 636 (Colo App 2010) (finding an abuse of discretion by a judge who deviates downwards to preserve paternal grandparents' eligibility for public daycare assistance benefits); *State v Oakley*, 629 NW 2d 200 (Wis 2001), cert denied, 123 S Ct 74 (2002) (upholding the constitutionality of a condition prohibiting the father from procreating due to his financial unwillingness to support his previous children).

concerned the enforceability of support obligation for unmarried partners, are clearly animated by a desire, with a neoliberal flavour, to privatise care. The most vulnerable party is protected and the state is relieved of the duty of support: everyone is happy (apart from whoever is paying for this).

Not only is a privatisation of care a legitimate state interest, but family and civil courts in the US also tend to excessively emphasise it, the result being quite distasteful. For instance, in *State v Oakley*, a Wisconsin court of appeals upheld the constitutionality of a rule prohibiting a father from procreating due to his unwillingness to pay child support.[67] In so doing, the Court discussed at length the paramount importance of the interest in protecting the public 'fisc'. The assumption is that if the father does not pay child support, the child would become a public charge, thereby undermining scarce public resources. In any such case, the state has a clear interest in shifting the burden of care from the state to private parties. Legal arguments seeking to expand access to private law entitlements would thus emphasise the undisputed state interest in protecting public resources and contextually de-emphasise the interest in protecting/preserving marriage, based on the state-of-the-art liberty jurisprudence.

By contrast, the very same interest cuts against extending public benefits to non-conjugal families. A desire to protect the public purse severely weighs against expanding access to public benefits. These benefits are costly for the state. In this context, an even more problematic interest that the state could put forward is the prevention of fraud. Preventing frauds refers to the risk that the claim to access public law benefits is driven by mere financial convenience. The implicit assumption is that some persons would call themselves family simply for the sake of getting benefits, without being in a genuine family relationship. Such argument is commonplace in discourses on the subject of family policy. Accusations of fraud are trickier to the extent that they are a variant on the undisputed state interest in protecting public resources. I will sketch out below a potential response to this argument.

ii. Is There a Rational Connection between the Means and the Purpose?

The second step requires inquiring into whether the law is rationally connected to the goal it pursues; in other words, there must be a causal connection between the law and its intended outcome.[68]

The *Moreno* case is an emblematic example where the Supreme Court struck down a provision excluding an extended family by applying a mere rational basis standard.[69] The Court was called upon to scrutinise an amendment to the Food

[67] *Oakley* (n 66).

[68] RH Fallon, The Dynamic Constitution: An Introduction to American Constitutional Law and Practice (Cambridge, Cambridge University Press, 2004) 112.

[69] *Department of Agriculture v Moreno*, 413 US 528 (1973).

Stamp Act. The Act once established eligibility based on household. 'Household' was defined as a 'group of related or nonrelated individuals, not residents of an institution or boarding house'. In addition to cohabitation, the law required that members of the household live as one economic unit, share common cooking facilities and purchase food in common. After Congress removed 'unrelated' from the eligibility conditions, a group of poor unrelated people brought a constitutional challenge to the law. This group qualified as a non-conjugal family of more than two persons as its members lived under the same roof, shared expenses and were committed to supporting each other.

The Court found a violation of equality, protected under the Fifth Amendment. In applying the rational basis test, it first identified the goals the new law was seeking to effectuate. The first of these purposes – excluding 'hippies' – was not valid. The Supreme Court did not have to delve far from the Declaration of Policy of the Act, where Congress clearly stated such a purpose.[70] The interest boiled down to a bare desire to harm a politically unpopular group. The Court concluded that this could not be considered a legitimate state interest.

Second, the state argued that the law intended to minimise the risk of fraud. The argument stressed that households with unrelated people are more likely to commit a fraudulent conduct by failing to report income or by intentionally remaining poor. They are also more unstable, making it difficult to detect frauds. A prophylactic rule was thus necessary to prevent anomalous outcomes. With respect to this argument, the Court noted that while the purpose is valid in the abstract, there were ad hoc provisions aimed at minimising the risk of fraud. Therefore, the measure adopted by Congress was not related to the stated goal. The existence of ad hoc provisions is a paradigmatic example of where a measure cannot be said to be rationally connected to the goal.

Most commonly, under-inclusiveness and over-inclusiveness determine a failure to establishing a rational connection between means and purpose. A law will not pass muster when it is under-inclusive, as it does not include within its scope a situation that would warrant inclusion. Also, it will not pass muster when it is over-inclusive, as it covers situations that should not be included. Clearly, the deferential nature of the standard tolerates a substantial degree of under-inclusiveness or over-inclusiveness.[71] Therefore, this line of argument has a more limited likelihood of success except for manifestly unjust under-inclusiveness or over-inclusiveness.

To conclude, despite doubts as to what a rational basis test entails, it is clear what a rational basis test does not entail. First, courts cannot invent a valid interest.[72] This requires state actors to always make an effort to proffer a reasonable justification for their action. Second, in order for a state interest to be valid, it

[70] AS Perlin, '*United States Department of Agriculture v Moreno*: The "Red Herring" of Social Welfare' (1974) 23 *DePaul Law Review* 1485, 1495.

[71] Fallon (n 68) 113.

[72] CT Dienes, 'To Feed the Hungry: Judicial Retrenchment in Welfare Adjudication' (1970) 58 *California Law Review* 555.

cannot coincide with bare hostility towards a certain group. *Moreno* had the merit of framing the 'animus' exception to a legitimate government interest. This exception proved decisive in *Romer v Evans*, where the Court struck down Colorado's constitutional amendment preventing the inclusion of homosexuality and bisexuality as prohibited grounds of discrimination. Ultimately, a valid justification does not warrant automatic deference. The *Moreno* decision demonstrates that, though fraud prevention is a valid state interest, the Court is still willing to move to the next step. At this second stage, despite the standard being fairly deferential, a lack of rational connection can still lead to the invalidation of the measure.

Understandably, some researchers have downplayed the *Moreno* decision as not impacting on the usual reluctance to uphold welfare rights. The decision seemed to rest on the impermissible motives driving the legislature, which saw 'hippies' as offensive.[73] However, the decision conferred a constitutional *imprimatur* to equal protection claims of non-conjugal families of more than two persons. It also contains important passages rejecting the contention that *any* purpose or *any* stated connection will pass muster.

For all these reasons, I conclude that the equal protection 'route' is not barred; however, a deferential rational basis test is likely to apply.

II. Due Process

The due process clause under the Fifth or Fourteenth Amendment[74] – depending on whether state or federal law is engaged – has an elusive meaning in constitutional doctrine. Its aim is to protect the most fundamental liberties of all individuals. Such liberties are 'so rooted in the traditions and conscience of our people as to be ranked as fundamental' and therefore cannot be infringed upon without compelling reasons for doing so.[75]

The clause has both a procedural and a substantive component. At the very least, it constitutes a procedural safeguard against arbitrary deprivations of life, liberty and property. However, as procedural safeguards are notoriously insufficient, it also protects individuals against the risk of legislation arbitrary in its substance, which results in a deprivation of personal freedoms. As Justice Harlan's dissenting opinion in *Poe* puts it:

> Were due process merely a procedural safeguard it would fail to reach those situations where the deprivation of life, liberty or property was accomplished by legislation which by operating in the future could, given even the fairest possible procedure in application to individuals, nevertheless destroy the enjoyment of all three … Thus the guaranties of

[73] *Moreno* (n 69) 534–35.

[74] To oversimplify, when fundamental liberties are infringed by a federal state actor, the Fifth Amendment applies. By contrast, when such liberties are infringed by state actors, the Fourteenth Amendment applies. See *Bolling v Sharpe*, 347 US 497 (1954).

[75] *Snyder v Massachusetts*, 291 US 97, 105 (1934).

> due process, though having their roots in Magna Carta's 'per legem terrae' and considered as procedural safeguards 'against executive usurpation and tyranny', have in this country 'become bulwarks also against arbitrary legislation'.[76]

Courts held that heterogeneous entitlements fall within the purview of the clause. These range from a parent's fundamental right to custody over their children to a negative liberty which shields economic activities from government interference.[77] Recently, in *Obergefell*, the Supreme Court removed all doubts as to whether the right to marry can be considered fundamental.[78] Marriage is the association with the noblest purpose in society, the Court reasoned, and an ability to access marriage is inherent in the concept of individual autonomy.[79] The right to marry is indeed one of the most 'vital personal rights'. As such, an exclusion from marriage can only be justified on compelling grounds.

LGBTQ litigators argued that the right to same-sex marriage is a subset of the broader fundamental right to marry. They marshalled evidence showing the functional equivalence of same-sex families with respect to cis-sex families: the same ability to love, engage in intimacy, raise children, responsibly allocate financial responsibilities etc. Should a group of new families be interested in marriage, this litigation offers a detailed blueprint. A line of argument based on due process has indeed been envisioned by a prominent US expert in polyamory when describing the various approaches poly advocates could adopt to introduce plural marriage.[80]

Consistent with the remedy outlined in section 3 above, however, this section focuses on specific entitlements rather than marriage or non-marital regimes. In this regard, it should be noted that whenever applicants wish to extend the relevant family definition in order to access these entitlements, they will be confronted with the constraints that constitutional liberalism imposes on requests to uphold affirmative rights. Yet, there is an interpretation of due process that leaves room for cautious optimism in specific circumstances. If the due process clause is applied to the relationship at stake rather than the legal-regulatory regime, the protection of a subset of non-conjugal families is warranted under the Constitution: relatives.

The boundaries of substantive due process are drawn based on history. Extended families were a widespread family model in the pre-industrialisation era.[81] Aware of the predominance of extended families before industrialisation, the Supreme Court in *Moore*[82] struck down a zone ordinance excluding two cohabiting relatives – a grandmother and a grandson – from the relevant definition of family

[76] *Poe v Ullman*, 367 US 497, 540–41 (1961).

[77] E Chemerinsky, 'Substantive Due Process' (1999) 15 *Touro Law Review* 1501, 1501–02.

[78] *Loving v Virginia*, 388 US 1, 12 (1967) (casting the right in terms of a 'vital personal right essential to the orderly pursuit of happiness by free men').

[79] *Obergefell* (n 38).

[80] Aviram and Leachman (n 3) 315.

[81] But see P Laslett (ed), *Household and Family in Past Time* (Cambridge, Cambridge University Press, 1972) (arguing that the predominance of extended families in the preindustrial era is a myth, since the nuclear family was already the predominant model).

[82] *Moore v City of East Cleveland*, 431 US 494 (1977).

for purposes of living together in a housing unit. In so doing, it held that the nation's history and tradition warrant a larger notion of family which goes beyond the nuclear family:

> Ours is by no means a tradition limited to respect for the bonds uniting the members of the nuclear family. The tradition of uncles, aunts, cousins, and especially grandparents sharing a household along with parents and children has roots equally venerable and equally deserving of constitutional recognition … Even if conditions of modern society have brought about a decline in extended family households, they have not erased the accumulated wisdom of civilization, gained over the centuries and honored throughout our history, that supports a *larger conception of the family*.[83] (Emphasis added)

Moore thus supports a larger conception of family. This conception includes households with 'uncles, aunts, cousins, and especially grandparents'.

There is a further string of cases which also supports a broader conception. These concern childrearing by grandparents and uncles,[84] so they do not directly bear on the topic discussed in this book. It is worth recalling that the focus of this work is horizontal relationships. Horizontal relationships refer to the relationship formed between consenting adults, while vertical relationships refer to the relationship between adults and minors. Despite non-directly bearing on the issue of extending benefits to adult–adult non-conjugal families, these cases corroborate the idea that the US legal system recognises a larger conception of the family in other areas as well. In questioning the existence of an 'average American family' and recalling that 'the composition of families varies greatly from household to household',[85] these decisions offer valuable doctrinal underpinnings to argue that extended families merit legal protection.

To conclude, if focus is redirected onto the relationship at stake, the due process clause might warrant an extension of entitlements to non-conjugal families composed of uncles, aunts, cousins and/or grandparents.

III. Freedom of Association

The third line of argument concerns freedom of association. As anticipated, I find it unpersuasive. Legal arguments invoking association freedoms under the First Amendment clash with the quintessentially negative nature of this freedom. As a negative liberty, freedom of association is inherently unable to compel states to expand the coverage of benefits.

Some litigants attempted to fashion an argument on the basis of freedom of association. Two cases explored above have a freedom of association component. First, in *Moreno*, Justice Douglas' concurring opinion adopted a broader

[83] ibid 502–05.

[84] See, eg, *Troxel v Granville*, 530 US 57 (2000) (on a grandparent's visitation rights) and the strand of cases on non-biological parenting – eg, *Bethany v Jones*, 67, 378 SW 3d 731 (Ark 2011).

[85] *Troxel* (n 84) 63.

understanding of freedom of association to protect 'hippies'. Under the proposed construction, this freedom encompasses the 'right to invite the stranger into one's home' not only for 'entertainment' but also to join the household.[86] Second, in the *Belle Terre* case, the landlord also lamented a violation of freedom of association. Yet, only Justice Marshall, in his dissenting opinion, argued that this freedom had been violated. Marshall read freedom of association in conjunction with the right to privacy under the Fourteenth Amendment to lay stress on the existence of a longstanding right to establish a home.[87]

Of course, if one could make a case that state action – excluding non-conjugal families from legal protection – violates freedom of association, the standard of scrutiny would be much stricter. The impugned law could pass muster 'only upon a clear showing that the burden imposed is necessary to protect a compelling and substantial governmental interest'.[88] This conjures up the issue of what falls within the remit of this important freedom. In *Belle Terre*, for instance, Justice Marshall pondered whether it includes the right to invite someone to join the household and offered reasons to respond in the affirmative. However, the problem with arguments based on this freedom is not how broadly freedom of association is defined; the fundamental problem is that freedom of association, as a First Amendment freedom, is one of the negative liberties *par excellence*. As such, it cannot back claims targeting affirmative entitlements either directly or indirectly. It is no surprise that this argument only featured in a handful of concurring and dissenting opinions.

5. Legal Arguments in Family Law Litigation

Venue	Family or civil court dealing with the family law matter at stake (in the case of ALJs, the civil court hearing an appeal)
Remedy	Extension of specific family benefits
Legal arguments	1. Judicial updating 2. Under-inclusiveness and over-inclusiveness of marriage

Family law litigation holds more potential compared to constitutional litigation. Here the preferred remedy is also an area-specific approach. Two legal arguments can be suitable to this end: first, a claimant can argue that a judicial updating of the relevant family definition in the governing statute is needed; and, second, they could argue for the inadequacy of marriage as the basis for allocating family benefits when a statute explicitly confines eligibility to spouses, which is a likely

[86] *Moreno*, (n 69) 538–45 (Douglas, J, concurring).
[87] *Belle Terre* (n 64) 15, 18.
[88] ibid 18, citing *Shapiro v Thompson*, 394 US 618, 634 (1969).

occurrence. The second argument is also a form of judicial updating, but is specific to spousal benefits.

Both lines of argument aim to replace current narrow family definitions with functional ones accounting for the reality of family lives. For instance, a workable functional definition of family will be drawn from a minority approach to regulating post-breakdown 'spousal' support. When it comes to post-breakdown support, a handful of states adopt a definition pivoting on the following criteria: continuous cohabitation, the duration of the relationship, the purpose of the relationship, the pooling of resources and services for joint projects, and the intention of the parties. This is a workable variant of a functional definition that might include non-conjugal families within its ambit.

I. Judicial Updating

Once a benefit from which a non-conjugal family is excluded is identified, the first step of the first proposed argument requires an assessment of whether there is room for judicial updating.

I use the term 'judicial updating' to refer to both an outcome and a means. Under the first meaning, the term designates the result of a judicial interpretation that results in 'updating' a definition through various techniques (typically purposive canons of interpretation) to anchor it in contemporary values or practices. Under the second meaning, it refers to an interpretative canon per se. When substantial changes occur at the legal, factual or scientific level, statutory terms that are out of touch with the new reality should be interpreted in order to align with it. In the US, this technique is usually adopted when the matter at hand is governed by the common law.

In either case, it is indispensable to account for the rules governing statutory interpretation. Different statutory interpretation rules apply depending on whether (i) there is a governing statute or (ii) the matter is governed by the common law.

(i) *Governing statute*. In the case under condition (i), there is a statutory definition of family (eg, 'for the purposes of this statute "family" means spouses and *cohabiting partners*'). In any such case, statutory interpretation is more 'rigid'; claimants should be aware of a taxonomy of interpretative canons to predict the likelihood of success of their claim. Textual interpretation is by far the preferred approach to interpreting laws in the US. When a statutory definition is ambiguous, the judge will often first look at dictionaries and then at the legislative history of the text when an intended effect evidence is available.

Other rules of interpretation include textual context. Sometimes, if the judge is not satisfied with dictionaries (or legislative history), they will look at the broader textual context (is there a list of beneficiaries that can help understand what family means in that sentence?) or at the whole act or code (assuming that identical words throughout the act or code have a similar meaning, what is the meaning of the same word in different contexts?).

Purpose usually comes after the above-mentioned techniques to break a tie of two reasonable meanings. Judges can ascertain the purpose of a definition by either inferring it from the text or the legislative history, or by taking judicial notice of a meaning developed outside the courts. The use of purposive interpretative techniques is usually associated with judicial activism, as it commonly leads to judicial updating, but its use is hardly predictable. While in principle judges should resort to this canon only after textual canons, ambiguities can often be 'created' (and dictionaries discarded as unsatisfactory) by progressive judges willing to adopt a purposive approach to interpreting statutes. Thus, it is not predictable in advance whether a court will resort to purposivism in a creative fashion.

In a nutshell, whenever there is a statutory definition of family carrying an unambiguous meaning (eg, 'for the purposes of this statute "family" means husband and wife'), the judge will have their hands tied and will likely stick with the statutory definition. When, by contrast, such a definition is ambiguous (regardless of whether the ambiguity is genuine or created), the judge will enjoy more interpretative leeway. They will first look at dictionaries and then at the legislative history. Some judges will also inquire into the broader textual context. 'Activist' judges will soon move to inquire into the purpose of the law in order to update it.

This is to say that interpretative updating is not easy to pursue when there is a governing statute (as is the case under condition (i)) due to the relative rigidity of the taxonomy of statutory canons of interpretation. Yet, interpretative updating is not barred either. It is not barred when the statute contains an ambiguous definition of family; moreover, it is also not barred when the statute mentions the term 'family' without defining it.

It could well be the case that a statute lacks a definition and that the judge concludes that the legislative history does not command a specific meaning. Important developments in family law followed this pattern. In 1989, a New York court dealing with inheritance rights in a rent-controlled apartment construed the term 'family' under the rent control code so as to encompass two cohabiting conjugal partners.[89] In *Braschi*, the Court stated that there was no statutory definition of family and that legislative history offered insufficient evidence to construe the term. It thus moved to adopt purposive canons to recognise the relationship of two lifetime partners characterised by 'emotional and financial interdependency' as family under the statute.

In assessing the objective of the law, the Court concluded that the intended protection against sudden eviction should not rest on legal fictions, such as a marriage certificate or an adoption order. The Court set forth several criteria to go beyond 'fictitious legal distinctions' and account for the 'reality of family life',

[89] *Braschi v Stahl Associates Co*, 74 NY 2d 201 (NY 1989).

amongst which are 'the exclusivity and longevity of the relationship, the level of emotional and financial commitment, the manner in which the parties have conducted their everyday lives and held themselves out to society, and the reliance placed upon one another for daily family services'.[90] The test is an objective one. It is also a test where the totality of the circumstances is controlling. Thus, the absence of one or more of the listed markers of family is not dispositive.[91] Interestingly, the New York court justified this outcome by applying ordinary meaning as the controlling canon of construction. To that end, it quoted the (unusual?) *Webster's Dictionary* definition of family as 'a group of people united by certain convictions or common affiliation'.

A subsequent case, *Blake v Stradford*,[92] seemed to cast doubt on this doctrinal development. Yet, thereafter, the principle that '[p]rotections against sudden eviction should not be determined by genetic history, but should instead be based on the reality of family life'[93] was continuously re-affirmed in the state of New York.[94] This functional definition of family has then been codified in various provisions of the Rent Stabilization Code and in the implementing regulations.[95]

Although the applicants in *Braschi* were two conjugal partners, all the foregoing attributes are applicable to two non-conjugal family members. Therefore, non-conjugal couples can emphasise their ability to meet the conditions identified by the courts as relevant in the State of New York, especially the duration and intensity of their commitment. Overall, the decision in *Braschi* constitutes a good blueprint for a persuasive argument. First, it rightly redirects attention towards the purpose of the benefit. I offer a method for identifying the purpose of the programme in the next section.[96] In *Braschi*, the purpose of the scheme was the need to prevent the sudden eviction of a family member upon the death of the partner. Second, its placing stress on the importance to go beyond 'fictitious legal distinctions' and account for the 'reality of family life' is critical. This supplies an opportunity for a person in a non-conjugal relationship to describe the relationship at length and persuade the court of the seriousness of their commitment (eg, by showing joint bank accounts, shared residence and other relevant signposts of interdependence). It further supplies an opportunity to describe how supportive they and the other person have been to each other and how their mutual dependence, both financial and emotional, have unfolded over time and have reached a significant degree of intensity.

I should like to offer a second example of a benefit whose eligibility can be expanded via judicial updating. This concerns social security benefits. At the federal level, these benefits are administered by the Social Security Administration (SSA).

[90] ibid 213.
[91] ibid 212.
[92] *Blake v Stradford*, 725 NYS 2d 189 (Dist Ct 2001).
[93] *Williams v Williams*, 2006 NY Slip Op 26302, 822 NYS 2d 415 (Civ Ct).
[94] ibid; see also *DeJesus v Rodriguez*, 768 NYS 2d 126 (Civ Ct 2003).
[95] *Hazel Towers Co, LP v González*, 2013 NY Slip Op 51937(U), 981 NYS 2d 635 (Civ Ct).
[96] See s 5.II below.

The governing regulations adopt a notion of family which is broad compared to other public benefits. SSA benefits extend not only to spouses, but also to common law partners. They might also extend to same-sex couples in a civil union, domestic partnership or designated/reciprocal beneficiary scheme, subject to the condition that the relevant non-marital regime includes inheritance rights within its scope.

In the wake of same-sex couples' judicial victories – especially *Windsor*, striking down DOMA,[97] and *Obergefell*, recognising same-sex marriage nationwide[98] – the Social Security Administration (SSA) started enlarging the notion of family through interpretative guidance. Effective from February 2016, social security employees apply an internal guidance called Program Operations Manual System (POMS). The relevant POMS rule is entitled 'Same-Sex Relationships – Non-Marital Legal Relationships'. It purports to extend social security benefits to same-sex partners in a non-marital union.[99] By 'non-marital legal relationship' (NMLR), the rule refers to parties to a civil union, domestic partnership, designated or reciprocal beneficiary regime. Eligibility is conditional upon the legal regime at hand conferring inheritance rights, as a clue for its being comparable to marriage.[100]

The new rule grants NMLR partners the social security benefits under Title II, namely retirement, and survivor's or disability insurance. It also grants Medicare enrolments.

I contend that this new framework is ambiguous as to whether it includes non-conjugal families. Take the example of two relatives who registered under a designated beneficiary scheme where available. As previously seen, state schemes, such as designated or reciprocal beneficiary schemes and domestic partnerships, sometimes allow non-conjugal pairs to register.[101] This is case in Colorado, Hawaii, Maryland, Maine, District of Columbia (and Vermont until 2013). Within this group, many of these states allow registered couples to enjoy inheritance rights. Nonetheless, it is unclear whether a non-conjugal family could claim social security benefits and Medicare under the POMS rule.

As a matter of language employed, non-conjugal couples that have registered in these states can be included in the notion of NMLR. The 'only' problem is the reference in the title of the POMS rule to 'same-sex relationships'. Yet, it is unclear whether this entails a willingness to exclude registered non-conjugal couples. It seems that the administration had simply not foreseen the applicability of the scheme to non-conjugal couples. Hence, it is reasonable to conclude that at

[97] *Windsor* (n 34).

[98] *Obergefell* (n 38). After *Obergefell*, the President instructed the Cabinet to review over 1,000 federal statutes. Likewise, the decision also exerted a profound impact on states and their domestic laws.

[99] 42 USCS § 216(h)(1)(A)(ii) (Social Security Act); 20 CFR § 404.345 (1979); Soc Sec Admin., Program Operations Manual System (POMS), GN 00210.004 – Non-Marital Legal Relationships (Such as Civil Unions and Domestic Partnerships) (2016), https://secure.ssa.gov/poms.nsf/lnx/0200210004.

[100] Eligibility is granted only if the domicile of the number holder (NH) would allow the claimant to inherit a spouse's share of their personal property should the NH die without a will. See GN 00210.004 – Non-Marital Legal Relationships.

[101] See s 1 above.

present, non-conjugal families are not envisaged by the policy and that room for action exists.

However, this is a peculiar situation. The ambiguity is contained in an interpretative guidance. Agencies adopt interpretative rules when they aim to clarify the meaning of a statute or regulation they are called to implement. The administration enjoys a nearly unfettered discretion in interpreting its own rules, including guidance documents. Therefore, should the administration refuse to include non-conjugal families in the policy, there is only a route/argumentative move left: first, arguing that the rule is legislative rather than interpretative, since it is innovating the legal framework; and, second, requiring a judicial review of the rule and arguing for the absurdity of an interpretation that excludes non-conjugal families.[102] In the end, despite its situation being not envisaged by the law, a registered non-conjugal couple checks all the boxes.

(ii) *The matter is governed by the common law.* At other times, the matter is governed by the common law. In any such case, judges enjoy ample leeway in terms of updating definitions.

This occurs if there is either a common law statute or a statute which adopts common law concepts. In relation to the first category, for instance, tort recovery is an area governed by the common law. Hence, non-conjugal couples do not need to comply with strict statutory interpretation rules to innovate definitions – it is the case law itself which shapes the relevant definitions. In relation to the second category, in some cases the matter is governed by a 'common law statute' in the sense that the concepts contained therein are fairly abstract (as fashioned in a deliberately vague common law-like language) or that a substantial delegation of authority to lay out definitions and standards to common law adjudicators can be inferred from the text.[103]

In both cases, it is possible to point to changes that have occurred at the legal, factual or scientific level by responding to the following questions: have subsequent judicial decisions eroded the force of an old judicial interpretation? Have subsequent facts/theories/science eroded its force? Has subsequent legislation eroded it? The changes that have occurred in family structures and law as outlined in this chapter offer solid grounds on which to argue that definitions warrant judicial updating. This line of argument is especially suited to the area of tort recovery. State courts often adopt a functional definition of family to allow someone to receive a compensation for the wrongful death of a family member or in the context of other common law torts.

[102] If the court finds that the rule is legislative in its substance rather than interpretative, it will subject it to the ordinary scrutiny given to administrative rules. On the so-called Chevron Step Zero doctrine see *United States v Mead Corp*, 533 US 218 (2001); on the distinction between the two types of rules see PL Strauss, 'The Rulemaking Continuum' (1992) 41 Duke Law Journal 1463, 1478–79.

[103] *Leegin Creative Leather Products, Inc v PSKS, Inc*, 551 US 877 (2007).

The most illustrative area is likely that of recovery of damages for the infliction of emotional distress. This common law tort allows someone to be compensated under certain circumstances when an accident to a close family member occurs. Following the pioneering decision in *Graves v Estabrook*,[104] New Hampshire courts have adopted a functional notion of family in defining the third requirement of the foreseeability test (that the parties be 'closely related'). Along with a showing that the applicant was near the scene of the accident and that the shock resulted from direct observance of the accident, the third condition requires that the party be 'closely related'. In grappling with the condition, the Court rejected the 'bright-line' rule put forward by the defendant, according to whom 'closely related' shall be construed as meaning two individuals related by blood or marriage.[105] The Court, by contrast, adopted a 'flexible approach designed to account for factual nuances'. The appropriate inquiry is whether, regardless of labels, the parties are in a 'stable, enduring, substantial, and mutually supportive' relationship:

> [T]o foreclose [an unmarried cohabitant] from making a claim based upon emotional harm because her relationship with the injured person does not carry a particular label is to work a potential injustice … where the emotional injury is genuine and substantial and is based upon a relationship of significant duration that … is deep, lasting and genuinely intimate.[106]

The approach has subsequently been adopted in Hawaii,[107] Nebraska,[108] Ohio,[109] Tennessee,[110] West Virginia,[111] Pennsylvania[112] and, to a more limited extent, New Jersey.[113]

Again, a persuasive line of argument would stress the importance of overcoming 'labels' and accounting for the reality of family ties. The first step is to identify the objective of the law. In this case, the aim is compensating someone for the emotional harm they have sustained. It then becomes key to stress the importance of going beyond fictitious legal definitions to achieve the aim in question. This will give a non-conjugal family an opportunity to describe the relationship so as to convince the court of the seriousness and intensity of the reciprocal commitment, on the assumption that commitment rather than formal ties is the proper benchmark to be used in allocating the benefit.

[104] *Graves v Estabrook*, 818 A 2d 1255 (NH 2003).
[105] *Elden v Sheldon*, 758 P 2d 582 (Cal 1988).
[106] *Graves* (n 104) 1261–62, citing *Dunphy v Gregor*, 642 A 2d 372, 378 (NJ 1994).
[107] *Leong v Takasaki*, 520 P 2d 758 (Haw 1974) (permitting a step-grandmother to recover for negligent infliction of emotional distress).
[108] *James v Lieb*, 375 NW 2d 109 (Neb 1985).
[109] *Paugh v Hanks*, 451 NE 2d 759 (Oh 1983).
[110] *Thurmon v Sellers*, 62 SW 3d 145 (Tenn Ct App 2001).
[111] *Heldreth v Marrs*, 425 S.E 2d 157 (WVa 1992).
[112] *Sinn v Burd*, 404 A 2d 672 (Pa 1979).
[113] *Dunphy v Gregor*, 642 A 2d 372 (NJ 1994).

II. The Over-Inclusiveness and Under-Inclusiveness of Marriage

Following a second line of argument, I lay out a methodology allowing courts to re-assess government programmes which confine legal protections to spouses. I observe that marriage can be both under-inclusive and over-inclusive when it comes to identifying the relevant definition of 'family' which deserves the protection of the law.

This argument capitalises on various critiques of marriage as the basis for allocating government benefits. When family benefits are only conferred upon spouses, non-conjugal families can demonstrate that a similar allocation is obsolete in light of the developments that have occurred in family law and family structures. The developments in the field of family law and family structures were outlined in section 1 above. In addition to these findings, the present section draws on: (i) empirical research on caretaking duties and resource pooling; and (ii) judicial decisions or legislative reforms adopting a larger conception of family in order to extend access to specific benefits.

In relation to the former, empirical findings suggest that nowadays marriage can be an under-inclusive and over-inclusive mechanism in terms of allocating benefits and privileges in several situations. As a consequence, each government programme could be re-assessed with a view to understanding if a valid state interest exists and whether such an interest can be better effectuated by extending eligibility requirements so as to include other families. A number of judicial opinions and legislative reforms were conducive to enlarging family definitions – for instance, in some areas, states introduced a functional notion which does not pivot on conjugality, that is, on a sexual component.

This section offers the conceptual tools to conclude that when a government programme restricts eligibility to marital families (which occurs quite often!),[114]

[114] Detecting a marital privilege is a complex task. Definitions of family for the purposes of conferring family benefits change across jurisdictions and across areas, such as welfare and tax. One can also sometimes find a different definition within the same area. It is thus neither possible nor advisable to offer a complete overview of these eligibility requirements. As such, I will only offer some illustrative examples. For instance, evidentiary privileges offer the narrowest definition of family (that is, the married family). See Fed. R. Evid. 501. They can sometimes be extended to domestic partners, where this is recognised by state rules of evidence (see, eg, the District of Columbia), which is often not the case. Tax law seems to retain a marital privilege. After Trump's reforms, marital status no longer carries a serious penalty if the couple comprises equal-earners. The major tax privileges gained as a result of being married derive from the personal exemptions and credits in the context of income tax; see KA Ryan, 'EITC as Income (In)Stability?' (2014) 15 *Florida Tax Review* 583. Estate tax rules (or wealth transfer taxation) also rely heavily on marriage. At the federal level, the most well-known example is the rule permitting spouses to transfer by means of inter vivos gifts or, upon death, assets free of any gift tax or estate tax (so-called marital deduction) (26 USCS §§ 2056(a), 2523(a)). Another major spousal privilege is gift splitting. Each spouse is granted an annual exception ($14,000 as of 2017) to make tax-free gifts to third parties (26 USC § 1041). The privilege consists of allowing spouses to make a gift to third parties which is considered as being made from one-half of each spouse's allowance, thereby doubling the amount of the exception; see L Kahng, 'The Not-So-Merry Wives of Windsor: The Taxation of Women in Same-Sex Marriages' (2016) 101 *Cornell Law Review* 325, 364. Additional key tax benefits of

marriage is an under-inclusive and/or over-inclusive benchmark in many respects. I propose a two-step approach to verify whether the current family definitions based on marriage are 'accurate'. The two steps germane to verifying their accuracy can be framed as two questions:

(i) What is the purpose of the programme? Is it valid?
(ii) If there is a valid purpose, does an inclusion of non-conjugal families within the definition of 'family' better achieve such a purpose?

(i) *Purpose of the law*. This step aims to assess the purpose a government programme is set to achieve. This is a highly context-specific inquiry. The purpose that this step refers to is not the purpose of the family definition, but of the programme, ie, of the family benefit. One should be alert to the fact that the inherent purpose of the programme and the state interest in adopting a certain family definition do not always overlap. Take the example of welfare benefits. The state interests in adopting a narrow definition of family often boils down to avoiding the situation where people become public charges, as well as a well-known interest in a privatisation of care; these interests, as argued above, severely curtail the likelihood of success of legal arguments aimed at obtaining public benefits. However, I suggest redirecting focus onto the purpose of the *programme*. The purpose of, say, a social security plan is to compensate the other member of the relationship for the informal and unpaid care they have provided. Thus, a state pays you a survivor's pension owing to the fact that you provided unformal and unpaid care in favour of a family member who was once active on the job market.

At other times, the distinction between the purpose of the programme and the state interest in adopting a certain family definition is more blurred. Take the example of evidentiary privileges. Spousal immunity allows someone not to take the stand against their spouse. This rule is a relic of the past stemming from the doctrine of coverture.[115] The ostensible aim of such immunity is to allow spouses to talk freely without fear of being forced to take the stand in a way that

being married include: (a) the higher maximum limitation to enjoy the exclusion of gain from sale of principal residence; (b) tax-free healthcare coverage provided by the spouse's employer; and (c) an 'ability to shift the tax burden on alimony at divorce'. See PA Cain, 'Legal Guidance for Same-Sex Couples Considering Marriage' (2016) 35 *ABA Tax Times* 1, 1–3. In the field of social security, federal employees also enjoy many spousal benefits. The following benefits flow automatically from marital status: the Federal Retirement Thrift Savings Plan (FRTSP), the Federal Employees Health Benefits Program (FEHB), the Federal Employees Group Life Insurance (FEGLI), the Federal Employees Dental and Vision Program (FEDVIP), the Federal Long-Term Care (FLTCIP) and the Federal Flexible Spending Account (FSAFEDS). There are multiple benefits enjoyed by military personnel due to marriage, such as retirement and medical spousal benefits, family separation allowance when the spouse is on duty, and a host of 'perks' such as shopping privileges at the commissary. Similarly, there are many veteran benefits conferred upon spouses, such as spousal benefits in the event of death or disability, healthcare, home loan assistance and educational benefits. The spouse is also entitled to a gratuity of $100,000 in the event of the death of active-duty personnel, and only where there is no surviving spouse will the gratuity be conferred to the next of kin (which could be a parent or a sibling). See SE Squillace, *Whether to Wed: A Legal and Tax Guide for Gay and Lesbian Couples* (Boston, Squillace & Associates, 2014) 48.

[115] W Blackstone, *Commentaries on the Law of England* (Chicago, University of Chicago Press, 1979 [1725]) 442.

could be detrimental to the other partner. These privileges largely rest on reasons of humanity, such as protecting the sacred precincts of marriage and the marital bedroom.[116] However, in any such case, it is not clear whether protecting the precincts of marriage is the purpose of the programme per se or whether it is instead a post hoc rationalisation for having adopted a certain definition of family (one pivoting on marriage).

(ii) *Does the purpose warrant an extension of eligibility requirements?* The purpose having been identified, the question arises as to which definition of 'family' better effectuates it.

The marital couple is the focus of the majority of US public and private law entitlements.[117] When redirecting focus onto the purpose of the scheme, marriage is unlikely to pass muster at this stage. Definitions based on marriage are unlikely to pass muster in that they can be both under-inclusive and over-inclusive.

Let us consider social security law. I argued above that the purpose of a social security plan is to compensate the other member of the relationship for the private informal and unpaid care they have provided. As such, a pension scheme that grants a survivor's pension to a person who either married two months before the partner's death or who did not actually provide care would be irrational and unable to fulfil this purpose. In this sense, marriage is over-inclusive: it grants protection to a host of spouses who did not support each other in a sufficiently solid way to deserve state assistance. At the same time, marriage is under-inclusive, as many interdependent adults who actually performed informal and unpaid care in favour of a family member slip under the radar of the law. Interdependent non-conjugal adults can be ascribed to this category.

Let us move on now to analysing tax regimes. The state could argue that the purpose of tax exemptions, credits and favourable brackets is a bare desire to incentivise marriage. Yet, on closer examination, the purpose is nudging people into mutually supportive relationships since the 'first and most important justification is economic unity'.[118] The favourable treatment marital families enjoy is in fact founded on a presumption that they share assets and pool resources. Nevertheless, the relevant notion of family is over-inclusive in the sense that it recognises all married families as economic units. This is an undemonstrated claim, which recent empirical research tends to repudiate.[119] In particular, social scientists have

[116] Instrumental justifications, by contrast, fell into disuse. Such justifications were unrealistically assuming that spouses would not communicate in the absence of such an immunity. See CA Wright and KW Graham, Jr, *Federal Practice and Procedure: Evidence § 5572* (St Paul, West Publishing Co, 1989), cited in JH Wigmore, EJ Imwinkelried and RD Friedman, *The New Wigmore: A Treatise on Evidence*, 2nd edn (New York, Aspen Publishers, 2010) 506–09.

[117] See the accompanying text to n 114.

[118] ME Kornhauser, 'Love, Money and the IRS: Family, Income Sharing and the Joint Return' (1993) 45 *Hastings Law Journal* 63, 96.

[119] Institute for Family Studies, 'The Case for Merging Finances in Marriage' (26 May 2015), https://ifstudies.org/blog/the-case-for-merging-finances-in-marriage (reporting that '31 percent of married or cohabiting couples have separate checking accounts, and 23 percent keep separate personal savings accounts' and that 'closer to half of couples with joint accounts also maintain separate accounts').

shown that when it comes to marital families, joint returns, asset pooling and control sharing are arguably a myth.[120] These researchers suggest that a significant percentage of marital couples (30–50 per cent) do not share or pool resources.[121] For instance, a subset of married couples (ie, married couples living apart) rarely do so. Spouses living apart are nonetheless able to file taxes jointly and to enjoy tax exemptions and credits. In a similar vein, the notion of family adopted in the field of tax is under-inclusive. This notion does not fully account for non-conjugal families or all other family networks sharing resources in innovative ways.[122]

Hence, an argument can be made that the preferential treatment marital families enjoy is an injustice to all non-conjugal families pooling resources and sharing assets. Despite their demonstrable interdependence, non-conjugal families will not be able to file a joint tax return. This is mainly a critique of the filing status, but the whole tax architecture (and set of exemptions) is based on similar assumptions, *rectius* presumptions concerning joint returns, asset pooling and control sharing. At present, these presumptions only attach to marital families. A policy choice to retain the marital family as the benchmark overlooks empirical research to the contrary. Hence, an argument can be made that the relevant definition should be expanded to confer more favourable tax brackets and exemptions upon non-conjugal families.

A third example concerns legal standing to sue under wrongful death statutes. Wrongful death statutes allow a person to recover damages for the death of a family member resulting from negligence or misconduct. The victim's family can recover loss of support and/or income, funeral expenses, out-of-pocket expenses and non-economic damages. Legal standing to bring these lawsuits is established at the state level. Some states confer legal standing upon a person who is 'dependent' on the deceased; these include New Jersey, Virginia, Wyoming and California.[123] The majority of states also confer legal standing upon a broad array of persons holding kinship to the deceased, such as domestic partners or designated beneficiaries, grandchildren, parents, siblings and those entitled to inherit under state law. Although the presumption of dependence only applies to spouses,[124] the notion of family adopted therein is much larger and more 'functional' than in other areas of law.

According to Professor Polikoff, the emphasis these statutes place on proof of dependency provides a good occasion to reflect on the objective of the law. In her view, the aim is to compensate someone for the loss of an economic provider.[125]

[120] Kornhauser (n 117) 105.

[121] Institute for Family Studies (n 118); see also AC Infanti, 'Decentralizing Family: An Inclusive Proposal for Individual Tax Filing in the United States' (2010) *Utah Law Review* 605, 617.

[122] Kornhauser (n 117) 104–09.

[123] In the case of California, the dependant must also reside in the deceased's dwelling.

[124] Note that Michigan, Illinois and Maryland require proof of dependency by the spouse as well.

[125] ND Polikoff, *Beyond (Straight and Gay) Marriage: Valuing All Families under the Law* (Boston, Beacon Press, 2009) 99.

With this purpose in mind, one should find definitions carefully tailored to achieve this aim. For instance, the presumption of dependency that a spouse enjoys in many states disregards the fact that some married couples do not live together or are not financially interdependent, and therefore do not need to be compensated.

While eligibility requirements from time to time extend to non-conjugal families – especially those units made up of relatives, or registered friends or relatives in states where this is possible – only spouses usually enjoy a presumption of dependency. This presumption is not grounded in reality and marriage turns out to be over-inclusive in many cases, as previously illustrated. In light of the inclusion of relatives as family members in these statutes, the problem is not one of egregious under-inclusiveness. A subset of non-conjugal families does have legal standing to recover damages for the loss of an economic provider. These persons only encounter an additional burden consisting of the need to prove their economic dependence. The issue here could virtually entail discrimination; as such, it should be addressed through constitutional litigation, namely through an equal protection challenge.

In the end, while no general answer can be provided, the proposed two-step analysis to assessing government programmes shows that marriage can often be under-inclusive and/or over-inclusive. A second important lesson is that the state potential objection that functional definitions are unworkable is untenable. An extensive string of judicial opinions, some of which I have explored above, illustrate that functional definitions can and do work. This is to say that there are plenty of models to draw upon. These models demonstrate that administrative reasons can be easily rejected as an insufficient ground to continue privileging traditional marital families over non-conjugal families.

Conclusion

The chapter has examined the different approaches to the problem of the invisibility of non-conjugal families in the US. While falling short of offering a complete overview of the vast universe of legal benefits, it supplies a theoretical framework and a critical methodology for re-assessing government programmes in such a way to include non-conjugal families.

If one wants to distil some takeaways from the analysis, the first one would be a disenchantment with constitutional litigation – that is, the traditional avenue litigators pursue to innovate the legal framework. With (extremely) cautious optimism, one could only resort to the due process-based line of argument, which embeds a conceptually 'larger conception of family'. A second potential line of argument is an equal protection approach, despite the applicable standard being one of minimum rationality. When this standard applies, the chances are high that state action will be upheld unless it is found to be manifestly irrational.

A second, more promising – and yet overlooked – avenue to tackle the exclusion of non-conjugal families is family law litigation. Two main arguments can profit non-conjugal pairs: one aiming at the judicial updating of family definitions and the other at demonstrating that marriage is over-inclusive and under-inclusive when taken as a benchmark. Both arguments endeavour to replace current family definitions based on marriage or other formal family ties with a functional test which identifies family definitions that better effectuate the purpose of the law. When it comes to functional tests, with their emphasis on actual rather than presumed caretaking activities, interdependent non-conjugal families are not only suited for inclusion, but are perhaps second to none in the hypothetical ranking of those that should be included.

4

Canada

Introduction

Canada is a fertile terrain for family law policy reforms, for many reasons. Canadian demographics are unique in the sense that they reveal a stunning variety of family arrangements. The general public have also had a significant level of exposure to progressive ideas on family recognition (compared to other parts of the world), usually incubated and developed in legal academia. Further, in the last two decades, a trend towards the legal recognition of new families has been registered, such as unmarried conjugal couples or, in some cases, non-conjugal couples.

Consistent with the overarching purpose of this book, this chapter seeks to predict how non-conjugal couples might gain legal recognition in Canadian courtrooms, the arguments that can be used and the potential hindrances to be overcome in relation to this. Looking at same-sex couples' litigation, which is the most pertinent analogy, two types of arguments have been mobilised: one based on human rights legislation and the other on the Canadian Charter of Rights and Freedoms (hereinafter 'the Charter').[1] Human rights codes are statutes of quasi-constitutional nature that specialise in preventing discrimination against citizens in certain social settings, such as housing and employment. The Charter is the federal constitutional bill of rights.

Substantively, the arguments that this chapter expounds are all equality-based. This decision is the product of both the relative weakness of autonomy-based arguments applicable to new families and of the robust anti-discrimination apparatus in force in the country. There is an arsenal of provisions substantiating the right to equality, fair treatment, equal opportunity and non-discrimination in Canada. These include, inter alia, the Charter, the Canadian Bill of Rights,[2] federal and provincial human rights codes, and the rights and freedoms guaranteed under the common law. This is likely the reason why, historically, the extension of protections to non-marital families resulted from a litigation strategy claiming equality with respect to marital couples.

[1] Canadian Charter of Rights and Freedoms, 1982 (Schedule B to the Canada Act, 1982 (UK)), c 11, repr RSC 1985.

[2] Canadian Bill of Rights, SC 1960, c 44.

In the following sections, I will first illustrate the most recent evolutions affecting family patterns and family legislation. I will then proceed to elucidate the two venues where constitutional litigation and human rights litigation are conducted. In section 3, I will sketch out the type of remedy that can be sought in each context. Ultimately, I will outline the lines of arguments that I consider to be more persuasive.

1. The Changed Landscape of Family Structures and Family Law in Canada

The last available census in Canada nicely captures a fluid reality with a growing incidence of new families.[3] Such a reality comprises married couples, common law marriages, multi-generational families with grandparents, parents and children, and skip-generation families with grandparents and grandchildren. Yet, it also excludes other family grids due to the fact that demographers often lack the conceptual categories to detect them. Families that slipped under the radar include, inter alia, friends in a non-conjugal relationship, and polyamorous relationships.

We have seen in Chapter 3 how the rate of marriages is decreasing in the US.[4] Crude marriage rates in Canada are even lower compared to those in the US[5] and a further, constant decline is under way.[6] Cohabitation, by contrast, is becoming increasingly appealing as a form of intimate connection, with Québec having one of the highest cohabitation rates in the world – 31.5 per cent of all census couples in 2011 fell into this category.[7] I realised the significance of this figure when an academic fellow in Montréal told me that it was quite normal for Québécois to have unmarried parents. You can imagine how striking that would sound to someone born and raised in Catholic southern Italy. My grandma still cannot come to terms with the fact that I – a woman in her thirties – am not married.

In addition, Canadian family structures keep evolving and achieving new levels of complexity.[8] Recently, multi-generational households rose to 404,000, becoming the 'fastest-growing household type since 2001 (+38%)'.[9] One-person households also reached their peak in 2016 (28.2 per cent of all households), the

[3] Statistics Canada, 'Families, Households and Marital Status: Key Results from the 2016 Census' (2 August 2017), https://www150.statcan.gc.ca/n1/daily-quotidien/170802/dq170802a-eng.htm.

[4] See ch 3, s 1.

[5] In Canada, the crude marriage rate in 2008 – when the last statistics were collected – was 4.4 per 1,000 of the population, while in the US in 2011, it was 6.8 per 1,000 of the population. See Institute for Family Studies, 'Increasing Cohabitation is Destabilizing the Canadian Family' (23 August 2017), https://ifstudies.org/blog/increasing-cohabitation-is-destabilizing-the-canadian-family.

[6] JD Payne and MA Payne, *Canadian Family Law*, 6th edn (Toronto, Irwin Law, 2015) 2 ff.

[7] Institute for Family Studies (n 5).

[8] Vanier Institute of the Family, 'A Snapshot of Family Diversity in Canada' (February 2018), www.vanierinstitute.ca/snapshot-family-diversity-canada-february-2018.

[9] ibid.

highest share since the birth of the Canadian Confederation.[10] These changes also resonate with the social perception of the phenomenon: Canadians believe that there is no such thing as a 'typical family' – at least not anymore.[11]

The second rationale for considering Canada a receptive place for 'progressive' family policy is the considerable traction these themes have had in legal academia. Among family law scholars, there is a lucid awareness that the current legal framework does not reflect the sociological reality of family formations and that it should be reformed accordingly. Indeed, in Canada, it seems that feminist and queer studies have arguably higher prevalence in this domain of legal scholarship than any other. By contrast, in continental Europe, similar topics receive comparatively less traction, with research in this field even being discarded as 'non-legal' by traditionalist fringes in academia in Italy, France and Germany.

At least since the 1990s, family law researchers in Canada have been treating the misalignment between the legal framework and the many different forms of family as a compelling problem. For instance, in 1998, a study by the British Columbia Law Institute voiced concerns around the dangers associated with such misalignment and recommended the introduction of a registration scheme that would be open to conjugal and non-conjugal relationships alike.[12] Most importantly, in 2001, the Law Commission of Canada, an independent federal law reform agency, released a report entitled 'Beyond Conjugality',[13] the focus of which was non-conjugal caregiving.[14] The report has circulated globally and is routinely cited as the benchmark study in fora where the topic is discussed.[15]

The aim of the Law Commission study was to propose a principled approach to re-assessing all existing laws and regimes employing relational terms to allocate duties, responsibilities or privileges – usually laws distributing benefits based on marriage.[16] The proposed approach consists of a four-step analysis, whereby policy-makers ask in turn whether:

(i) the objectives of the law are legitimate;
(ii) the relationship on which distribution is based is relevant to the achievement of the objective;
(iii) the law allows for the self-designation of the beneficiary;

[10] Statistics Canada (n 3).

[11] Vanier Institute of the Family, 'Families Count: Profiling Canada's Families IV' (2010) 26, cited in Alberta Law Reform Institute, *Property Division: Common Law Couples and Adults Interdependent Partners* (Final Report 112, 2018) fn 135.

[12] British Columbia Law Institute, *Report on Recognition of Spousal and Family Status* (1998), www.bcli.org/sites/default/files/5-Report-Report_on_Recognition_of_Spousal_and_Family_Support.pdf.

[13] Law Commission of Canada, 'Beyond Conjugality: Recognizing and Supporting Close Personal Adult Relationships' (2001) 37.

[14] While acknowledging the limits of the methodological decision of leaving out polyamorous relationships, the drafters were persuaded that it was premature to push for any reform in that sense.

[15] K Brook, 'Cameos from the Margins of Conjugality' in R Leckey (ed), *After Legal Equality: Family, Sex, Kinship* (Abingdon, Routledge, 2015) (calling it a 'watershed' in the development of the socio-legal understanding of family).

[16] Law Commission of Canada (n 13) xii.

(iv) should self-designation not be possible/appropriate, there is a better way to include the relevant functional relationship.[17]

One telling example concerns the rollover provision in the tax field for transfers of property. The Commission's proposal was to reframe it so as to include all persons in an economically interdependent relationship. The Commission established that the purpose of the law is to encourage transfers of property within the family without excessive scrutiny on the nature of their relationship. Once a thus-framed purpose is identified, the statutory conditions for eligibility (marriage or common law marriage) end up being irrelevant to the achievement of the objective.[18] By contrast, a broader definition of family that refers to parties to an economically interdependent relationships better serves it.

In addition to laying out the four-step approach to retrospectively recalibrate existing benefits, the report pushes the analysis further to find the most suitable mechanism to recognise new families. After outlining the limits of marriage, the contractual model and ascription, the Commission proposes the introduction of a registration scheme open to conjugal and non-conjugal pairs. Yet, the Department of Justice laconically dismissed the question. To this effect, it submitted that 'further study would be needed before Parliament can decide whether it is appropriate to treat non-conjugal relationships in the same way as spouses or common-law partners in all federal laws'.[19] On a more positive note, although the Department of Justice did not follow through with the reform, the report helped the seeds of change to sprout by laying the ground for a debate that more aptly focuses on self-definition, autonomy and radical pluralism in the realm of the family, both in Canada and abroad.

Ultimately, a third reason as to why Canada is an ideal site of inquiry is the variety of legal reforms that have been enacted to recognise a wider range of families. Take unmarried conjugal couples, which are labelled common law couples in common law provinces and de facto couples in Québec. The available menu of options for these couples, both cis-sex and same-sex, is varied. They have the option of: (i) getting married; (ii) registering in a civil union; (iii) qualifying for common law marriage in common law provinces; and (iv) qualifying as a de facto couple in Québec.

There is a *décalage* of protections associated with each option. Civil unions are usually offered the same primary regime of marriage with few exceptions; common law couples need not marry to gain access to several legal protections

[17] ibid xii–xiii.
[18] ibid xv.
[19] Canadian Department of Justice, *Marriage and the Legal Recognition of Same-Sex Unions: A Discussion Paper* (no 14, November 2002) fn 4, https://silo.tips/download/s-e-r-v-i-n-g-c-a-n-a-d-i-a-n-s.

(support obligations, compensatory allowances etc);[20] de facto couples in Québec are mostly legal strangers, except when children are involved. Unlike other provinces, Québec did not extend the same protections afforded to civil unions and marriage to de facto couples. Cohabitants can only resort to contracts to govern their patrimonial regime and bring an action for unjust enrichment if they are wronged following the breakdown of the relationship.[21] For limited purposes – eg, in some social statutes – de facto couples are equated to married and civil partners.[22] Yet, these remedies fall far short of what such partners may presumptively obtain.

Along with same-sex marriage, Québec allows same-sex and opposite-sex couples to register in a civil union. Registration schemes are also in force in Nova Scotia and Manitoba. The remaining provinces and territories adhere to an ascription model whereby unmarried couples gain the same rights and obligations as married couples, with some exceptions concerning the post-breakdown distribution of property.

Interestingly, two legal schemes in force in the country officially recognise non-conjugal families. Reference is made to the Adult Interdependent Relationships Act (AIRA) in Alberta[23] and to the Family Services Act in New Brunswick. AIRA comes in the form of a comprehensive registration scheme; by contrast, the Brunswick law only regards support obligations.

Alberta's scheme is open to any two adults in an interdependent relationship. It was enacted in response to the decisions of the Supreme Court of Canada, which held that discrimination based on sexual orientation was constitutionally impermissible,[24] and a cognate decision of Alberta's Court of Queen's Bench.[25] These judgments fuelled a mobilisation by socially conservative Christian movements, seeking to mitigate the symbolic value of same-sex couples' recognition.

The phrase 'adult interdependent partners' (AIPs) is now added to laws and provincial programmes previously reserved to spouses.[26] The system is a mixed one – both contractual and ascriptive. To become AIPs, the parties can either sign an agreement or seek the ascription of status after three years of an interdependent relationship – or a relationship 'of some permanence' when children are involved.

[20] Some differences persist in the field of private law, especially vis-a-vis the distribution of property. See ND Polikoff, *Beyond (Straight and Gay) Marriage: Valuing All Families under the Law* (Boston, Beacon Press, 2009) 113.

[21] R Leckey, 'L'enrichissement injustifié, l'union de fait et l'emprunt à la common law dans le droit mixte du Québec' (2018) 59 *Les Cahiers de droit* 585, 598–600.

[22] For instance, they can consent to care and treatment in the case of incapacity of the partner under art 15 of the Code Civile du Québec (CCQ) or bring a direct action in liability in case of wrongful death (abolition of the rule in art 1056 of the Civil Code of Lower Canada (CCLC).

[23] Adult Interdependent Relationships Act, Statutes of Alberta 2002, c A-4.5 (AIRA).

[24] *M v H* [1999] 2 SCR 3.

[25] *Johnson v Sand*, 2001 ABQB 253 (CanLII), citing *M v H* (ibid).

[26] These include statutes conferring healthcare benefits where one partner's age is above 65, workers' compensation death benefits, spousal support and inheritance rights, including a right to inherit a share of estate assigned by law, irrespective of the content of the will.

However, to palliate the adverse impact on the freedom of choice of relatives, which constitutes the majority of long-term cohabiting non-conjugal adults, status is not ascribed to this category: relatives must take affirmative steps to become AIPs by signing an agreement. By contrast, close friends and roommates meeting the eligibility conditions can have this status ascribed.

The definition of 'relationship of interdependence' is material to attributing status. Parties must: (i) share lives; (ii) be emotionally committed; and (iii) 'function as an economic and domestic unit'.[27] The last condition, which has the most elusive meaning, must be found by employing a totality of the circumstances test. Such a test takes into account several factors, including whether the parties are in a 'conjugal' (*sic*) relationship, are exclusive, hold out as a couple, eat together, share living expenses, property, and finances.

Thus, in order for non-conjugal couples to be ascribed status, they must be conjugal. However, the irony in this conclusion is mitigated by Canadian courts in common law provinces adopting a totality of circumstances test. The test was outlined in *Molodowich v Penttinen*, and then 'approved' by the Supreme Court in *M v H*. In *Molodowich*, an Ontario's court listed 7 indicia to detect conjugality amongst which is the arrangements for shelter the parties make, their arrangements for domestic services, their sexual behaviour, the community's attitude towards the couple etc. Based on the test, if one condition is not met (eg, sex), this is not dispositive.

The choice to employ typical signposts of the marital family was bound to impact on the capability of the scheme to attract non-conjugal families. A recent survey conducted by the Alberta Law Reform Institute confirms that non-conjugal couples have not registered – or at least have not sought to enforce their rights in court.[28] The same situation occurred in New Brunswick. The Family Services Act extends spousal-like support obligations to anyone in a family relationship of at least three years who is 'substantially dependent upon the other for support'. The relevant definition of 'family' potentially encompasses non-conjugal couples.[29] Yet, in the case law analysis I conducted, I was not able to detect a single lawsuit brought by a non-conjugal family.

Despite non-conjugal couples having not registered, the laws created a possibility for them to conceive of themselves as family. A recent case on interdependent siblings in Alberta is instructive in this sense. The applicants were a non-conjugal pair seeking an extension of the federal Canada Pension Plan (CPP) survivor's pension before the Social Security Tribunal.[30] Although rejected on jurisdictional grounds, the case epitomises the new possibility for non-conjugal families to emerge from the shadow of the extra-legal.

[27] AIRA, s 1(1)(f).
[28] Alberta Law Reform Institute (n 11) [215].
[29] Article 112(3) of the Family Services Act, SNB 1980, c F-2.2.
[30] *EH v Minister of Employment and Social Development*, 2017 CanLII 30681 (Soc Sec Trib).

2. Venue

Constitutional and human rights litigation have taken centre stage in Canada as the two key avenues for the recognition of new families. This section maps the differences between the two contexts.

I. Constitutional Litigation

It is much less straightforward to understand what the constitution is in Canada compared to the other jurisdictions under examination. The Constitution of Canada comprises a political component (of constitutional conventions, which courts might ascertain yet not enforce) and a legal one. In turn, the 'legal' constitution can be found in both written and unwritten norms.[31] Unlike US states, Canadian provinces do not have their own written constitutions. Only British Columbia has a written 'constitution', which is nevertheless statutory in nature and therefore can be amended through parliamentary law. Provinces have their own unwritten constitutions, but these are perceived as 'too opaque, oblique, and inchoate to rouse much interest, let alone passion'.[32] The supremacy of the federal constitution is, by contrast, undisputed. Textually, such supremacy is set forth in section 52(1) of the Constitution Act, 1982, which states that any law inconsistent with the Canadian Constitution 'is, to the extent of the inconsistency, of no force or effect'.[33]

The key parameter for assessing the compliance with human rights of family laws is the Charter. This constitutes the first part of the Constitution Act, 1982. Although before the Charter, some courts had made an effort to shape an 'implied bill of rights' in order to curb government action, it was the advent of this document that marked a watershed moment. Enacted in 1982, the Charter empowered courts to protect fundamental rights and freedoms throughout the nation through 'wide and unfettered discretion'.[34]

As to 'where' constitutional litigation occurs, Canada adopts a decentralised model of constitutional review ('judicial review').[35] Consistent with this

[31] P Oliver, P Macklem and N Des Rosiers, 'Introduction' in P Oliver, P Macklem and N Des Rosiers, *The Oxford Handbook of the Canadian Constitution* (Oxford, Oxford University Press, 2017) 1–2. See also M St-Hilaire and L Bich-Carrière, 'La constitution juridique et politique du Canada : notions, sources et principes' in *Droit constitutionnel* (Montréal, LexisNexis Canada, 2011) fasc 1.

[32] N Wiseman, 'Clarifying Provincial Constitutions' (1996) 6 *National Journal of Constitutional Law* 270.

[33] Section 52(1) of the Constitution Act, 1982 (UK), being sched B to the Canada Act, 1982 (UK), 1982, c 11.

[34] The formula 'wide and unfettered discretion' frequently appears in scholarly pieces on s 24(1) of the Charter, which concerns the remedies that can be granted to rectify a breach of Charter rights. See, eg, DM McAllister, 'Charter Remedies and Jurisdiction to Grant Them: The Evolution of Section 24(1) and Section 52(1)' (2005) 25 *Supreme Court Law Review* 62.

[35] R Hirschl, 'The Judicialization of Politics' in KE Whittington, RD Kelemen and GA Caldeira (eds), *The Oxford Handbook of Law and Politics* (Oxford, Oxford University Press, 2008) 131.

model, all ordinary courts have the power to carry out an a posteriori review of legislation in relation to nearly all types of controversies. Unlike in continental European jurisdictions, there is no specialised constitutional court. As is the case in the US, the Supreme Court is not an ad hoc body established to resolve constitutional disputes. The Court sits at the apex of the judicial system and thus in addition to reviewing the constitutionality of legislation, it also acts as the court of last resort in criminal and civil matters.

As a consequence, the analysis offered below only focuses on the federal constitution, as applied by all courts of justice before which a constitutional challenge is brought.

II. Human Rights Litigation

Both the federal government of Canada and the provincial governments have enacted human rights codes or acts (hereinafter 'codes'). This legislation aims to combat discriminatory acts and patterns of inequality stemming from discrimination in the public and contractual sphere. The settings usually covered by human rights codes include employment, accommodation, services or facilities available to the public (schools, hospitals, stores etc), housing, wages, purchase of property, and unions and associations. Compared to the Charter, codes have a different personal scope: they mainly apply to private actors and their relationships. However, they can also apply to governmental actors as their reach extends to public services. In relation to the type of prohibited discrimination, human rights codes adopt roughly the same grounds of discrimination as the Charter, with some additions concerning discrimination perpetrated by private actors, such as 'source of income'.

Despite their formal status as statutes, codes are considered as having a quasi-constitutional nature in light of their content.[36] This heightened rank has major implications. Primarily, judges must follow special rules of statutory interpretation. Due to its special content, the code as a norm ought to be construed purposively, while limitations ought to be construed narrowly. Their quasi-constitutional stature also reverberates in their relationship with other sources of law. Quasi-constitutional statutes are considered 'more important than other laws'.[37] Therefore, when a conflict with a statute arises, the code shall 'supersede' the statute, except, clearly, when the conflicting statute is also quasi-constitutional.

[36] See, eg, *Insurance Corporation of British Columbia v Heerspink* [1982] 2 SCR 145.
[37] ibid para 178.

Each human rights code establishes its own enforcement mechanism and vests administrative bodies with a mandate to implement the equality mandate they enshrine. These bodies are usually quasi-judicial in the sense that they utilise court-like procedures, such as hearings, to decide cases. However, they are also less formal compared to a court of justice, as well as faster, less costly and more conciliatory in nature. At the federal level, the relevant code is the Canadian Human Rights Act (CHRA) of 1977. This establishes a two-tier system with the Canadian Human Rights Commission (CHRC) at the bottom and the Canadian Human Rights Tribunal (CHRT) at the top, reviewing cases referred to it by the Commission. The Commission investigates complaints and helps the parties reach an agreement, but without ruling on cases. The provinces feature a one-tier system. The name of the competent administrative body should not mislead us: despite jurisdictions like Ontario and British Columbia calling it 'tribunal', and Saskatchewan, Manitoba, New Brunswick, Québec and Nova Scotia calling it 'commission', the purpose of the body does not change. For the sake of clarity and simplicity, I will use the term 'commission' when referring to the administrative body established under provincial codes, and 'Commission' when referring to the federal CHRC.

3. Remedy

The term 'remedy' refers to the ultimate goal a claimant seeks to achieve through litigation. This could be a share of estate or pension or 'spousal' support, or access to a family regime. In light of the wide variety of benefits that can be sought, this book uses two overarching categories: an area-specific approach, targeting specific entitlements, and a comprehensive approach, targeting a family regime (eg, civil partnerships).

I. Constitutional Litigation: An Area-Specific Approach

Unmarried couples and same-sex couples first gained recognition by focusing on specific entitlements. Adopting This tack is reasonable. It avoids broad, loaded, value-laden generalisations as to which family the state should officially recognise. It more aptly focuses attention on the objective of the relevant legislation and on whether policy-makers are allotting benefits in a discriminatory manner. For instance, the justification proffered for excluding same-sex couples or unmarried conjugal couples from certain entitlements at some point became simply untenable. Distinctions between these couples and spouses became less justifiable in light of factors such as the social acceptance of these non-marital formations, legal developments that occurred in human rights fora, and empirical findings concerning their ability to 'function' as family.

In the case of same-sex couples, this area-specific approach was part and parcel of a broader plan culminating in the liberalisation of the institution of marriage. The plan can be described as following an inductive pattern which went from the specific to the general. It involved gathering sufficient elements – ie, legal precedents on sectorial issues – to infer at a later time that same-sex couples deserved comprehensive recognition through a full-fledged comprehensive regime. The area-specific could draw criticism from scholars emphasing its contribution to a systemic failure of courts to detect endemic inequalities.[38] While I share this criticism, in the area of family law, the chosen piecemeal approach has been successful in rejecting the idea that same-sex couples could not function as a family. This was achieved by rightly homing in on whether such couples could be family for purposes of that specific entitlement, thereby avoiding broad generalisations. Hence, if viewed as a stepping-stone to comprehensive recognition, this approach is not only useful but also arguably indispensable to the cause of non-conjugal families.

A separate issue is whether non-conjugal families can successfully follow the pattern illustrated above. I argue that they can. It is notable how courts changed their minds in such a short space of time, moving from a celebration of the 'heterosexual difference' to full acceptance of sameness. The functional equivalent of the 'heterosexual difference' for non-conjugal couples is the 'conjugal difference'. The term refers to the popular belief that only sexually intimate relationships can properly function as a family.

M v H provides a salient example of the extent to which, back then, the heterosexual family was taken for granted. In its defence, the government of Canada did not even 'bother' saying that it was protecting the vulnerable member of a *heterosexual* family; it merely referred to a general protection of 'intimate relationships'. The implicit assumption was that the boundaries of intimacy necessarily overlap with those of heterosexual intimacy. Predictably, the same obliteration of non-conjugal families will occur when defending schemes which exclude non-conjugal families. Family definitions do not usually mention the modifier 'conjugal', nor will the government argue that it is defending the conjugal family, but merely the family. In any such case, it is critical to unveil the strategic erasure of conjugality which aims at surrounding family definitions with an aura of inevitability.

The chances are relatively high that the conjugal difference can be debunked. Non-conjugal couples attract lower resistance compared to same-sex couples. This is especially due to the absence of the sexual component, which has been at the centre of much government attention, and to unions of care being praiseworthy and socially endorsed.

[38] F Faraday, 'One Step Forward, Two Steps Back? Substantive Equality, Systemic Discrimination and Pay Equity at the Supreme Court of Canada' (2020) 94 *Supreme Court Law Review* (forthcoming) (exposing the gap between the Supreme Court paying lip service to fighting systemic discrimination and its scattered approach to only tackling 'isolated provisions in single statutes').

II. Human Rights Litigation: An Area-Specific Approach

By the time the Supreme Court recognised marital status as an analogous ground of discrimination, most provinces had already done so through their human rights codes. Despite the Charter being a watershed moment, one could legitimately doubt that the axis of litigation has ever shifted from human rights claims to constitutional equality claims. Human rights commissions and tribunals tend to be preferred over ordinary courts because they are a less costly and faster means of protection. In addition, these bodies are specialised in human rights law and are more acquainted with theories of equality and related concepts. This specialist knowledge is often key to upholding complex anti-discrimination claims.

Yet, human rights litigation is not a complete surrogate for constitutional litigation. In fairness to the courts, they receive the hard cases challenging legislation as opposed to discriminatory practices in services or employment. Moreover, when inequality is embedded in a statute, it is one thing to strike down the law, but quite another to expand access to some services on a case-by-case basis. At some point, the difference between the two venues became blurred. Until recently, a rather expansive interpretation of 'service' has been conducive to framing 'Charter-like' claims under the codes. This generated a partial overlap between constitutional litigation and ligation based on human rights instruments.[39] However, in 2018, the Supreme Court clarified that the notion of 'service' cannot be stretched to the point of becoming synonymous with 'law'.[40] This reasoning came across as a friendly reminder that human rights tribunals cannot strike down laws and that decisions yielding this effect in practice would unduly stretch the letter of human rights legislation. A third reason why human rights litigation is not a surrogate for constitutional litigation is that systematic inequalities are not easily discernible in cases addressed by human rights bodies; they are part and parcel of a larger phenomenon concerning the way in which structures of power function and affect the lives of individuals. Hence, the most appropriate forum to disentangle these subtle and pervasive inequalities is ordinary courts vested with the power of constitutional review.

Yet human rights litigation does play a unique role: the role of stimulating policy change in the field of equality.[41] The case of LGBTQ rights is not only instructive but also encouraging in this respect. The Canadian Human Rights Commission, established under the CHRA, was a key advocate of sexual orientation equality rights at a time when such rights were not only not recognised but also vehemently opposed. In 1981, only one-third of Canadians were supportive of equal

[39] C Mummé, 'At the Crossroads in Discrimination Law: How the Human Rights Codes Overtook the Charter in Canadian Government Services Cases' (2012) 9 *Journal of Law and Equality* 103.

[40] *Canada (Canadian Human Rights Commission) v Canada (Attorney General)* [2018] 2 SCR 230.

[41] A Nierobisz, M Searl and C Théroux, 'Human Rights Commissions and Public Policy: The Role of the Canadian Human Rights Commission in Advancing Sexual Orientation Equality Rights in Canada' (2008) 51 *Canadian Journal of Public Administration* 239, 241.

rights for all sexual orientations.[42] However, hostile public sentiment did not keep the Commission from pursuing its mandate as the shaper of public opinion. This was achieved through annual reports and intense lobbying activity throughout the 1980s. What is especially encouraging is that a comparable public hostility is not present in the case of non-conjugal families.

An additional approach was that of accepting claims of same-sex couples even before Parliament introduced the ground of sexual orientation in the CHRA in order to speed up the amendment process. This would not be even necessary in the case of non-conjugal families. All codes already provide for the grounds of family status and/or marital status. In some cases, what they do not envisage is a more expansive application of family and marital status to cover non-conjugal families.

Next, once Parliament introduced the ground of sexual orientation in the CHRA, which did not occur until 1996, the Commission became even more active in tackling the exclusion of same-sex couples. While since 2000 it also became an advocate for same-sex marriage, in the first phase it played a crucial role in extending benefits, with a major focus on employment-related benefits. Its activity was carried out on various fronts: it received complaints by same-sex couples concerning a broad range of issues, such as health coverage, tax credits, family leave and survivor's pensions; it deferred cases to the federal human rights tribunal; and it intervened in major equality cases brought before the courts. Furthermore, it successfully mobilised employee organisations and raised public awareness on the importance of recognising same-sex unions.[43]

For all these reasons, I believe that human rights litigation plays a critical role in family policy reform. In Canada, convincing human rights commissions that non-conjugal families are the next frontier in family law could prove indispensable if one wants to raise awareness amongst the general public, employers and legislators – an awareness which at present is lacking.

Looking at past litigation, the most appropriate approach before human rights commissions is an area-specific approach. Human rights litigation is structured in such a way that claimants challenge a discriminatory exclusion from benefits or services. Thus, they usually seek an order whereby access to these benefits is obtained, and potentially other remedies such as a cease and desist order, a declaratory order saying that the conduct is discriminatory, or compensation for losses or expenses. By contrast, human rights fora are unsuitable in terms of opening up comprehensive schemes to new beneficiaries. But again, one should recall that commissions are powerful vehicles through which to raise awareness and lobby other actors to pursue legislative change, including comprehensive family law regimes.

[42] Canadian Human Rights Commission, *Canadians and Discrimination: An Analysis of the 1981 Opinion Poll* (Ottawa, Research and Special Studies, Canadian Human Rights Commission, 1982) 11.

[43] Nierobisz, Searl and Théroux (n 41) 250.

4. Legal Arguments in Constitutional Litigation

Venue	Any court performing a judicial review of laws under the Constitution
Remedy	Extension of specific familial benefits
Legal arguments	1. Marital status discrimination 2. Family status discrimination

The most compelling lines of argument in constitutional litigation are equality-based. The constitutional provision shielding individuals from discrimination is section 15 of the Charter, which reads as follows:

> Every individual is equal before and under the law and has the right to the equal protection and equal benefit of the law without discrimination and, in particular, without discrimination based on race, national or ethnic origin, colour, religion, sex, age or mental or physical disability.

Section 15 guarantees equality 'before the law', in continuity with the Canadian Bill of Rights of 1960. It also guarantees equality 'under the law', which encompasses both questions of discriminatory administration of the law and substantive inequality. It then ensures the 'equal benefit of the law', meaning a fair administration of government benefits. Ultimately, it ensures the 'equal protection of the law', a wording that purportedly conjures up the Fourteenth Amendment of the US Constitution and its jurisprudence.[44] The provision embeds a 'broad range of values':[45] Its reach extends to all cases where a person's essential dignity risks being attacked or a person is at risk of being treated as 'less worthy'.[46]

However, equality-based claims also have their limits. These are twofold in nature:

(i) the periodic reluctance of the Supreme Court to uphold them; and
(ii) their unpredictability, due largely to the instability of the equality legal test as it has been developed by courts.

In the first years of the Charter jurisprudence, Canadian courts were hesitant to let claims on equality grounds move forward. Dispositions of section 15 claims in courts dropped from 190 in the 1990–94 period to 69 in the 2010–13 period.[47] The success rate oscillated between an average of 15 per cent in 1990–94, 21 per cent in 1995–99 and 2000–04, and 7.2 per cent in 2010–13.[48] However, lately it seems that

[44] PW Hogg, *Constitutional Law of Canada*, 5th edn (Toronto, Carswell, 2007).
[45] *Andrews v Law Society of British Columbia*, [1989] 1 SCR 143, para 171.
[46] *Gosselin v Québec (Attorney General)* [2002] 4 SCR 429, para 20.
[47] B Ryder, 'The Strange Double Life of Canadian Equality Rights' (2013) 62 *Supreme Court Law Review* 261, 271.
[48] ibid 271.

courts are more willing to adjudicate equality claims.[49] Hence, it is not possible to identify a unified trend in section 15 cases, but the intermittent reluctance to dispose of and uphold such claims is a potential obstacle to bear in mind. Some tentative reasons for the relative marginality of equality in constitutional jurisprudence can be teased out.

For one thing, Parliament and the provincial legislatures have passed laws in voluntary compliance with the equality guarantee, without litigation becoming necessary. In order to streamline this process and give governments time to bring their legislation into compliance with equality rights, the effective date of section 15 was delayed by three years (to 1985). Governments then amended a host of laws to remove the most egregious forms of discrimination. Subsequently, once the Supreme Court recognised marital status[50] and sexual orientation[51] as analogous grounds of discrimination to the grounds listed in section 15(1), a similar pattern was followed: governments amended hundreds of statutes and regulations in order to comply with the Court's rulings.

A second reason for the relative marginality of equality jurisprudence could be that the Court is more familiar with 'individualistic' rights rather than group-based rights. Comparatively, section 7 claims – implicating a breach of the right to the security of the person – raised along with equality claims proved much more successful. A case in point in this respect is *Carter*,[52] a leading case that decriminalised medical assistance in dying. The claim was originally framed both in terms of discrimination on the basis of disability and in terms of an infringement of the right to life and security of the person. However, the Supreme Court did not consider the equality claim. In a similar vein, when a violation of equality rights and a violation of freedom of association under section 2(d) were simultaneously raised, the Court upheld freedom of association over equality rights.[53]

A final tentative reason could be the continued relevance of statutory claims under human rights codes, which I have previously described.[54] This is likely the key reason behind the marginality of the section 15 jurisprudence.

The second complicating factor which is listed above is unpredictability. Unpredictability especially derives from the non-linearity of the section 15 legal test, which has been continuously (re)shaped by the Supreme Court. The fact that the test keeps changing excludes the opportunity to make predictions as to the likelihood of the success of equality claims and keeps litigators in a permanent state of uncertainty.

[49] This point was raised by Bruce Ryder during the conference 'Italo-Canadian Conference: Celebrating the 150th anniversary of the Canadian Constitution', held at the University of Toronto on 17 September 2017.

[50] *Miron v Trudel* [1995] 2 SCR 418.

[51] *M v H* (n 24).

[52] *Carter v Canada (Attorney General)* [2015] 1 SCR 331. See also *Alberta v Hutterian Brethren of Wilson Colony* [2009] 2 SCR 567.

[53] *Health Services and Support – Facilities Subsector Bargaining Association v British Columbia* [2007] 2 SCR 391.

[54] See s 3.II above.

In a nutshell, unlike the US, in Canada the legal test is unified. Regardless of whether discrimination occurs based on race, sex, sexual orientation etc, the same standard applies. Further, the test is essentially two-pronged, comprising an infringement prong and a justification prong. First, a claimant must show a denial of 'equal protection' or 'equal benefit' of the law, compared with some other group, and that this constitutes discrimination based on a prohibited ground (known as the infringement or section 15 prong). Next, the onus shifts to the defendant to justify the discrimination under section 1 (the justification or section 1 prong).

Under the current approach to the infringement prong, courts are required to inquire whether:

(1) the law or government action creates a distinction based on a ground; and
(2) the distinction is discriminatory in the substantive sense.

(1) *Distinction linked to a ground.* The first step is to ascertain that a law or action makes a distinction or produces an adverse impact on someone because of a personal characteristic. Omissions can also be relevant if the law or action fails to account for the disadvantaged positioning of a group in society.

Section 15 prohibits discrimination based on the grounds of race, national or ethnic origin, colour, religion, sex, age or mental or physical disability. The section has been construed to also include 'analogous grounds' – ie, it contains an open list of prohibited bases of discrimination. The centrality of the Charter's prohibited grounds of discrimination in Canadian jurisprudence is undeniable.[55] The grounds turned out to be the stage where courts defined the categories worth protecting and screened out trivial claims.[56] In other words, Canadian courts used grounds as a threshold requirement to satisfy before moving to the equality analysis. In the midst of the discordance provoked by a famous trilogy of decisions on equality rights,[57] Justice L'Heureux-Dubé was the only member of the Supreme Court championing an 'approach that looks to groups rather than grounds'.[58] This move was meant to allow claimants to refer to these personal characteristics only in a descriptive sense in order to help convey their personal experience of discrimination. Yet, the L'Heureux-Dubé approach has never garnered the support of the Court. Eventually, it was abandoned by the Justice herself.

This rigid grounds-based approach to equality had various effects on the equality test. The most conspicuous effect was shutting the door to claims that merely attacked 'irrational' or 'arbitrary' laws, as would be possible under a US-style rational basis test. In Canada, questions of reasonableness are usually dealt with

[55] *Withler v Canada (Attorney General)* [2011] 1 SCR 396, para 33 (stating that grounds are 'constant markers of suspect decision making or potential discrimination'). See N Palazzo, 'Equality in Canada: A Tale of Non-normative Groups Struggling with Grounds of Discrimination' (2020) 10 *Oñati Socio-Legal Series* 88.

[56] S Grammond, *Identity Captured by Law: Membership in Canada's Indigenous Peoples and Linguistic Minorities* (Montréal, McGill-Queen's University Press, 2009) 54.

[57] *Egan v Canada* [1995] 2 SCR 513; *Thibaudeau v Canada* [1995] 2 SCR 627; *Miron* (n 50).

[58] *Egan* (n 57) 552.

under the section 1 prong, where the Supreme Court assesses whether an infringement can be subject to justifiable limitations.

The need to invoke grounds also has implications for non-conjugal pairs and their litigation strategy. In order to move forward in the equality analysis, non-conjugal claimants must demonstrate that they align with one of the existing grounds. Alternatively, they must argue that their circumstances reveal a ground that has not yet been identified (a so-called analogous ground). As to which ground can be invoked in our case, The two arguments I outline do this: they distinguish between non-conjugal families able to invoke 'marital status' and those needing to introduce a new ground, 'family status', which is not yet protected at the constitutional level.

(2) *Substantive discrimination.* The second step of the infringement prong requires a showing of substantive discrimination. It looks at whether there has been an imposition of disadvantage. The related case law is a nightmare for Canadian scholars and litigators. The Supreme Court has repeatedly shifted opinion, most recently in May 2018, with the two companion decisions on Québec's pay equity legislation.[59]

The relevant test was first established in *Andrews.*[60] The initial approach gave primary weight to the actual circumstances and to the disadvantage suffered by the complainant. The Court was not willing to uphold claims coming from socially or economically advantaged groups, thereby adopting a relational-status theory of grounds.

Next, the test was radically changed at least five times: in the above-mentioned trilogy of decisions, the justices established three different approaches, none of which gained sufficient support.[61] Overall, the 1995 trilogy had the effect of discarding the disadvantage test in favour of the so-called relevance and stereotyping test. This resulted in shifting the focus away from the circumstances of the claimant to the kind of decision being made.

In *Law*, the Supreme Court introduced a human dignity approach.[62] Despite the intention being the protection of the dignity of claimants, the new approach became problematic. It imposed an additional burden on claimants: that of showing that their personal dignity had been violated as a consequence of discrimination. After *Law* came *Kapp*, which reinstated a version of the first test under *Andrews.*[63] On that occasion, the Court laid down a more coherent approach by shifting the focus from human dignity to distinctions 'that create a disadvantage by perpetuating prejudice or stereotyping'.[64] This approach was not without its critics either. In particular, its requiring a showing that discrimination ensues from prejudice or

[59] *Québec (Attorney General) v Alliance du personnel professionnel et technique de la santé et des services sociaux* [2018] 1 SCR 464; *Centrale des syndicats du Québec v Québec (Attorney General)* [2018] 1 SCR 522 [*CSQ*].

[60] *Andrews* (n 45).

[61] See n 57 above.

[62] *Law v Canada (Minister of Employment and Immigration)* [1999] 1 SCR 497, para 88.

[63] *R v Kapp* [2008] 2 SCR 483 [*Kapp*].

[64] ibid para 17.

stereotypes became a 'formidable barrier for claimants' and 'the fulcrum on which many Section 15 claims have turned'.[65]

Québec (Attorney General) v A, and later *Taypotat*, called for a flexible inquiry over:

> [*A*]*rbitrary – or discriminatory – disadvantage*, that is whether the impugned law fails to respond to the actual capacities and needs of the members of the group and instead imposes burden or denies a benefit in a manner that has the effect of reinforcing, perpetuating or exacerbating their disadvantage. (Emphasis added)[66]

A major change related to the Supreme Court's submission that prejudice and stereotyping were not a test per se, but only 'useful guides'.[67] Nonetheless, it was not easy to make sense of this different wording. Some scholars maintained that the new standard risked being more exacting: while on the one had prejudice and stereotypes had become potential clues for discriminatory treatment rather than discrete elements to prove, on the other reference to arbitrariness – ie the need to prove that the decision is based on evidence and reason – could prove onerous for claimants.[68]

The Supreme Court adjusted its approach lately, in May 2018, in the two companion decisions on Québec's pay equity legislation. In these, it laconically referred to whether the law 'burdens or denies a benefit in a manner that has the effect of reinforcing, perpetuating, or exacerbating … disadvantage'.[69] The legal reasoning in both cases omitted any reference to:

(i) arbitrary – or discriminatory – disadvantage, and
(ii) the responsiveness to the capacities and needs of the members of the group.

What are the implications of this omission? In all probability, its welcomed consequence is to lower the burden of proof for claimants. For instance, arbitrariness placed too much emphasis on the intention of the legislature rather than the actual effects on the group. This unduly shifted the burden on the claimant to prove arbitrariness and imported considerations pertaining to section 1 into the section 15 analysis.[70]

Moving on to see how claimants can prove they have suffered a disadvantage, a contextual analysis that looks at the following factors is required: (i) the preexisting disadvantage of the claimant group; (ii) the degree of correspondence between the differential treatment and the claimant group's reality; and (iii) the

[65] Ryder (n 47) 265.

[66] *Kahkewistahaw First Nation v Taypotat* [2015] 2 SCR 548, paras 19–20.

[67] *Québec (Attorney General) v A* [2013] 1 SCR 61, paras 325–31 and 418.

[68] JW Hamilton and J Koshan, 'Kahkewistahaw First Nation v. Taypotat: An Arbitrary Approach to Discrimination' (2016) 76 *The Supreme Court Law Review* 243.

[69] *Alliance du personnel professionnel* (n 59) and *Centrale des syndicats du Québec* (n 59). The latter case only added 'including historical disadvantage' at the end of the test as a way to further clarify what 'disadvantage' means.

[70] J Koshan and JW Hamilton, 'The Supreme Court's Latest Equality Rights Decision: An Emphasis on Arbitrariness' *ABlawg.ca* (29 May 2015), www.ablawg.ca/2015/05/29/the-supreme-courts-latest-equality-rights-decision-an-emphasis-on-arbitrariness.

nature of the interest affected. I will elaborate on each factor in the next section in an attempt to illustrate how it applies to non-conjugal families.

This short overview should have clarified how fluctuating the equality jurisprudence is. After this 'no responsibility' disclaimer for non-linear parts of the equality analysis in this chapter, I will outline two lines of argument. The first line is based on marital status discrimination and the second on family status discrimination.

I. Marital Status Discrimination

Marital status discrimination was recognised as an analogous ground in *M v H*. Since then, the legislature has encountered constitutional constraints in terms of shaping family law policy. By virtue of the prohibition, legislatures cannot distribute benefits in a discriminatory manner and the relative decisions are subject to constitutional scrutiny.

Yet, in this domain, the line between legitimate constitutional review and improper judicial second-guessing of social policy is more blurred than ever. To err on the side of caution, the Court stressed that in the absence of evidence of an evolution in the fundamental values of society 'by a clear consensus', the matter is left to the legislature.[71] As was seen in section 1 above, non-conjugal claimants can point to both empirical evolutions in family structures and a normative shift towards self-authorship and radical pluralism in family matters.

In addition, constitutional interpretative canons work to the advantage of non-conjugal families. Although much less attention is paid to canons of interpretation compared to the situation in the US and only seldom do interpretative fault lines arise between Canadian justices, the prevalent approach is grounded in the so-called living tree doctrine.[72] The doctrine suggests giving a 'liberal and large', 'purposive', 'remedial' interpretation to the Charter. The practice is so rooted that even when rare originalist turns are taken, there is still a 'ritual nod' to these interpretative 'pieties'.[73] In other words, constitutional dynamism, with its firm rejection of frozen rights, is at the core of constitutional interpretative enterprises.

It is worth recalling that in order for a discrimination claim to be upheld, it is first necessary to demonstrate that the lamented distinction is based on a prohibited ground and then that the distinction constitutes discrimination in the substantive sense.

[71] *Miron* (n 50).

[72] *Edwards v Attorney General for Canada* [1930] AC 124, 136.

[73] BJ Oliphant, 'Bobbitt's Paradise: Canadian Constitutional Interpretation and Public Meaning Originalism' (2017) 31 *DPCE Online* 617, 619.

i. Distinction Based on Marital Status

The first step in the equality analysis requires ascertaining that the impugned legislation draws a distinction between the claimant and one or more groups. When it comes to exclusion from family benefits, the distinction is quite 'straightforward':[74] usually, it is sufficient to point out an exclusion from a default associated with marriage.

Next, the distinction must be linked to a ground. Most family benefits are distributed based on marriage – that is, on marital status. But what does 'marital status' mean in practice? To whom does it apply? Marital status is the status of being married and applies to distinctions drawn between married and unmarried partners. As a personal characteristic, it shares little with other grounds because it is based on a consensual decision to gain status by entering into marriage. The prevailing construction of the ground is strongly steeped in the doctrine of voluntarism. Its influence is only partially mitigated by an acknowledgement that the decision to marry is not genuinely 'free', for there can be a plethora of factors at play which might influence it.[75] For instance, people often have no choice but to live in extra-marital arrangements.[76] But the gist of 'marital status' remains the fact that, unlike other grounds, people 'choose' to marry. By entering into this contract – as the common law tradition frames it – they 'choose' to assume the burdens and benefits attendant to it.

As a consequence of this prevalent understanding, only those who could marry in the abstract but did not are considered as potential victims of marital status discrimination. Indeed, the current constitutional doctrine places emphasis on the invidiousness of discrimination that flows from the decision not to marry. Scholars, moving within this paradigm, advocate for a 'true choice system'[77] that 'respect[s] the different reasons why couples choose not to marry'.[78] However, the implicit assumption is that people can marry in the first place.

In principle, the ground could thus apply to non-conjugal couples of friends or relatives outside the prohibited degrees of consanguinity. This would be possible if only conjugality were not so deeply ingrained in case law and legal thinking. My instinct is that judges might be reluctant to allow non-conjugal pairs to claim marital status discrimination. Nonetheless, I believe that there are reasons to maintain that the ground of marital status should apply to friends and relatives who are eligible to marry in the abstract. Both the non-consummation doctrine and sham marriage doctrine lend support to this view. Let us take friends

[74] *Withler* (n 55) para 64.
[75] See *Nova Scotia (Attorney General) v Walsh* [2002] 4 SCR 325, para 43.
[76] *Miron* (n 50).
[77] Alberta Law Reform Institute (n 11) [160].
[78] ibid [160].

as an example. A marriage entered by two friends would be legally valid based on the following grounds:

(i) Annulment on the grounds of non-consummation can only be granted where one party has a physical incapacity preventing them from consummating the marriage. It cannot be granted if 'failure to consummate is a wilful refusal not to partake in intercourse'.[79] In other words, neither party to the relationship could at some point invalidate a marriage for a failure to engage in sexual intercourse.

(ii) There is no sham marriage doctrine that is conducive to invalidating marriage. The sham marriage doctrine is only relevant for immigration purposes. Unlike the situation in the US, there is no doctrine applicable across the board which warrants a termination of marital benefits (or criminal sanctions) where a marriage is purposefully entered into in order to gain such benefits by US citizens. The doctrine of marriage fraud is much narrower in Canada compared to the US; it only applies in the field of immigration law where one of the spouses is a non-citizen who tries to play the system through a marriage of convenience.[80] Hence, it seems that friends or relatives with Canadian citizenship can enter into a valid (sham!) marriage and cannot be held liable if they wish to do so.

Non-conjugal families that are ineligible to marry warrant a separate discussion. Think of non-conjugal relatives within the prohibited degrees of consanguinity and affinity.[81] Based on the current doctrines, they might not be able to invoke marital status discrimination. I argue that they should not invoke it and should focus on family status discrimination instead. Hence, their situation is addressed separately in the next section.

Once a distinction is identified and linked to marital status, one is left with the question of whether such distinction is discriminatory.

ii. Substantive Discrimination

Clearly, not all distinctions based on marital status are discriminatory. Should all distinctions be impermissible, the very possibility to enact differentiated family regimes would not stand – there could be, say, no common law marriages or civil partnerships. This would hardly pay heed to the rationale of the prohibition, which does not seem to mandate the erasure of plural family regimes.

The Supreme Court offers some guidance on how to distinguish discriminatory and permissible distinctions. The first two useful decisions in this regard

[79] *Heil v Heil* [1942] SCR 160.

[80] On which see R Challborn and L Harder, 'Sex and the genuine marriage:consummation and conjugality in Canadian citizenship', (2019) 23 Citizenship Studies 407.

[81] In Canada, the category of ineligible relatives includes persons 'related linearly, or as brother or sister or half-brother or half-sister, including by adoption'. See the Marriage Prohibited Degrees Act, SC 1990, c 46.

are *Miron* and *M v H*, where the Court found that marital status is an analogous ground of discrimination. In *Miron*, it focused on the benefits under an automobile insurance.[82] It held that, through the Insurance Act,[83] the Ontario legislature excluded common law spouses from such benefits without reasonable justification. In *M v H*, an Ontario's statute limiting post-breakdown support to heterosexual common law couples[84] was invalidated, but on the grounds of sexual orientation discrimination.[85]

These two cases became the wellspring of a conspicuous body of decisions in common law provinces. Judicial decisions gradually struck down the main distinctions between married and unmarried couples in fields as varied as succession,[86] alimony[87] and the division of property, such as the allocation of the matrimonial home.[88] Yet, striking down all distinctions would have rendered the decision to marry completely irrelevant. In 2002, the Court thus strove to draw a line between the impermissible exclusion of protected groups and the acceptable modulation of different legal regimes – though the boundaries are still conceptually blurred. In *Walsh*, the Supreme Court rejected an argument that by limiting the presumption of equal division of property to married couples, the Matrimonial Property Act of Nova Scotia discriminated on the basis of marital status.[89] Protecting the freedom of choice of the parties is paramount, the Court reasoned. The conclusion was further buttressed by the absence of a traceable discriminatory purpose or impact on the dignity of the claimants. Furthermore, the parties already enjoyed some form of protection, such as the possibility to claim post-breakdown support. The Act was merely 'defining the legal content of the different forms of conjugal relationships' by taking notice of the decision to not marry and to not subject the patrimonial relationship to the mandatory statutory framework of marriage.[90]

A coherent analytical framework for inquiries on substantive discrimination comes from *Withler*. The decision embodies the current approach to making a finding of discrimination. The following contextual factors must be considered:[91]

(i) The claimant's historical position of disadvantage. Here, emphasis is placed on whether the group is a 'discrete and insular minority' which has been

[82] *Miron* (n 50).
[83] Insurance Act, RSO 1980, c 218.
[84] Family Law Act, RSO 1990, c F.3.
[85] *M v H* (n 24).
[86] *Grigg v Berg*, 2000 BCSC 858 (CanLII).
[87] *Rossu v Taylor*, 1998 ABCA 193 (CanLII).
[88] *Watch v Watch*, 1999 CanLII 12842 (SK QB).
[89] *Walsh* (n 75).
[90] *Québec v A* (n 67) para 218.
[91] *Withler* (n 55).

historically disadvantaged from a political, social or legal perspective.[92] To tick this box, one should consider inter alia whether the group has suffered from prejudice or stereotypes, or endured legal restrictions. Examples include exclusion from family regimes or from entering into enforceable contracts.

In many decisions, the Supreme Court considered unmarried conjugal partners as a historically disadvantaged group. This occurred notwithstanding the fact that their positioning in society has substantially improved in recent years. In the past, their lifestyle was considered 'less worthy of respect than that of married persons'.[93] In most cases, the decision to withhold the benefit of access to social protections from them was based on stigma. This is no longer the case.[94] However, improvements in social perception do not affect their status as a historically disadvantaged group. As the Court put it: 'The disadvantage this exclusion perpetuates is a historic one: it continues to deprive de facto spouses access to economic remedies they have always been deprived of.'[95]

Based on this snapshot of historical disadvantage, are non-conjugal families a historically disadvantaged group? The main hurdle to arguing yes to this question is the possibility of finding that they are an insular and discrete group in the first place. The reason is that, unlike same-sex couples and unmarried conjugal couples, non-conjugal families often lack a sense of self-awareness. This is best exemplified by their absence in the political arena.[96]

As to whether they might have suffered from social stigma, one should acknowledge that their societal perception is not one of overt hostility. The 'man on the Clapham omnibus' would presumably approve non-conjugal coupledom. As was argued in Chapter 1, unions of mutual care are socially endorsed. The absence of sex within these relationships, which has been the focus of most biopolitical efforts in the last decades, is also a plus.

Regardless, a failure to demonstrate historical disadvantage is not necessarily a hindrance. A group can be discriminated even without this being the instantiation of a history of disadvantage. As stated by the Supreme Court:

> [I]t is conceivable that a group that has not historically experienced disadvantage may find itself the subject of conduct that, if permitted to continue, would create a discriminatory impact on members of the group. If it is shown that the impugned law imposes a disadvantage by stereotyping members of the group, s. 15 may be found to be violated even in the absence of proof of historic disadvantage.[97]

[92] *R v Turpin* [1989] 1 SCR 1296, 1333.
[93] *Québec v A* (n 67) para 385.
[94] In recent times, stigmatisation of cohabitants and their children has receded; see R Probert, *The Changing Legal Regulation of Cohabitation* (Cambridge, Cambridge University Press, 2012) 277.
[95] *Québec v A* (n 67) para 349.
[96] See ch 1, s 2.II.
[97] *Withler* (n 55) para 36.

Historical disadvantage is a good marker of discrimination since the 'existence of a pre-existing or historical disadvantage will make it easier to prove prejudice or a stereotype.'[98] However, it does not amount to a *sine qua non*.

(ii) The nature of the affected interest. The more important the nature of the affected interest, the higher the chance of discrimination occurring. To tick this box, one must ask which interest is affected by a decision to leave non-conjugal families out of a scheme. Looking at the case law, the interest affected by the legislation on spousal support in *M v H* consisted of ensuring that a person meets their basic financial needs after a relationship breakdown. This interest was recognised as 'fundamental' by the Supreme Court. In *Walsh*, the Court went one step further and recognised something whose fundamental nature was less obvious: the interest protected by a prima facie right to the equal division of property.[99]

In order to assess the calibre of the interest protected by the law, a judge must consider whether 'the distinction in question restricts access to a fundamental social institution, or affects a basic aspect of full membership in Canadian society, or constitutes a complete non-recognition of a particular group'.[100] The second and third aspects are especially engaged in the case of non-conjugal families. Without difficulty, these families might demonstrate 'the undeniable importance to them of the benefits accorded by the statute'. In so doing, they can point out the ways in which their exclusion restricts full citizenship and results in a blanket policy of non-recognition that is hurtful to the group.

(iii) Stereotyping or prejudice. In order to meet this condition, a claimant must seek evidence that shows that the law perpetuates stereotypes or prejudice. These two drives must also objectively worsen the situation of the group. To show that legislation is based on stereotypical views of the group, the question becomes whether there is 'correspondence with the claimants' actual characteristics or circumstances'.[101] This factor was the argumentative fulcrum in *M v H*, invalidating unmarried same-sex couples' exclusion from spousal support. There, the Court found that the gender-neutral formulation of the Act suggests that the proper benchmark to allocate support obligations is the economically interdependent couple. As such, not only does it defy logic to exclude same-sex couples, but exclusion of same-sex partners from the benefit also problematically 'impl[ies] that they are judged to be incapable of forming intimate relationships of economic interdependence, without regard to their actual circumstances'.[102]

[98] *Québec v A* (n 67).
[99] *Walsh* (n 75) para 104.
[100] *M v H* (n 24) para 72.
[101] ibid para 38.
[102] ibid para 3.

> This has potential for new families. It could indeed have paved the way for the recognition of all interdependent family dyads if only the Court had not used language pointing to the relevance of sexual intimacy. More explicitly, in an effort to set good forms of relationships apart from bad ones, it added that: 'Being in a same-sex relationship does not mean that it is an impermanent or a nonconjugal relationship.'[103] This passage draws anew the boundaries of normalcy. The move relegated non-conjugal families to the realm of deviance through a well-known technique. The technique consists of a boundary-setting exercise furthering acceptance of new groups by entrenching discrimination towards other groups.

The challenge ahead is thus exposing the many holes in the 'conjugal difference' narrative without resorting to this technique. Arguably, it would be strategically powerful to set non-conjugal pairs apart from polyamorous unions. This would make it possible to capitalise on the contrast that their markedly diverse social acceptance creates. This approach was followed by LGBTQ litigators, who attempted to ameliorate the reduced social acceptance of gay couples by, inter alia, fuelling social condemnation of plural relationships. However, this strategy is deplorable. Language that purports to obtain legal recognition of non-conjugal families at the expense of other new families should be avoided.

A recent case illustrates how the third factor, stereotyping or prejudice, operates in practice. In *Québec (Attorney General) v A* – best known as *Eric v Lola* – the Court scrutinised Québec's distinctions between married and unmarried couples relating to property divisions and spousal support. Justice Abella, writing for the majority, found an infringement. She first traced a history of exclusion from economic remedies (a factor under point (i) above)[104] and then placed under scrutiny the belief that de facto couples could not function as a family (a factor under point (iii) above). She stressed that many de facto couples exhibited the same functional attributes as married couples. Notably, they display the same capability to function as an economic unit, and the same potential to experience economic vulnerability following the breakdown of the relationship. To corroborate this conclusion, she cited to various reforms at the provincial level and case law officially recognising their functional equivalence.

The functional similarity prong is squarely applicable to non-conjugal families. *Québec (Attorney General) v A* offers guidance on building a persuasive argument to this effect. First, like conjugal couples, non-conjugal couples can point to reforms at the provincial level thanks to which they are now recognised as family unions. The key example in this respect is Alberta's AIRA. A further example is the New Brunswick Act, which allocates spousal support based on a mere 'substantial dependency' criterion. 'Beyond Conjugality', the report of the Law Commission of Canada, is also a precious resource. As a federal law reform agency, its finding that

[103] ibid.
[104] *Québec v A* (n 67) para 349.

non-conjugal families can be functionally identical to (interdependent) married couples is especially authoritative.[105]

The case law is, by contrast, less helpful. There is a rich string of cases on unmarried conjugal couples being functionally similar to married couples. Predictably, however, they place strong emphasis on 'conjugality' and 'intimacy'.[106] There is no comparable string of cases on non-conjugal coupledom. Even in Alberta, the only Canadian jurisdiction which has enacted a comprehensive regime to recognise them, a case law analysis reveals that non-conjugal couples do not seek redress in courts.[107]

Yet, what is striking is how elusive the meaning of conjugality is in constitutional and statutory case law in Canada. This could eventually profit non-conjugal families. In *M v H*, the Court balked somewhat at defining conjugality, while acknowledging the intrinsic difficulty in understanding what it stands for.[108] On that occasion, it clarified that sexual activity is not required. No one would deny that a conjugal couple involving, say, two elderly people does not qualify once they stop engaging in sexual intercourse.[109]

Lower courts gradually aligned themselves with the Supreme Court decision to do away with sexual intercourse as a necessary condition of conjugality.[110] Bruce Ryder and Brenda Cossman reported courts steering away from a strict functional approach, requiring couples to mimic an ideal marital couple to gain recognition. They welcomed this trend by noting that '[t]aking sex into account at all is wrong-headed and offensive'.[111] It is wrong-headed since sex is unrelated to the accomplishment of legitimate state objectives. It is offensive as it intrudes on the most intimate decisions a person can make, which ought not to be disclosed to administrative or judicial bodies.

The interpretation of conjugality in tax courts is even more instructive. Kim Brook, in her essay 'Cameos from the Margins of Conjugality', stresses how sexual intimacy need not always be present – with courts finding a 'conjugal' relationship even though the couple in question engaged in sexual intercourse only sporadically or did not engage in it at all for protracted periods (eg, people living apart).[112] She also notes extreme judicial discretion in discerning when the requirement is met. At present, it seems that it does not always require mutual care or care towards the

[105] Law Commission of Canada (n 13) 113–14.

[106] See, eg, *Pettkus v Becker* [1980] 2 SCR 834.

[107] See s 1 above.

[108] *M v H* (n 24) paras 58–59.

[109] CA Thomas, 'The Roles of Registered Partnerships and Conjugality in Canadian Family Law' (2006) 22 *Canadian Journal of Family Law* 223, 238.

[110] B Cossman and B Ryder, 'What is Marriage-Like Like? The Irrelevance of Conjugality' (2001) 18 *Canadian Journal of Family Law* 269, 294–300, especially 298.

[111] ibid 326.

[112] Brook (n 15). See, eg, *Astley v The Queen*, 2012 TCC 155 (CanLII).

children, nor that the couple be perceived as such by the community.[113] The two must also not live under the same roof[114] or sleep in the same room.[115]

Case law sheds light on how ephemeral the distinction between conjugal and non-conjugal couples is in practice. Crucially, it constitutes an important occasion for lawyers and courts to reflect on the conjugal difference, its significance and implications. With conjugality wearing thin, drawing the line between deserving and non-deserving families proves to be more complicated. All which is left to mark the 'boundaries of normalcy' seems to be a bare desire to preserve the traditional hallmarks of family.

iii. The Justification Prong

Section 1 of the Charter contains a general limitation clause. In section 1, the rights and freedoms enshrined in the Charter warrant protection 'only to such reasonable limits prescribed by law as can be demonstrably justified in a free and democratic society'.

Therefore, rights infringements can still pass muster if they are justified. This is the stage where the government argues for the reasonableness of the discriminatory distinction and attempts to salvage it. In short, the government first must point out a valid state interest or purpose of the law. It must then establish a rational connection – even a tenuous one – between the means employed and the purpose. Third, the law must pass the so-called minimal impairment test.[116] According to the test, the infringement shall be 'as little as is reasonably possible' – that is, proportional.[117] The latter stage focuses on the two conflicting dimensions of the impact of the law on the enjoyment of the right on the one hand and the 'broader public benefits'[118] that the measure is seeking to achieve on the other hand.

In *Québec (Attorney General) v A*, the Court eventually upheld the exclusion of de facto couples in Québec from the presumptive protections of marriage. The Supreme Court found the promotion of autonomy (of unmarried couples) to be a pressing and substantial state interest. Thus, courts must pay heed to their decision not to marry. In her dissent, Justice Abella, while conceding that the mentioned interest is valid, argued that the law did not pass muster at the proportionality stage; she opined that an opting-out system, where couples decide to contract out of familial obligations, instead of the current opting-in system, where they agree to such obligations, was more compatible with the equality mandate.

Protecting the autonomy of the will of the parties has long been recognised as a valid purpose.[119] The received wisdom has it that couples 'choose' to be

[113] *Hendricken v The Queen*, 2008 TCC 48 (CanLII).
[114] *Richard v R*, 2003 CCI 774 (informal procedure).
[115] *Hamel v R*, 2004 TCC 315 (informal procedure).
[116] *R v Oakes* [1986] 1 SCR 103.
[117] *R v Edwards Books and Art Ltd* [1986] 2 SCR 713, 772.
[118] *Québec v A* (n 67).
[119] *Walsh* (n 75).

discriminated against because a lack of protections is counterbalanced by a lack of obligations.[120] However, the majority opinion regarding the section 15 analysis rightly pointed to the decision to marry being a non-decision. A myriad of factors influences it and often people have no choice but to live in extra-marital arrangements.[121] The above-mentioned interest in protecting choice is even more untenable in the case of non-conjugal couples. Marriage is no choice at all for non-conjugal families even if they could opt for it.[122] I would not want to marry my cohabiting cousin just because I can. Marriage would signal something which is not the case: a relationship marked by sexual intimacy. Marriage for non-conjugal couples is simply not an option. Therefore, when the interest at stake is furthering the autonomy of claimants, non-conjugal couples can reject it on these grounds.

In one of the few successful section 15 challenges, *M v H*, the Court determined that the means – excluding same-sex couples from post-breakdown support – were not rationally connected to the purposes.[123] The main stated purposes for Ontario's regime were: (i) the equitable resolution of economic disputes arising between financially interdependent individuals in an 'intimate relationship' upon its breakdown; and (ii) the alleviation of the burden on the public purse.[124] Such alleviation is achieved by shifting the obligation of supporting economically vulnerable persons from the state to families. However, the Court notes, the intentions are betrayed by the fact that those very reasons call for extending the benefit to same-sex couples rather than withholding it. It is the inclusion of same-sex couples that better serves the stated objectives. The conclusion is warranted upon considering the functional attributes of these couples. In both cases, the law would want to prevent one party from simply walking away at the end of a relationship of interdependence, with no consequences whatsoever arising from this.

The case law illustrates that when it comes to private familial obligations, there is no shortage of valid interests in terms of imposing them on family members. Rather, when these benefits are pursued, the Supreme Court becomes an activist in extending them. In any such case, the protection from vulnerability and a neoliberal interest in privatising care are the doctrinal underpinnings for the extension. Both interests equally apply to private law obligations in the case of non-conjugal families. When private pockets are at stake, the proffered state interests in *M v H* apply. What has sex to do with the vulnerability a family member can experience upon separation? What has it to do with the oft-sanctified interest in avoiding the situation where family members become public charges?

The lack of a rational connection is the most powerful analytical passage to debunk stereotypes around conceptions of family. This is where one can discern

[120] R Leckey, 'Chosen Discrimination' (2002) 18 *Supreme Court Law Review* 445, 458.
[121] *Miron* (n 50).
[122] See ch 2, s 1.I.
[123] *M v H* (n 24). It should be recalled that observations now pertaining to s 1 were dealt with at the s 15 stage before *Kapp*.
[124] ibid para 93.

that the impugned legislation is under-inclusive or over-inclusive. To follow up on the earlier example, if the purpose of the law is to alleviate the economic fallout of a breakdown, marriage is an under-inclusive basis for allocating the protection. This the Court has been willing to concede; what it has not been willing to concede is that the conjugal relationship is also an under-inclusive benchmark. As the Law Commission powerfully demonstrates, across a number of contexts, the ideal proxy is the emotionally and economically interdependent couple. Unmarried conjugal cohabitants were recognised at first precisely because their mutual support and interdependence bear witness to their ability to form an 'economic unit', like married couples. As empirical findings show, non-conjugal pairs are also able to form economic and emotional units just like conjugal couples. Empirical research on gay and lesbian friendship networks are a major resource for buttressing this claim. Often rejected by their own 'families' of origin, homosexuals have structured their daily interactions around friendships which they came to consciously define as family.[125] In so doing, they became 'enmeshed in complex networks of intimacy and care, and had strong commitments and connections to others'.[126] In informal unions of friends, individuals might provide and receive both material and economic support to a significant extent.[127] Hence, a non-conjugal couple can display all the attributes relevant to presuming that the abrupt end of the relationship will produce economic and emotional fallout.

Public law entitlements are, by contrast, more difficult to obtain. Decisions refusing to extend the reach of public familial entitlements are countless.[128] These cases resonate well with the neoliberal shift and its tendency to multiply private shoulders on which is placed the burden of caregiving.[129] However, a legal precedent in Ontario lays stress on the fact that when the policy-makers choose a private law definition of 'spouse', they cannot choose a different definition for a related purpose, such as social assistance.[130] The case in question is *Falkiner*. On that occasion, the Court of Appeal for Ontario was called to assess the constitutionality of the 'spouse in the house' rule, which established a rebuttable presumption that opposite-sex people living together were spouses. Following the application of the rule by the government of Ontario, thousands were cut off from welfare assistance. The applicant, who was allegedly in a 'trial run' relationship with her partner, also had her social assistance terminated. The Court, in striking down the 'spouse in

[125] S Roseneil, 'Why We Should Care about Friends: An Argument for Queering the Care Imaginary in Social Policy' (2004) 3 *Social Policy and Society* 409.

[126] ibid 413.

[127] B Gusmano, 'Subvertir la heteronorma a través de la amistad. Convivencia y redes de cuidado en la precariedad' (2018) 14 *TransVersos* 90.

[128] See eg *Egan* (n 57); *Hodge v Canada (Minister of Human Resources Development)* [2004] 3 SCR 357.

[129] H Lessard, 'Charter Gridlock: Equality Formalism and Marriage Fundamentalism' in S Rodgers and S McIntyre (eds), *Diminishing Returns: Inequality and the Canadian Charter of Rights and Freedoms* (Markham, LexisNexis Canada, 2006) 304.

[130] *Falkiner v Ontario (Minister of Community and Social Services)*, 2002 CanLII 44902 (ON CA).

the house' rule, reasoned that when policy-makers choose a private law definition of 'spouse', the same definition should be used for related purposes. The Court concluded that it is especially inadvisable to use different family definitions across various contexts when the different definition at hand yields an adverse impact on a vulnerable group.

This decision regards a specific case of what Erez Aloni tags deprivative recognition.[131] The term refers to courts' penchant for recognising 'more' families only for the purposes of terminating benefits or privileges. I contend that the same rationale applies to not conferring benefits in the first place. In public law, the decision to terminate means-tested public outlays through recognising more families (the larger the notion of family, presumably the higher the income and thus the higher the chance of benefits being terminated) is tantamount to a decision to not confer public benefits in terms of economic rationale. The decision cited above thus lends support to the view that this double-standards attitude is constitutionally unacceptable, regardless of whether it occurs through *ex post* termination or *ex ante* exclusion. However, one cannot ignore the neoliberal turn in government policy in Canada. Discourses and practices of a neoliberal flavour are socially absorbed and politically normalised to such an extent that the likelihood of success of this line of argument is inexorably low.

To conclude, private law protections are more likely to be expanded compared to public law ones. Yet, expanding access to private law benefits creates legal precedents bearing witness to non-conjugal couples' ability to function as family. At the same time, it could stimulate the expansion of public law benefits if the (now weak) line of argument denouncing scattered recognition as constitutionally impermissible is accepted.

II. Family Status Discrimination

This section deals with non-conjugal relationships that are ineligible for marriage under the current law, such as siblings. These persons may not be able to invoke the ground of marital status. It is worth recalling that if claimants are unable to invoke a ground, they will fall through the cracks of the equality guarantee. Therefore, this section briefly outlines a line of argument pursuant to which these non-conjugal families can invoke a different ground: family status. Such a ground is not yet recognised at the constitutional level, although it is protected in human rights legislation.

However, before doing that, I would like to note that family status better captures the discrimination suffered by 'all' non-conjugal families. I especially concur with the definition provided by Justice L'Heureux-Dubé in her dissenting opinion in *Mossop*,[132] who defined family status discrimination as discrimination occurring

[131] E Aloni, 'Deprivative Recognition' (2014) 61 *UCLA Law Review* 1276.
[132] *Canada (Attorney General) v Mossop* [1993] 1 SCR 554.

because the relationship someone had with their companion was not recognised as a family relationship.[133] This version is preferable. It correctly places emphasis on the likely occurrence that lack of recognition per se produces discrimination in terms of accessing social goods, resources and benefits in society. Think of a landlord deciding not to rent their apartment to two friends in a long-term interdependent relationship because they incorrectly believe that stability is more aptly associated with married couples.

As to how a new ground can be introduced, the Court has recognised as analogous grounds the following: marital status,[134] sexual orientation,[135] non-citizenship[136] and aboriginality-residence.[137] It has laid out alternative approaches to determining whether an analogous ground is present: (1) the target group suffers from historical disadvantage;[138] (2) the target group forms a discrete and insular minority which lacks political power and does not fully participate in the political process;[139] and (3) the distinction is based on a personal characteristic which is either immutable or constructively immutable.[140]

The prevailing approach is approach (3). This was set out in *Corbiere*, where grounds became synonymous with characteristics that one cannot change (immutable) or 'that the government has no legitimate interest in expecting us to change to receive equal treatment under the law' (constructively immutable).[141] According to this approach, courts must assess whether someone's status can only be changed at unacceptable personal expense, eg, through changing one's religion or sexual orientation, or one's marital status from 'unmarried' to 'married'. As with marital status, family status would not be immutable in a strong sense. One can 'virtually' decide to change it. The issue arises as to whether a state's request to change it is legitimate or comes at unacceptable personal expense.

At the outset, the Court refused to recognise new grounds unless the group had suffered legal, social or political disadvantage.[142] The most interesting recent claims concern groups of workers. Some workers mobilised to recognise occupational status as an analogous ground. The occupational status saga is useful as it bears many similarities to our case. Nowadays, groups of workers lack a coherent identity and their mobilisation is eminently based on the material interest being pursued. I have argued elsewhere that this shift from identity to the material interest pursued is consistent with the key tenets of queer theory.[143]

[133] ibid 702.
[134] *Miron* (n 50).
[135] *Egan* (n 57); *Vriend v Alberta* [1998] 1 SCR 493; *M v H* (n 24); *Little Sisters Book and Art Emporium v Canada (Minister of Justice)* [2000] 2 SCR 1120.
[136] *Andrews* (n 45); *Lavoie v Canada* [2002] 1 SCR 769.
[137] *Corbiere v Canada (Minister of Indian and Northern Affairs)* [1999] 2 SCR 203.
[138] ibid.
[139] *Andrews* (n 45).
[140] *Miron* (n 50).
[141] *Corbiere* (n 137) para 13.
[142] *Turpin* (n 92).
[143] Palazzo (n 55) 112–14.

The Court consistently rejected the contention that the occupational status of farm workers is an analogous ground.[144] Lately, in *Fraser*, a case concerning the protection of Ontario's farm workers governed by a separate labour relations regime, it defined the section 15 claim as 'premature'.[145] There was, in the Court's view, an insufficient evidentiary record showing that the new law produced an adverse impact on farm workers. Yet, this is not tantamount to discarding the claim on the grounds that occupational status is not a prohibited ground, as the concurring opinion of Justices Charron and Rothstein would have.[146] Thus, a robust evidentiary record showing an adverse impact on non-conjugal families could balance out the current restrictive approach to finding new grounds.

Once the ground of family status is introduced, the same lines of arguments outlined in the context of marital status discrimination apply.

5. Legal Arguments in Human Rights Litigation

Venue	Human rights tribunal or commission, established under the relevant human rights code
Remedy	Extension of specific familial benefits
Legal arguments	Family or civil status discrimination, depending on the jurisdiction

Constitutional equality law and human rights law stand in a position of reciprocal interference and cross-fertilisation. Since its first Charter-based decisions, the Supreme Court has attempted to harmonise the interpretation of the human rights codes and section 15 of the Charter. This was made on the assumption that both aim at combating substantive inequality.[147] Due to their shared objective, the same principles should apply.

Yet, the differences in terms of the analytical framework remain obvious, especially when it comes to the claimant's burden of proof. The burden of proof is more linear in the case of human rights law and more 'fluctuating, verbose, demanding'[148] in the case of constitutional litigation. Under human rights codes, the claimant must (only) prove an adverse distinction that can be linked to a prohibited ground – and thus no human dignity violation, disadvantage stemming from prejudice and stereotype or other sophisticated formulations of disadvantage. In addition,

[144] See, eg, *Baier v Alberta* [2007] 2 SCR 673; *Dunmore v Ontario (Attorney General)* [2001] 3 SCR 1016.

[145] *Ontario (Attorney General) v Fraser* [2011] 2 SCR 3.

[146] C Sheppard, 'Bread and Roses: Economic Justice and Constitutional Rights' (2015) 5 *Oñati Socio-Legal Series* 225.

[147] *Andrews* (n 45) para 172.

[148] Ryder (n 47) 268.

anti-discrimination legislation does not contain a general limitation clause akin to that enshrined in section 1 of the Charter. Therefore, a finding of discrimination can never be salvaged. Looking at the complaint form of the Canadian Human Rights Commission, one finds that the claimant should simply tell their personal story of discrimination without too many formalities. They should succinctly respond to the following questions: 'How and when were you treated differently, based on each ground of discrimination you have identified?' and 'How did these events have a negative effect on you?'

The codes prohibit discrimination roughly on the same grounds as the Charter. Yet, exceptions concern some additional grounds that are not applicable to discrimination perpetrated by the government – which is relevant to the present analysis – and different defensive claims. Further, the lack of a prohibited ground of discrimination in the code is not dispositive. The Supreme Court has not refrained from reading in grounds that it viewed as constitutionally mandated, such as 'sexual orientation'.[149]

At an argumentative level, since the Charter is superior law, constitutional law can corroborate arguments under human rights legislation. The opposite is not true: courts are sceptical about reaching a conclusion at the level of constitutional interpretation simply because human rights legislation supports it. This is to say that the constitutional material discussed in the previous section applies here.

In human rights litigation, the most compelling line of argument harnesses the prohibition against family status discrimination in common law provinces and against civil status discrimination in Québec.

I. Family and Civil Status Discrimination

As noted above, human rights commissions are key actors in terms of moulding public opinion. They are also important allies in lobbying courts and legislators to adopt a broader conception of family. The case of the Canadian Commission of Human Rights (CCHR) is instructive. The CCHR has been particularly obstinate in its advocacy for the recognition of same-sex couples since the 1980s.

I am convinced that the federal Commission and other provincial human rights bodies are ideally suited to the task of promoting awareness of non-conjugal families and the importance of their legal recognition. The same arsenal of tacks employed in the past can be utilised to further the cause of such families – the complaint mechanism, intervention in court proceedings, annual reports and so on. In addition, there is a substantial likelihood that commissions could be sympathetic to the claims of non-conjugal couples. To follow up on my earlier example on the CCHR, the notion of family it adopted in various annual reports to persuade Parliament to recognise homosexual couples was especially broad.

[149] *Vriend* (n 135).

On various occasions, the Commission rightly placed emphasis on autonomy, arguing that: 'It is the Commission's business … to ensure that our legal and administrative systems do not permit discrimination against persons who happen to live together in situations that differ from those of the majority.'[150] Further, it rightly placed stress on functional attributes: 'if benefits are to be extended to individuals in a stable, interdependent relationship, such benefits should be made available to everyone who satisfies the criteria.'[151] In both cases, it can be easily noticed how these definitions, pivoting on autonomy and functional attributes, are broad enough to encompass non-conjugal families. These words were pronounced in the 90s. Hence, there could be no insurmountable opposition to getting the Commission on board.

This subsection first highlights the formulation of the grounds of marital, family and civil status in human rights codes, including the 'rare' variants that incidentally protect non-conjugal families. It then offers a primer on their implementation by commissions and courts.

All human rights codes and acts throughout Canada protect individuals against discriminations based on marital status and family status. Likewise, in Québec, the relevant act refers to 'civil status', which is a mix of family and marital status.[152] The definition of marital status tends to be roughly the same across provinces. In Ontario and Alberta, it refers to the state of being 'married, single, widowed, divorced or separated'.[153] In both cases, it includes common law marriage, which is defined as a conjugal relationship outside marriage. Saskatchewan replicates Ontario and Alberta's definition while adding 'the state of being engaged to be married' to the list.[154]

As to family status, in Ontario and Saskatchewan, this is defined as the 'status of being in a parent–child relationship'. By contrast, Alberta defines it as the 'status of being related to another person by blood, marriage or adoption'.[155] Alberta's definition is thus broad enough to incidentally include non-conjugal families composed of relatives by blood or adoption. In the Québec Charter of Rights and Freedoms, 'civil status' is broadly defined as encompassing discrimination occurring because one is single, married, in a civil union, adopted, divorced or a member of a single-parent family. Importantly, it also includes discrimination linked to any family tie or affinity with another person.

Both marital and family status are prohibited grounds for discrimination in Manitoba and British Columbia. However, they lack a formal definition. New

[150] Canadian Human Rights Commission, *Annual Report 1991* (Ottawa, Cat No HR1-1991, 1992) 43.
[151] Canadian Human Rights Commission, *Annual Report 1992* (Ottawa, Cat No HR1-1992, 1993) 55.
[152] *Fundamentals of Human Rights Law in Canada* (Toronto, Carswell, 2017) 46–52.
[153] Human Rights Code, RSO 1990, c H19, s 10(1) 'marital status' [am 2005, c 5, s 32(8)]; Alberta Human Rights Act, RSA 2000, c A-25.5, s 44(1)(g) 'marital status' [am 2009, c 26, s 30 (b) (i), (ii)].
[154] Saskatchewan Human Rights Code, SS, 1979, c S-24.1, s 2(1)(i.01) 'marital status' [en 2000, c 26, s 3(4)].
[155] Alberta Human Rights Act, RSA 2000, c A-25.5, s 44(1)(g) 'family status'.

Brunswick, by contrast, is the only jurisdiction that does not encompass family status in its code. However, there is an ongoing discussion suggesting that the ground will be added at some point.

From the above, it appears that helpful definitions are found in Alberta and Québec, where the ground of family/civil status prohibits discrimination that occurs respectively because someone is 'related to another person by blood' or because of a family tie or affinity with another person. The definition used in Alberta has the potential to at least encompass discrimination against non-conjugal unions made up by relatives or siblings, such as multi-generational families. Québec's definition, by contrast, is sufficiently broad to potentially encompass all non-conjugal families.

Except for these two cases, if one looks at formal definitions of family and marital status, non-conjugal couples seem to be barred from the protection under both umbrellas. Leaving aside 'the status of being single', the relational part of marital status refers either to formal relationships such as marriage or civil union or to *conjugal* relationships outside of marriage. To err on the side of caution, Saskatchewan expressly precludes the term from being used when there is 'discrimination on the basis of a relationship with a particular person'. Likewise, 'family status' is unserviceable in most jurisdictions as it only takes into account vertical relationships, ie, parent–child relationships.

Amongst the two grounds (marital status and family status), it seems that marital status is more hermeneutically 'rigid' compared to family status. Definitions of family status, where present, leave slightly broader interpretative leeway. They are also closer to the type of discrimination experienced by non-conjugal families. However, the application of the code by human rights bodies and ordinary courts is not encouraging. The majority of the jurisdictions employing family status concluded that it captures (only) discrimination based on pregnancy,[156] parenthood[157] and the status of being the child of a certain parent.[158]

More interestingly, federal courts interpreted it as also including discrimination deriving from the obligation to care for a member of an extended family, such as an elderly person.[159] Such a version, which is conducive to protecting elderly parent care, is also expressly provided by the applicable code in Nova Scotia. However, what these versions imply is that *asymmetrical* relationships with particularly vulnerable persons call for special protection. They by no means question the traditional understanding of horizontal, adult–adult relationships.

[156] *Peterson v Anderson*, 1991 15 CHRR D/1 (Ont Bd of Inquiry). Some codes, such as the Canadian Human Rights Act, expressly provide that discrimination based on pregnancy shall be deemed as discrimination based on sex.

[157] See, eg, *Brown v Canada (Department of Natural Revenue – Customs and Excise)*, 1993 19 CHRR D/39 (Can Human Rights Trib); *Flamand v DGN Investments*, 2005 52 CHRR D/142 (Ont Human Rights Trib); *Stephenson v Sooke Lake Modular Home Co-operative Association (No 1)* (2007) BCHRT 341 (BC Human Rights Trib).

[158] *Fundamentals of Human Rights Law* (n 152) 51.

[159] *Patterson v Canada (Revenue Agency)*, 2011 FC 1398 (CanLII); *Canada (Attorney General) v Hicks*, 2015 FC 599 (CanLII).

A more interesting construction can be found in British Columbia. The Human Rights Tribunal in British Columbia has taken family status discrimination to be inclusive of all forms of discrimination relating to the status of being in a specific type of family. Examples include being a couple, a single-parent family or a two-parent family.[160] This is one of the rare instances where a provincial jurisdiction conceptually detaches the label 'family status' from the vertical axis of a relationship. This construction is broad enough to account for a vast array of horizontal or mixed (vertical and horizontal) relationships as sources of discrimination. However, its implementation is less encouraging: most cases revolve around a conflict between work and childcare obligations.[161]

Turning to the interpretation of family status provided by the Supreme Court, its reluctance to embrace a larger conception of family is the main takeaway. In *Mossop*, the Court was called upon to rule whether same-sex couples could invoke family status discrimination under the CHRA. More precisely, it was called to rule upon whether their exclusion from bereavement leave could fall within the meaning of family status discrimination. Contrary to the decision of the human rights tribunal, which answered the question in the affirmative, the Supreme Court said no. As a matter of statutory interpretation – no Charter claim was raised – a group of three justices concluded that there was a clear legislative intent barring the judicial addition of the ground of sexual orientation. Likewise, a group of two justices stated that ordinary meaning, context or purpose did not suggest including same-sex couples within the meaning of family status. However, I believe that the vantage point of Justice L'Heureux-Dubé, writing a dissenting opinion, is conceptually solid and persuasive. According to L'Heureux-Dubé:

> Concepts of equality and liberty which appear in human rights documents are not bounded by the precise understanding of those who drafted them. The enumerated grounds of discrimination must be examined in the context of contemporary values, not in a vacuum. Their meaning is not frozen in time and the scope of each ground may evolve. Textual context should not detract from the purposive approach mandated by human rights documents.[162]

When family status is left undefined, she submits, there is a clear legislative intent that the term's meaning is left for human rights bodies to define. Furthermore, I think that an argument can be made that the holding in *Mossop* does not apply to a non-conjugal family. The decision could be set aside on the grounds that there is no comparable characteristic that would be surreptitiously introduced, as was the case with sexual orientation in *Mossop*. Family status is already present in all jurisdictions (but one). Marital status is also protected. All courts should do is to interpret them in a more liberal and large way.

[160] See eg *Nelson v Bodwell High School*, 2015 BCHRT 183 (CanLII).
[161] Lately, see *Envirocon Environmental Services, ULC v Suen*, 2019 BCCA 46 (CanLII).
[162] *Mossop* (n 132) paras 621–22.

A second important decision of the Supreme Court is *B v Ontario (Human Rights Commission)*.[163] Thereby, both grounds were construed so as to cover discrimination due to a particular identity. The semantic reach of 'marital status' and 'family status' is broad enough, the Court argued, to apply to situations where an adverse distinction is drawn based on the particular identity of a claimant's spouse or family member. This often occurs on the assumption that family members think or act alike. This construction is not directly relevant to the cause of non-conjugal families. Their discrimination is not related to the particular 'identity' of someone they are in a relationship with, but to the very nature of their relationship – what the majority decision refers to as 'membership in a class or group'.

However, to reach this conclusion, the justices use language to the effect of adopting a liberal interpretation of the grounds that could be helpful for non-conjugal families. The Court first reiterated that human rights legislation has a quasi-constitutional nature. As such, liberal and purposive canons of interpretations should be adopted so as to advance the broad policy considerations underlying it. Second, it referred to its far-reaching goals, 'namely preventing the drawing of negative distinctions based on irrelevant personal characteristics',[164] which is furthered by adopting a more inclusive interpretation of the grounds in question. Most importantly, the Court reiterated that the purpose of human rights legislation is to protect individuals. Looking at the preamble of Ontario's Code, with its emphasis on 'the dignity and worth of each person' and on the importance that 'each person feels a part of the community', the Court submits that there is no need to demonstrate membership to an identifiable subgroup within the listed ground.[165] Non-conjugal couples – in addition to stressing the far-reaching goals of human rights legislation – might capitalise on this passage if they are unable to make a case that they belong to an identifiable group.

In the end, the Supreme Court adopted a narrow interpretation when faced with the issue of adding a new group within the meaning of family status (same-sex couples). By contrast, it resorted to an expansive interpretation when faced with the issue of individuals suffering discrimination broadly related to family status, but who did not belong to an identifiable group. Unlike the Supreme Court, human rights bodies were extremely sympathetic to the claims of same-sex couples from the get-go. Surely, this is a warning that human rights litigation can be curtailed by the judicial courts' reluctance to defer to their interpretation. However, historical developments seem to show that the human rights litigation proved useful in the end. Therefore, despite possible setbacks in courts, the potential of human rights bodies to mould public opinion and further legal reform remains significant.

[163] *B v Ontario (Human Rights Commission)* [2002] 3 SCR 403.
[164] ibid para 4.
[165] ibid para 57.

Conclusion

To conclude, the most persuasive lines of arguments can be inferred from past human rights litigation and constitutional litigation. These two routes have benefited same-sex couples and unmarried conjugal couples, and there are reasons to believe that if any family will follow suit this will be a non-conjugal family.

On the one hand, human rights commissions hold a strong potential to mould public sentiments and persuade both courts (through interventions) and legislators (through public statements and annual reports) to expand family definitions. This type of litigation is structurally aimed at extending access to familial benefits. Major employment-related benefits and 'services' such as pensions were obtained in human rights fora in the case of same-sex couples. On the other hand, constitutional litigation has proven especially effective in enlarging statutory notions of family by including first common law spouses and then same-sex couples.

Both avenues have their pitfalls. In the case of human rights litigation, no ground included in human rights codes expressly or clearly protects non-conjugal couples. Furthermore, should human rights commissions be willing to tackle what I call the conjugal difference, there could be setbacks in the courts. Courts seem to be comparatively more 'conservative' when it comes to interpreting codes so as to protect a wider range of families.

In relation to constitutional litigation, the verbosity and unpredictability of the equality test is the main hurdle that prevents us from predicting the 'likelihood of success' of non-conjugal couples' claims. In addition, it seems that the litigation of same-sex couples had the ill-fated effect of entrenching discrimination for non-conjugal families. This was especially achieved by conveying the idea that non-conjugality is synonymous with impermanence of the relationship.

However, taking a step back and looking at the big picture allows us to see the remarkable steps forward that Canada has taken in this domain. Especially remarkable is its constitutional jurisprudence embracing the concern that functional rather than formal attributes are key signposts for family. Further, if one considers how robust its anti-discrimination apparatus is, how vivid the academic debate on the issue is and how this debate has from time to time morphed into legal reform, it can be concluded that the potential to make strides in terms of the recognition of non-conjugal families in Canada is high.

5

The European Convention on Human Rights

Introduction

The object of this chapter is not a state. Nor is it a continent with clearly defined geographical, cultural and political boundaries. Hence, I should preliminarily stipulate a working definition of Europe. By 'Europe' I refer to the current 27 EU Member States; I do not refer to the Member States of the Council of Europe, the international organisation administering the European Convention on Human Rights (hereinafter 'the Convention' or 'ECHR'). The geographical extension of the Council of Europe is broader: It comprises 47 states, including shores and lands in Central Asian and Caucasian territories. While the conclusions reached in the context of the Convention are in principle applicable to all Contracting States, by 'Europe' I hence refer to the overlapping set of 27 states that participate in both the EU and the Council of Europe. In addition, though Norway is not part of the EU, it will be briefly discussed, for it supplies an interesting model for the recognition of new families.[1]

Chapters 5 and 6 expound, respectively, the framework of the ECHR, which is an international system, and the EU, which is a supranational system. For the sake of consistency, I refer to both as 'meta-national systems', for they operate 'beyond' and above nation state boundaries. The domestic laws of European states taking part in these meta-national projects are not the analytical focus of the chapters. However, domestic laws are not overlooked either. One cannot possibly deal with the EU or with the ECHR without accounting for the underlying national frameworks. It is the structure itself of the two systems which requires an in-depth inquiry into domestic law.

As regards the EU, it is worth recalling that there is no power to regulate substantive family law at the EU level.[2] In principle, Member States retain their

[1] This group of states includes Austria, Belgium, Bulgaria, Croatia, Cyprus, the Czech Republic, Denmark, Estonia, Finland, France, Germany, Greece, Hungary, Ireland, Italy, Latvia, Lithuania, Luxembourg, Malta, the Netherlands, Poland, Portugal, Romania, Slovakia, Slovenia, Spain and Sweden. The UK is not included in the list as it officially withdrew from the EU on 31 January 2020.

[2] K Kaesling, 'Family Life and EU Citizenship. The Discovery of the Substance of the EU Citizens' Rights and its Genuine Enjoyment' in K Boele-Woelki, N Dethloff and W Gephart (eds), *Family Law and Culture in Europe* (Cambridge, Intersentia, 2014) 293.

power to deal with most family law matters and when the EU does regulate family policy, it bows to national definitions. Furthermore, domestic laws and principles come into play when assessing the so-called common constitutional traditions that inform fundamental rights at the EU level.[3] Ultimately, the Treaty on European Union (TEU) establishes an obligation for the EU to respect the national identity of Member States, which again questions what constitutes the core of such an identity.[4]

Likewise, the Convention system necessitates the investigation of domestic law each time it conjures up the doctrine of European consensus. The European consensus is the main analytical tool employed by its judicial body to make doctrinal advancements. As an international court that cannot be equated with a full-fledged domestic court, the European Court of Human Rights (hereinafter 'ECtHR' or 'the Court') only acts under certain conditions. It usually grants a margin of appreciation to states in making substantive policy decisions, whose breadth depends on a host of factors, including a consensus amongst Contracting States on a given issue. The doctrine is quite inconsistent. It is not yet clear what 'consensus' refers to. Thus far, a consensus has been discerned by looking at national laws and principles, but also practices and even debates.[5] Regardless, it doubtlessly requires an in-depth inquiry into both national laws and legal and social discourses.

Having described how domestic legal regimes come into play, a caveat must be mentioned. A complete summary of legislation bearing upon the family in the 27 EU Member States would be beyond the remit of this book. States differ in terms of the constitutionalisation of marriage and family, the treatment of same-sex couples, the non-marital regimes in place, the legal treatment of informal cohabitation and so on. A quick look at such systems reveals a surprising diversity that does not lend itself to easy systematisation.[6]

Therefore, section 1 offers a mere primer on this complex legal landscape. The building blocks of the primer are the decentralisation of marriage within the family laws of Member States, and the degree of constitutionalisation of family and marriage across Europe. The chapter then moves to list the remedies that could be pursued before the ECtHR. In so doing, it distinguishes between two hypothetical stages. Based on the state-of-the-art jurisprudence of the Court, non-conjugal families can at present only seek to expand their access to familial benefits (stage 1). Yet, I predict that at a later stage, they might be able to claim access to a comprehensive means of recognition, such as a registered partnership (stage 2). The hypothesis is that stage 2 is reached once non-conjugal families have additional resources for arguing that a number of states protect them domestically or when

[3] Article 6(3) of the Treaty on European Union (TEU).
[4] ibid art 4(2).
[5] See s 4.I.iv below.
[6] JM Scherpe, *European Family Law Volume IV: The Present and Future of European Family Law* (Cheltenham, Edward Elgar, 2016) 42.

a broader public opinion movement that is favourable to their legal recognition is under way. In legal jargon, they might move to the next phase once they can point to an emerging or full-fledged European consensus on their legal recognition along the lines of what same-sex couples have done. The chapter ultimately proceeds to outline the most compelling lines of arguments which can be presented before the ECtHR. It expounds equality-based lines of argument, for equality and non-discrimination have become the doctrinal centrepiece of the Court's approach to new family recognition.

1. The Changed Landscape of Family Structures and Family Law in Europe

Changes in family patterns are uneven across Europe. They are entangled, inter alia, with processes of social change triggered by progressive movements, especially feminist and LGBTQ movements,[7] the concrete layout of welfare systems and the degree of women's participation in the labour market.

Yet, if a *fil rouge* in the way in which Europeans organise their intimate life can be found, this would be the increasing diversity in family arrangements. The 'Golden age of the family', whether it was mythological or real, characterised by the highest rates of marriage, birth at young ages and low rates of divorce, waned in the 1960s. Since then, not only are new family forms on the rise, but they are also considered prevalent by demographic researchers: this landscape comprises '[m]arried and cohabitating couples with or without children, single parents, step-families, blended families, childless couples and same-sex unions, just to mention a few'.[8] Migration flows dealt the 'fatal blow' to the traditional nuclear family, with a variety of ethnic minorities or religion-based families becoming more widespread.[9]

However, a common problem seems to be the scarcity of data concerning adult networks outside of traditional coupledom. These unions remain largely informal and are only seldom picked up by qualitative or quantitative research. Neither national statistics nor the European Union Census of 2011 capture a slight portion of this reality, with a notable exception concerning Belgium, where, as will be seen below, all committed adults, regardless of conjugality, can register.[10]

[7] On which see B Halsaa, S Roseneil and S Sümer (eds), *Remaking Citizenship in Multicultural Europe, Women's Movement, Gender and Diversity* (Basingstoke, Palgrave Macmillan, 2012) 67.

[8] D Vono de Vilhena and L Sz Oláh, *Family Diversity and its Challenges for Policy Makers in Europe* (Population Europe Discussion Papers Series no 5, April 2017) 2, www.jp-demographic.eu/wp-content/uploads/2017/04/famsoc_discussionpaper5_final_web.pdf.

[9] See, eg, R Grillo, *The Family in Question: Immigrant and Ethnic Minorities in Multicultural Europe* (Amsterdam, Amsterdam University Press, 2008).

[10] F Swennen, 'Un-coupling Family Law: The Legal Recognition and Protection of Adult Unions outside of Conjugal Coupledom' (2020) 28 *Feminist Legal Studies* 39, 44–45.

I. The Subconstitutional Landscape

Family laws vary significantly from state to state. Not only do European nations display distinct legal professional cultures, but they also stage distinct background social norms which infuse notions of family. Historically, European jurisdictions were marriage-centred, in the sense that family law tended to coincide with the law of marriage. As a sort of *Koiné* of relationship regulation,[11] the law of marriage was usually characterised by a similar material and personal scope: marriage came with the larger set of defaults[12] and in the form of a dyadic, exclusive, for-life union of a man and a woman. Yet, nowadays it would be reductive to equate family law with marriage law. Even in the states where marriage retains its undisputed social and institutional centrality – predominantly East-Central states – it would be misplaced to argue as much. The predominance of the marital family has been naturally challenged over time by informal relationships developing outside of wedlock. Same-sex relationships, whose recognition runs the gamut from complete invisibility to comprehensive protection through marriage, have also put a traditional understanding of family under pressure.[13] As of October 2020, out of the 27 Member States under examination, 13 legally recognise same-sex marriage: Austria, Belgium, Denmark, Finland, France, Germany, Ireland, Luxembourg, Malta, the Netherlands, Portugal, Spain and Sweden (plus Norway). On the other side of the spectrum lie states restricting the possibility of extending marriage to same-sex couples via bans enacted at the constitutional level. These restrictive provisions are mainly located in states in Central and Eastern Europe: Bulgaria, Croatia, Hungary, Latvia, Lithuania, Poland and Slovakia (though Croatia and Hungary do recognise same-sex civil partnerships). On 7 October 2018, Romania rejected a referendum planning to restrict the constitutional definition of marriage to cross-sex couples, due to a low turnout.

While these evolutions at the level of family norms did not sound the death knell for marriage, they had repercussions in relation to both the institution and the layout of the law of the family. Marriage as a social institution has changed dramatically. As in Canada and the US, parties have become free to personalise through self-created normativity the relationship and terminate it at will. Family law scholars speak of a 'privacy' approach[14] in order to stress the increasing retreat of the state from governing the marital relationship from the inception to the 'grave': clues for this retreat are the introduction of divorce in all

[11] MA Fineman, 'Masking Dependency: The Political Role of Family Rhetoric' (1995) 81 *Virginia Law Review* 2181, 2189.

[12] The characteristic of marriage as a relatively uniform institution surfaced in the debate surrounding the definition of 'spouse' under EU law in *Coman*. See Judgment of the Court (Grand Chamber) of 5 June 2018, *Relu Adrian Coman and Others v Inspectoratul General pentru Imigrări and Ministerul Afacerilor Interne*, C-673/16, EU:C:2018:385.

[13] Scherpe (n 6) 45–47.

[14] J Miles, 'Unmarried Cohabitation in a European Perspective' in JM Scherpe (ed), *European Family Law Volume III: Family Law in a European Perspective* (Cheltenham, Edward Elgar, 2016) 82–115.

European states,[15] the favourable treatment of marital agreements, including pre-nuptial, post-nuptial and separation agreements, and the decriminalisation of fornication and adultery.

Further, marriage is no longer the only option on the menu. A plurality of recognition means alongside marriage has been introduced in the last few decades, the main example being civil partnerships or civil unions.[16] For the sake of consistency, I shall call these schemes 'registered partnerships'. In a nutshell, Nordic countries, such as Denmark, Norway and Sweden, introduced registered partnerships as a functional equivalent to marriage, in the sense that the scheme was specifically designed for same-sex partners.[17] By contrast, Western European jurisdictions enacted registered partnerships as an alternative to marriage by making them available to both same-sex and cross-sex couples.[18] Italy is an exception to this as civil unions are reserved to same-sex partners.

Informal or de facto cohabitation is another phenomenon that has deeply affected the development of family law. A number of jurisdictions afford statutory protections to de facto couples, one paradigmatic example being Sweden.[19] In jurisdictions lacking comprehensive statutes, cohabitation still triggers legal consequences in specific areas. Alternatively, cohabitation can become legally relevant through the application of general principles or laws.[20] Sweden and Hungary offer a framework whereby de facto couples are recognised through functional recognition. Some Spanish territories, such as Catalonia, Navarre and Aragon, feature a peculiar model for recognising de facto families: a double-track system that combines registration with functional recognition through ascription.[21]

The accretion of social acceptability vis-a-vis cohabitation is reflected by doctrinal developments occurring in the two meta-national systems under consideration. As regards the Convention, since the 1980s,[22] the ECtHR has held that informal cohabitants enjoy the institution of 'family life' under Article 8 ECHR and the legal protections dependent on it. Yet, notwithstanding increasing recognition of informal cohabitation, there is no such thing as a 'common European trend' concerning its regulation.[23]

Looking at other subsets of new families and notably those outside of conjugal coupledom, only a handful of European states grant official recognition. Non-conjugal couples are officially recognised in Belgium (through a comprehensive

[15] In Europe, only the Holy See is an exception to this.

[16] C Sörgjerd, *Reconstructing Marriage: The Legal Status of Relationships in a Changing Society* (Cambridge, Intersentia, 2012).

[17] JM Scherpe and A Hayward (eds), *The Future of Registered Partnerships: Family Recognition Beyond Marriage?* (Cambridge, Intersentia, 2017), esp pt I.

[18] ibid, esp pt II.

[19] Other examples of cohabitation laws include those in Belgium, Croatia, France, Hungary, Norway, Scotland, Serbia, Slovenia, some regions in Spain and Ukraine. See WM Schrama, 'Marriage and Alternative Status Relationships in the Netherlands' in J Eekelaar and R George (eds), *Routledge Handbook of Family Law and Policy* (Abingdon, Routledge, 2014) fn 62.

[20] Scherpe (n 6) 69.

[21] Article 234(1) of the Catalan Civil Code. See also ch 2, s 2.IV.

[22] See, eg, *Johnston and Others v Ireland* (1986) 9 EHRR 203, especially para 55.

[23] Miles (n 14) 82 ff.

registration scheme) and in the Netherlands (through a contractual model). Norway recognises networks of cohabitants for a specific purpose – the purchase of the common household residence or goods at the end of the relationship while Slovakia recognizes all 'close persons' mainly to confer inheritance rights and protection against domestic abuse.

Belgium has arguably enacted the most protective regime amongst the three. The regime is known as *cohabitation légale*. This can be entered into by any two persons having made a formal declaration of common life,[24] regardless of the nature of their relationship. Following the critiques to only including same-sex couples levelled at the time of its enactment, the law covers both conjugal couples and pairs of friends and relatives. The latter category includes those in the first degree of the descending or collateral line, with the exception of minors.[25] The law comes in the form of a light regime as it displays a pared-down list of rules and does not have any effect on the civil status of the parties.

Fidelity duties and maintenance obligations are not included. Roughly speaking, *cohabitation légale* entails a basic level of solidarity.[26] The aspects covered are the duty to contribute to the expenses of the household and basic protections in the field of succession law, such as usufructuary rights on the common residence and tenancy rights upon the death of a partner. The regime, by contrast, falls short of conferring a reserved portion of the estate to the surviving partner. In the field of tax, the couple can now file a joint tax declaration, with the possibility of the wealthier partner enjoying lower taxation rates through the *quotient conjugal*[27] or the *attribution au conjoint aidant*.[28] The regime also provides matrimonial property rules, such as the presumption of joint property, representation and visitation rights,[29] and a number of social security and welfare rights.[30]

Yet, the law falls short of equating spouses with legal cohabitants. Important legal benefits, such as survivor's pensions, are excluded. In addition to the critique denouncing the fact that the equation is only partial, the law has been criticised for allowing only *two* persons to enter the scheme.[31] Most importantly, many social laws connected to the regime, such as those concerning residence rights, still adopt definitions requiring the couple to be in a sexual relationship.[32] Hence, the

[24] Article 1475(1) of the Civil Code of Belgium.

[25] Article 1475(2), 2° of the Civil Code of Belgium.

[26] G Willelms, 'Registered Partnerships in Belgium' in Scherpe and Hayward (n 17) 392.

[27] Articles 87–88 of the Code des Impôts sur le Revenu 1992 (Income Tax Code). This provision allows the allocation of a portion of the wealthier partner's income to the partner with the lower income.

[28] Article 86 of the Income Tax Code. This mechanism also allows the wealthier party to allocate a portion of its income to the assisting partner.

[29] See, eg, art 219 of the Civil Code on representation rights.

[30] These include social assistance, unemployment benefits, public health insurance and family allowance; see Willelms (n 26) 397.

[31] F Swennen, *Het personen-en familierecht* (Cambridge, Intersentia, 2014) 287; I Curry-Sumner, 'All's Well That Ends Registered?' in *The Substantive and Private International Law Aspects of Non-Marital Registered Relationships in Europe* (Antwerp, Intersentia, 2003) 33–72.

[32] Swennen (n 10) 41, citing S Eggermont, *De juridische bescherming van private relaties* (*The Legal Protection of Private Relationships*) (Antwerp, Intersentia, 2016).

legislature should make an effort to bring consistency across the relevant areas in order to avoid excluding non-conjugal families in a number of contexts.

The regime in the Netherlands is called a cohabitation agreement (*samenlevingsovereenkomst*). This is a contractual agreement entered into before a notary. There is no specific legal framework and the agreement is governed by the general rules on contracts. As such, it can be concluded by conjugal and non-conjugal families alike, including close relatives. It can even be entered into by more than two persons, regardless of whether they form a single household. However, in practice, it is extremely rare to see more than two persons entering into one such agreement.

The only areas open to regulation are those that are at the free disposition of the parties. The agreement can cover the property and financial aspects of cohabitation, the opportunity to have usufruct or tenancy rights upon the death of one party, and inheritance rights. It can also regulate the division of labour and duties with respect to family life and children, including maintenance obligations during or following the breakdown of the relationship.[33] Ultimately, when the parties stipulate a reciprocal duty of support (*zorgverplichting*), they automatically qualify for social benefits and for the important inheritance tax exemption threshold.[34] In 2010, 50 per cent of non-marital cohabiting couples entered into these agreements, many of which also included a duty of support.[35]

Norway also introduced some form of legal protection for all cohabiting relationships, including non-conjugal ones. The Norwegian Household Community Act 1991 applies to people living together in a household, provided that they are unmarried adults.[36] It thus applies to conjugal and non-conjugal families alike, including friends, roommates and non-dyadic networks. However, there is no corresponding comparably large material scope to this broad personal scope. The Act only offers the opportunity for any household member to purchase at market value both the common residence and goods therein when the household ceases to exist.

Slovakia recognizes 'close persons' (blízka osoba) for limited purposes as well, namely under succession law and criminal law under an ascriptive system. Regardless of registration, two people can gain these limited protections if they qualify as 'close'. Interestingly, this occurs if 'an injury inflicted to one of them is perceived by the other person as being inflicted to her'. Spouses, siblings, relatives, and 'persons in a relationship' can qualify.

[33] M Bonini Baraldi and M Oderkerk, 'Olanda' in F Brunetta D'Usseaux (ed), *Il Diritto di Famiglia nell'Unione Europea* (Padua, Cedam, 2005) 217.

[34] Article 24(2)(a) of Successiewet 1956 (Inheritance Tax Act 1956) As of January 2020, the threshold for spouses and registered partners is above €620,000.

[35] W Schrama, 'National Report: The Netherlands' in K Boele-Woelki, C Mol and E van Gelder (eds), *European Family Law in Action Volume V: Informal Relationships* (Cambridge, Intersentia, 2015), citing A De Graaf, 'Steeds meer samenwoners hebben een samenlevingscontract' *CBS Webmagazine* (The Hague, 10 February 2010).

[36] *Lov om rett til felles bolig og innbo når husstandsfellesskap opphører* or Norwegian Act relating to the right to the joint residence and household goods when a household community ceases to exist 1991 (the Norwegian Household Community Act).

Debates on the opportunity to extend registration schemes to non-conjugal couples were commonplace in Europe prior to the advent of same-sex marriage. A chief example comes from a former Member State of the EU, the UK. Access by siblings had long been at the centre of the debate surrounding the introduction of civil partnerships in 2004.[37] In particular, Edward Leigh MP advocated for such an extension in order to protect interdependent siblings in the event that one predeceases the other. Reference was made to the inheritance tax liability, a benefit reserved to spouses (and then civil partners) whose eligibility requirements were then challenged before the ECHR.[38] Leigh's amendment to the bill was labelled a 'wrecking amendment'.[39] Many commentators argued that its undeclared purpose was to derail the passage of the Civil Partnership Bill and impede the recognition of same-sex couples. Yet, others noted that, despite such non-laudable motives backing his proposal, 'extending rights to various forms of relationships … [remains] a worthwhile project from the perspective of equality and diversity'.[40]

Alistair Carmichael MP went one step further and challenged the contention that the relationship should be restricted to only two siblings. He further criticised the exclusion of parents and children from the list of eligible parties.[41] Lately, in 2017, Lord Lexden proposed an amendment to the Civil Partnerships Act to allow siblings over 30 years old, who have been in a cohabiting relationship for more than 12 years, to access civil partnerships. However, the Bill has not gained final approval in Parliament.[42]

Likewise, in France, the political debate leading up to the Pacte Civil de Solidarité (Pacs) featured positions in favour of the recognition of non-conjugal couples. The original proposal by Senator Mélenchon dates back to 1990. The proposal was meant to target any 'pair' and not necessarily a conjugal one; thus, it was open to almost all types of dyadic relationships.[43] A subsequent proposal shored up ascending and descending relatives from the cohort of eligible parties. A further proposal made explicit reference to *couples*. What lurked behind this attempt was harnessing the fact that the French term 'couple' is synonymous with conjugal couple.

[37] A Hayward, 'The Future of Civil Partnerships in England and Wales' in Scherpe and Hayward (n 17) 187.

[38] *Burden v UK* (2008) 47 EHRR 38.

[39] N Barker, 'After the Wedding, What Next? Conservatism and Conjugality' in N Barker and D Monk (eds), *From Civil Partnership to Same-Sex Marriage: Interdisciplinary Reflections* (Abingdon, Routledge, 2015) 224–41.

[40] A Gross, 'The *Burden* of Conjugality' in E Brems (ed), *Diversity and European Human Rights: Rewriting Judgments of the ECHR* (Cambridge, Cambridge University Press, 2003) 287–88.

[41] HB Deb 9 November 2004, vol 246, cols 729–30.

[42] Hayward (n 37) 556.

[43] J Halley, 'Recognition, Rights, Regulation, Normalization: Rhetorics of Justification of the Same-Sex Marriage Debate' in R Wintemute and M Andenas (eds), *The Legal Recognition of Same-Sex Partnerships: A Study of National, European and International Law* (Oxford, Hart Publishing, 2001) 101, citing D Borrillo, 'The "Pacte Civil de Solidarité" in France: Midway between Marriage and Cohabitation' in the same volume at 475.

The approved version of Pacs referred to two unrelated adults who are not married or *pacsés*. By entering into a Pacs, these two adults pledge to share a common legal residence and support each other through financial and material assistance.[44] Hence, seemingly neutral language has been used to describe the type of relationship in the relevant definition. This notwithstanding, the Conseil constitutionnel restricted the application of the law to relationships conducting 'une vie de couple' – that is, to sexual relationships[45] – thereby curtailing its potential to include non-conjugal relationships.

A further example concerns the so-called 'DICO' scheme. This was a legislative proposal presented and discussed in Italy in 2007 during Legislature XV. If approved, DICO would have supplied an option to register to any person in a stable cohabiting relationship, with limited exceptions concerning some prohibited degrees of consanguinity or affinity.[46] Despite such exceptions, the proposal was ambitious: it would have covered grandparents and non-minor children, siblings and other non-conjugal couples. Likewise, a bill presented in 2010 would have introduced an interesting *décalage* of family regimes.[47] These ranged from 'free unions' ('unioni libere'), ie, a marriage where the parties can opt out of all current marriage-related provisions and can agree on distinct, customised provisions, to 'solidarity agreements' ('intese di solidarietà'), which can be entered into by two or more persons who are not in sexual relationship and to which limited rights and obligations of mutual solidarity are attached. However, this ambitious bill has not even made it to the discussion stage in the Parliament.

However, this short overview attests to the extent to which non-conjugal coupledom is not an exotic issue for many European jurisdictions, nor is it extrinsic to the legal professional cultures therein.

II. The Constitutional Landscape

The constitutional treatment of family and marriage shows a variety of approaches. With the sole exception of four countries, the key takeaway from this section is that European states are most assuredly interested in regulating families and family roles.

Figure 5.1 below organises these approaches from the least intrusive to the most intrusive. States mentioning marriage and family in their constitutions adopt a variety of approaches that run the gamut from a mere privacy approach, where the public authority pledges to refrain from unlawful interference, to one that seemingly crystallises the family as a natural social institution antecedent to the state and superior to positive law.

[44] Loi n° 99-944 du 15 novembre 1999 relative au Pacte Civil de Solidarité.

[45] Conseil Constitutionnel, n° 99-419 DC du 9 novembre 1999.

[46] Art 1 ddl n 1339, 20 febbraio 2007, Senato della Repubblica, XV legislatura.

[47] Articles 330-*ter* to 330-*octies* (Unioni libere), arts 330-*novies* to 230-*quaterdecies*, ddl n 3607, 6 luglio 2010, Camera dei deputati, XVI legislatura.

Figure 5.1 The constitutional regulation of marriage and the family

Approach	State(s)	Relevant provisions
No reference to marriage/ family	The Netherlands; Denmark	• The Netherlands: monist system (international obligations concerning the family are directly applicable) • Denmark: the Succession to the Throne Act only contains rules on royal marriages and succession; dualist system (international obligations concerning the family must be 'domesticated')
Distribution of competences	Austria; Sweden	• Constitution of Austria: Art 10 (Federation's competence over matters pertaining to personal status) • Swedish Riksdag Act: ch 4, Part 6, Art 6 Supplementary Provision 4.6.5 (allocation of marriage-related matters to a specific Riksdag Committee) and ch 10, Part 8, Art 8 (approval/rejection by the Riksdag of the EU Commission's proposals on family laws with cross-border consequences)
Respect of one's private and family life	Belgium; Bulgaria; Croatia; Cyprus; the Czech Republic; Estonia; Greece; Hungary; Lithuania; Malta; Poland; Portugal; Romania; Slovakia; Spain	• Constitution of Belgium: Art 22 (private and family life); Constitution of Bulgaria: Art 32 (private or family affairs) • Constitution of Croatia: Art 35 (personal and family life) • Constitution of Cyprus: Art 15 (private and family life) • Czech Charter of Fundamental Rights and Basic Freedoms: Art 10(2) (private and family life) • Constitution of Estonia: Art 26 (private and family life) and Art 45 (private and family life as limits to the right to disseminate ideas) • Constitution of Greece: Art 9 (private and family life) • Constitution of Hungary: Art VI, (private and family life) • Constitution of Lithuania: Art 22 (private and family life) • Constitution of Malta: Art 32 (private and family life) • Constitution of Poland: Art 47 (private and family life)

(continued)

Figure 5.1 ***(Continued)***

Approach	State(s)	Relevant provisions
		• Constitution of Portugal: Art 26 (private and family life) • Constitution of Romania: Art 26 (private and family life) • Constitution of Slovakia: Art 19 (private and family life) • Constitution of Spain: S. 18 (personal and family life; protection of the family against the use of data processing)
Duty of care	Estonia; Latvia	• Constitution of Estonia: Art 27 (the family must care for its needy members) • Constitution of Latvia: Preamble (duty to take care of oneself, one's relatives and the common good of society)
'Empowering' role of the state	France	• Constitution of France: Preamble (the state provides the individual and the family with the conditions necessary for their development)
Procedural and substantive requisites of marriage	Belgium; Bulgaria; Croatia; Cyprus; Hungary; Ireland; Lithuania; Luxembourg; Poland; Romania; Slovakia; Slovenia; Spain	• Constitution of Belgium: Art 21 (civil wedding must precede blessing of marriage) • Constitution of Bulgaria: Art 46(1) (matrimony as the free union between a man and a woman; only civil marriage is legal) • Constitution of Croatia: Art 61 (marriage as a living union between a woman and a man; parliamentary legislation must regulate families and extra-marital unions) • Constitution of Cyprus: Art 22 (a person of nubile age is free to marry and to found a family) • Constitution of Hungary: Art L (union of a men and a woman, while family ties are based on marriage or the parent–child relationship) • Constitution of Ireland: Art 41(3) (divorce provisions; marriage as a union of two persons regardless of sex) • Constitution of Lithuania: Art 38(3) (marriage as the union between a man and a woman) • Constitution of Luxembourg: Art 21 (civil marriage must precede blessing of marriage) • Constitution of Poland: Art 18 (marriage as the union between a man and a woman)

(continued)

Figure 5.1 ***(Continued)***

Approach	State(s)	Relevant provisions
		• Constitution of Romania: Art 48(1) (family founded on freely consented marriage) and Art 48(2) (dissolution, nullity and civil marriage before religious wedding) • Constitution of Slovakia: Art 41 (union of a man and a woman) • Constitution of Slovenia: Art 53 (mandatory civil marriage; parliamentary legislation must regulate marriage, 'the legal relations within it and the family' and extra-marital unions) • Constitution of Spain: s 32 (parliamentary legislation must regulate marriage, dissolution and rights/duties of spouses)
Roles within marriage/ family	Bulgaria; Italy; Lithuania; Malta; Poland; Portugal; Romania; Slovenia	• Constitutions of Bulgaria, Lithuania, Poland, Romania and Slovenia ensure the equality of the spouses • Constitution of Italy: Art 37 (working conditions must allow women to fulfil their essential role in the family) and Art 29 (moral and legal equality of the spouses within the limit of the unity of the family) • Constitution of Malta: Art 45 (anti-discrimination does not apply to marriage, adoption, or succession law) • Constitution of Portugal: Art 59 (reconcile work and family life) and Art 36(3) (equality of spouses)
Special state protection to family/ marriage	Bulgaria; the Czech Republic; Estonia; Germany; Greece; Hungary; Ireland; Italy; Latvia; Lithuania; Poland; Portugal; Slovakia; Spain	• Constitution of Bulgaria: Art 14 (family, motherhood and children enjoy the protection of the State and society) • Czech Charter of Fundamental Rights and Basic Freedoms: Art 32(1) (protection to parenthood and the family) • Constitution of Estonia: Art 27, (family as fundamental to the preservation and growth of the nation and as the basis of society) • German Basic Law: Art 6 (protection to marriage and the family) • Constitution of Greece: Art 21 (protection to the family, as the cornerstone of the nation, as well as marriage, motherhood and childhood)

(continued)

Figure 5.1 ***(Continued)***

Approach	State(s)	Relevant provisions
		• Constitution of Hungary: Art L (protection to the family as the basis of the survival of the nation) • Constitution of Ireland: Art 41(2) (protection of the family as indispensable to the social order and welfare of the nation and the state) and Art 41(3) (the state offers special protection of marriage, on which the family is founded) • Constitution of Italy: Art 31 (the state facilitates the creation of the family, especially large families, and the fulfilment of its duties) • Constitution of Latvia: Art 110 (protection of the family, marriage, parents and children) and Preamble (the family as the foundation of a cohesive society) • Constitution of Lithuania: Art 38(1) (protection of the family as the basis of society and the state), Art 38(2) (protection of the family, motherhood, fatherhood and childhood) and Art 39 (duty to take care of families that raise children at home) • Constitution of Poland: Art 18 (protection of marriage, the family, motherhood and parenthood) and Art 71 (social and economic policies must 'account for the good of the family'; special assistance to needy families, especially those with children) • Constitution of Portugal: Art 36 (right to found a family and to marry under conditions of full equality), Art 67 (social and state protection of the family as a fundamental element in society) and a host of public assistance provisions, such as Art 65 (dwelling) and Art 59 (crèches, planned parenthood, taxes and social benefits etc) • Constitution of Slovakia: Art 41 (the state cherishes and protects marriage) • Constitution of Spain: s 39 (social, economic and legal protection of the family)

(continued)

Figure 5.1 ***(Continued)***

Approach	State(s)	Relevant provisions
Family as an institution antecedent to the state	Ireland; Italy; Luxembourg	• Constitution of Ireland: Art 41(1) (the family as the natural primary and fundamental unit of society and as a moral institution possessing inalienable and imprescriptible rights, antecedent and superior to all positive law) • Constitution of Italy: Art 29 (the family as a natural society founded on marriage) • Constitution of Luxembourg: Art 11 (the state guarantees the natural rights of the family)

The provisions in Figure 5.1 arise out of peculiar normative values informing family policy. For instance, a noticeable tension between individualism and communitarianism runs through the various state approaches.

Most European constitutions tend to protect the family as a social institution of its own. However, while the original provisions in Western European constitutions were often informed by a communitarian conception of family, judicial courts mitigated their bearing. Think of Article 29 of the Italian Constitution, which reads as follows: 'The Republic recognises the rights of the family as a natural society founded on marriage'. This natural law conception was meant to depict the family as a collective entity with essentialised features pre-dating the state. Despite the rather clear-cut wording, the Court of Cassation has consistently read the article in conjunction with Article 2, which protected social formations.[48] This link was instrumental to arguing that the family is not the locus where inviolable rights are compressed, but the site where individuals as such, preserving their essential features, can freely develop and fulfil their goals.

A minority approach does not take into account the family, but only the individuals within the family. This is the case in France. As argued by prominent legal scholar Jean Boulouis, in France the cornerstone of marriage is not the couple, but the individual.[49] The French Constitution of 1958 does not mention marriage, except for the purposes of the division of powers. Nor does it mention the family, except for the Preamble to the 1946 Constitution, which reads: 'La Nation assure à l'individu et à la famille les conditions nécessaires à leur développement' ('The Nation shall provide the individual and the family with the conditions necessary

[48] Cass, sez I civ, 10 maggio 2005, n 9801. This approach is also followed by the Italian Constitutional Court, according to which cohabiting same-sex couples were constitutionally protected social formations under art 2 of the Italian Constitution. See Corte cost, sentenza n 138/2010.

[49] J Boulouis, 'Famille et droit constitutionnel' in *Études offertes à Pierre Kaiser*, vol 1 (Aix-en-Provence, Presses Universitaires d'Aix-Marseille, 1979) 149 ('Reléguée sous surveillance dans l'ordre privé, la famille devient politiquement transparente. Cette transparence … doit permettre de n'apercevoir que l'individu').

for their development').[50] This should come as no surprise. The reticence to discuss family matters is consistent with the atomist conception of society inherited from the French Revolution.

A further variable concerns the degree of intrusiveness of state regulation. Based on such a variable, one could speak of a spectrum that runs the gamut from full privatisation to over-constitutionalisation of the family. The majority of states lean towards over-constitutionalisation. This stands in sharp contrast with the situation in the US, whose constitution does not mention marriage or family. In light of this, some academics have long questioned the existence of a jurisprudential fundamental right to marry in order to lay claim to the abolition of civil marriage.[51] The European approach also differs from the Canadian approach. In Canada, marriage is a legislative matter that is allocated to the competent level of government. However, it is worth recalling that the family has been gradually constitutionalised through subsequent case law, especially via the equality jurisprudence under the Canadian Charter of Rights and Freedoms.[52]

As Figure 5.1 shows, only two states omit any reference to the family: Denmark and the Netherlands. However, the protection of the family is achieved by way of incorporating international human rights treaties. Relevant instruments include the Convention and sectorial treaties specialising in the protection of women, the protection of children etc.[53]

A second cluster of states, including Austria and Sweden, only display provisions concerning the division of powers in family-related matters, much like Canada. A third group features constitutional provisions which shield families from unlawful interferences and includes 15 states. Yet, all such states include additional clauses setting forth the substantive and procedural conditions to enter into marriage, or granting enhanced protection to the family, or both. In other words, no polity in Europe adopts a pure privacy approach, whereby the only imperative for the state is to refrain from excessive intrusion into the private sphere.

This is consistent with modern European constitutions belonging to a phase of constitutionalism subsequent to that of liberal constitutions. The European legal tradition embraces a 'holistic' vision in the light of which constitutions aspire to inform the regulation of society as a whole, its formations and its constituent elements. These constitutions indirectly shape society in the sense that they are structured in such a way as to orient and accompany social change. In their

[50] Paragraph 10 of the Preamble to the French Constitution of 1946.

[51] See, eg, N Tebbe and DA Widiss, 'Equal Access and the Right to Marry' (2010) 158 *University of Pennsylvania Law Review* 1375; M Nussbaum, 'A Right to Marry?' (2010) 98 *California Law Review* 667; C Sunstein, 'The Right to Marry' (2004) 26 *Cardozo Law Review* 2081.

[52] B Baines, 'Using the Canadian Charter of Rights and Freedoms to Constitute Women' in B Baines and R Rubio-Marin (eds), *The Gender of Constitutional Jurisprudence* (Cambridge, Cambridge University Press, 2005).

[53] See, eg, Convention on the Elimination of All Forms of Discrimination Against Women (adopted 18 December 1979, entered into force 3 September 1981) 1249 UNTS 13.

shaping of power and indirectly society, they go beyond mere non-interference in relation to the natural rights of citizens.[54]

A logic outgrowth of this aspiration is socio-democratic rights. European constitutions assume a host of positive duties towards citizens. They hold fast to the conviction that it is the state's role to tackle the substantive inequalities hindering the development of human beings. Further, these constitutions yield indirect horizontal effects, after the German doctrine of the *mittelbare Drittwirkung*, meaning that they bind not only public authorities but also citizens in their daily interactions.[55] They do so by 'provid[ing] the basis for claims against public authorities to intervene on behalf of rights-claimants in response to threats from third parties'.[56] A thus-framed holistic vision of constitutionalism sits uneasily with a pure privacy approach, and factors into the over-constitutionalisation of family in Europe.

A fourth cluster gathers provisions whereby the government places on families a duty to care for their own members. Under this approach, care duties are 'privatised', as they are primarily placed upon family members themselves. Estonia and Latvia belong to this group. As with the previous group, in their complementing a privatisation approach to family care with a robust set of provisions granting special protection to 'the' family, these states offer food for thought: when privatisation of care is combined with a state-sponsored singular definition of family, privatisation becomes instrumental to entrenching such definitions and crystallising distinct family roles.

Another cluster of states – mostly East-Central ones – features provisions that set forth substantive and procedural requirements to enter into a valid marriage.[57] Procedurally, they display rules mandating that a civil marriage is to precede a religious ceremony, as well as rules relating to the procedures of divorce, separation and succession. The list then includes a reference to the substantive requirements for entering into marriage such as capacity and consent. Some constitutions substantively define marriage as the union of two persons regardless of sex. Others – Bulgaria, Croatia, Hungary, Latvia, Lithuania, Poland and Slovakia – define it as a union solely between a man and a woman. However, in Croatia and Hungary, the constitutional 'ban' has been interpreted as not preventing the introduction of same-sex civil partnerships. Hence, when it comes to same-sex marriage, the picture that emerges is of a fractured Europe, with a social and cultural cleavage visibly dividing the continent in two parts.

[54] C Pinelli, 'The Combination of Negative with Positive Constitutionalism in Europe' (2011) 13 *European Journal of Law Reform* 31, 37.

[55] The existence of horizontal effects is still debated in four states: Belgium, Croatia, Poland and Portugal. See I Chopin and C Germaine, European Commission, *A Comparative Analysis of Non-discrimination Law in Europe 2017* (Luxembourg, Publications Office of the European Union, 2017) 10.

[56] M Kumm, 'Who is Afraid of the Total Constitution? Constitutional Rights as Principles and the Constitutionalization of Private Law' (2016) 7 *German Law Journal* 341, 344.

[57] The states belonging to this group are Belgium, Bulgaria, Croatia, Cyprus, Hungary, Ireland, Lithuania, Luxembourg, Poland, Romania, Slovakia, Slovenia and Spain.

As regards other substantive definitions, only Croatia and Slovenia mention extra-marital unions to require that the matter be governed by parliamentary legislation. This provision is a legacy of the socialist Republic of Yugoslavia, which after the Second World War extended major forms of legal protection to informal cohabitants in order to reflect the social reality of families at the time.[58]

Another group of three states go beyond policing entrance into and exit from marriage. Such states go to the trouble of neatly defining the roles that spouses must assume. The Italian example is emblematic in this regard. The Italian Constitution requires the state to set working conditions so as to allow women to 'fulfil their essential role in the family'.[59] At the same time, it makes the moral and legal equality of the spouses contingent on 'the limit of the unity of the family'.[60]

Moreover, it is significant that almost two-thirds of the 27 Member States confer a special level of protection upon the family. Special protection is always premised on the contention that the family is a foundational institution that is integral to the preservation of society. This approach is adopted in the Baltic countries, where it is seen as the 'basis' or 'foundation' of society, and in states where it is pompously defined as 'the cornerstone of the preservation and the advancement of the Nation'[61] or 'the basis of the survival of the nation'[62] (respectively, Greece and Hungary).

Within this group are three states which seemingly depict the family as an institution grounded in natural law: Ireland, Italy and Luxembourg. At first glance, this conception entrenches the family as a social institution pre-dating the state. It has been harnessed by opponents of marriage equality to argue that its characteristics are immutable, despite nowadays the dominant opinion being that family is a historically variable and contingent concept.[63]

What is highly problematic for the purposes of our analysis is the conflation of marriage and the family in many states such as Bulgaria,[64] Lithuania[65] and Romania.[66] The trend is also apparent in Cyprus, where the right to found a family is granted according to the law on marriage,[67] in Hungary, where it is stated that '[f]amily ties shall be based on marriage and/or the relationship between parents

[58] P Šarćević, 'Cohabitation without Marriage: The Yugoslavian Experience' (1981) 29 *American Journal of Comparative Law* 315.

[59] Article 37 of the Italian Constitution of 2 June 1946.

[60] ibid art 29.

[61] Article 21 of the Greek Constitution of 8 December 1974.

[62] Article L, 1 ch 'Foundations' of the Constitution of Hungary of 18 April 2011.

[63] P Barcellona, voce 'Famiglia (dir. civ.)' in *Enciclopedia del diritto*, vol XVI (Milan, Giuffrè, 1967) 780 ff; F Caggia and A Zoppini, 'Art 29' in R Bifulco, A Celotto and M Olivetti (eds), *Commentario alla Costituzione*, vol I (Turin, Giappichelli, 2006) 605 ff.

[64] Article 46(2) of the Constitution of Bulgaria of 12 July 1991.

[65] Article 38(5) of the Constitution of Lithuania of 25 October 1992.

[66] Article 48(1) of the Constitution of Romania of 8 December 1991.

[67] Article 22 of the Constitution of Cyprus of 16 August 1960.

and children', and in Ireland and Italy, where it is explicitly submitted that the family is founded on marriage.[68] Other states, while not explicitly conflating marriage and family, tie them together in the relevant provisions.[69] There is a 'sandwich' provision, whereby the family is placed in between marriage and parent–child relationships, in Latvia[70] and Greece.[71] Where 'family' is given independent consideration, as in German constitutional case law, it usually designates the vertical relationship between children and parents, instead of other non-marital horizontal relationships. Non-marital cohabitation in Germany receives protection under the general clause guaranteeing the freedom of action, under Article 2(1) of the Basic Law.[72] Likewise, in Italy, cohabiting couples find their legal basis in Article 2 as 'social groups where human personality is expressed'.

To conclude, this snapshot of constitutional family law in Europe shows a variegated picture, with over-constitutionalisation being the common denominator of a large majority of approaches. One can confidently argue that European states tend to over-constitutionalise family and marriage. In terms of the impact of this approach on strategic litigation, constitutionalisation implies an ossification of the notions of family. In turn, an ossification forces new families to bargain change via constitutional litigation or constitutional amendments. With many states aggrandising the centrality of family to the point of linking it to the 'survival' or fabric of the nation, it seems reasonable to argue that the family is relevant to the core identity of many European nations. Hence, judicial decisions at the meta-national level which run counter to the constitutionally entrenched notions of family might lead to a political backlash domestically, potentially culminating in a withdrawal from the EU and the ECHR framework should it run roughshod over such notions.

2. Venue

The ECtHR is the judicial body which enforces the rights enshrined in the Convention. As argued above, the Convention is an international human rights treaty. However, it displays some peculiar characteristics that are worth emphasising.

[68] Article 41(3) of the Constitution of Ireland of 29 December 1937; and art 29 of the Italian Constitution. See G Di Rosa, 'Famiglia e matrimonio: consolidate tradizioni giuridiche, innovative discipline interne e attuale sistema comunitario' in B Montanari (ed), *La costruzione dell'identità europea: sicurezza collettiva, libertà individuali e modelli di regolazione sociale* (Turin, Giappichelli, 2013) 63.

[69] Article 36 of the Constitution of Portugal 2 April 1976 [Portuguese Const].

[70] Article 110 of the Constitution of Latvia of February 15, 1922 (as amended in 1998).

[71] Article 21 of the Greek Constitution.

[72] See, eg, Bundesverfassungsgericht, 03.04.1990 – 1 BvR 1186/89, 82, 6. The Federal Constitutional Court rejected a restrictive interpretation of art 6 as requiring a prohibition to extend marital protections to non-marital unions (the so-called distance rule or *Abstandsgebot*). See Bundesverfassungsgericht, 17.07.2002 – 1 BvF 1/01, 1 BvF 2/01, 105, 313, 347.

The Convention is the sole international treaty where individuals stand on an equal footing with states in the international legal order – with the partial exception of the Inter-American Human Rights System, where, however, individuals are mediated by a Commission.[73] In front of the ECtHR, individuals have the effective status of 'human rights bearer', without a need for contracting parties to mediate. Most importantly for the purposes of this analysis, unlike other international human rights treaties, the Convention provides for a strong enforcement mechanism. This mechanism is inclusive of an individual complaint mechanism. Individuals can thus access the ECtHR if they think that their rights, as enshrined in the Convention, have been breached. This is subject to an ability to show their status as victims – meaning that they have been personally affected by the alleged violation – and that they have exhausted all available domestic remedies.

The key advantage of this venue compared to the EU is its being a system specialised in the protection of human rights. The EU, by contrast, has at its core market freedoms. Starting from the mid-1980s, when a sharp increase in individual applications was registered, the ECtHR became a sort of court of last resort in human rights issues in the region. Its specialisation, acting in tandem with an ability to gain prestige, contributed to the Court becoming the authoritative voice in European human rights law. Interestingly, despite paying lip service to its 'subsidiary role', the ECtHR has ended up playing a salient role in delivering human rights protection across the continent, as this chapter will illustrate.

Yet, this venue also has its pitfalls. Judgments are mostly symbolic in that the remedy adjudicate by the ECtHR is a modest compensation (and other limited rewards). Further, while many laws and practices have been altered following successful individual applications, in the face of persistent violations of the Convention on the part of Member States, the Council of Europe has not managed to tackle them with bite.[74] Second, while its open-textured provisions warrant a prima facie large interpretation, their application is restricted by the Court's recourse to the doctrine of the margin of appreciation. This doctrine, whereby the Court grants a degree of latitude in balancing public interests with rights, reaches its peak in matters of social engineering. In these domains, the Court's scrutiny is particularly weak.

However, all things considered, the success of the system of the ECHR is there for all to see – again, especially compared to its other international counterparts. It is undeniable that the ECtHR has added momentum to the development of legal frameworks at the domestic level. When the time was ripe to make strides

[73] B Simma, 'The Sources of International Human Rights Law: Human Rights Treaties' in S Besson and J d'Aspremont (eds), *The Oxford Handbook of the Sources of International Law* (Oxford, Oxford University Press, 2017) 878–79.

[74] S Greer, 'What's Wrong with the European Convention on Human Rights?' (2008) 30 *Human Rights Quarterly* 680, 691.

in the area of family regulation, the Court was intransigent about accepting states' justifications for not updating their family laws or other laws breaching the Convention. Examples of this are numerous. The ECtHR's judgments triggered reforms in fields as varied as the recognition of same-sex couples in Italy,[75] legal gender recognition in the UK,[76] the rights of illegitimate children in France[77] etc. Hence, its potential to trigger legal innovation processes at the domestic level remains high, notwithstanding the limits outlined above. It is such potential that this chapter seeks to harness.

3. Remedy

An analysis of the Court's case law makes it possible to conclude that, at present, non-conjugal families can only seek access to singular family benefits; they cannot request access to family regimes, such as civil unions. However, I also anticipate that once non-conjugal couples have gained more legal recognition domestically, an argument can be made before the Court that they deserve a 'specific legal framework', such as a registration scheme.

I. Stage 1: An Area-Specific Approach

LGBTQ advocates at first approached the Court seeking to gain access to specific entitlements. In so doing, they obtained landmark victories that led to an extension of major forms of legal protection, including tenancy rights[78] and accident and sickness insurance.[79] Likewise, in the EU, they were especially successful in obtaining equal benefits in the workplace.[80]

By contrast, the chances of introducing a comprehensive recognition mechanism through the ECHR are slim, at least at present. The prognosis is negative since there are an insufficient number of states that have recognised non-conjugal families domestically. As a consequence, it is unlikely that the Court would find a European consensus, even in its attenuated form of an 'emerging consensus', on the issue as I illustrate below. A claim that a comprehensive regime is to be introduced would be 'abrupt' and would lack the contextual conditions that led to such a claim eventually being upheld for same-sex couples. As a result of the incessant lobbying

[75] *Oliari and Others v Italy* [2015] 65 EHRR 26.

[76] *Goodwin v UK* (2002) 35 EHRR 18, which led to the introduction of the Gender Recognition Act 2004.

[77] *Mazurek v France* (2006) 42 EHRR 9.

[78] *Karner v Austria* (2003) 38 EHRR 528; and *Kozak v Poland* (2010) 51 EHRR 16.

[79] *PB and JS v Austria* (2010) 55 EHRR 31, para 33.

[80] Judgment of the Court of 12 December 2013, *Frédéric Hay v Crédit agricole mutuel de Charente-Maritime et des Deux-Sèvres*, C-267/12, EU:C:2013:823.

activity of LGBTQ same-sex couples went from being seen as social outcasts to being known and accepted as normal partners in a committed relationship. In turn, social acceptance translated into legal reforms in the majority of the Member States of the Council of Europe under the impulse of such movements. It is against this backdrop that the ECtHR first conceded that same-sex families enjoy a private life. Next, it recognised that they enjoy the institution of family life. Ultimately, it concluded that they deserve a 'specific legal framework' for their legal recognition. Yet, in light of the sharp East/West divide on the issue, this doctrinal development did not occur until July 2015, when the Court remedied the protracted failure of Italy – the last 'reluctant' state in Western Europe – to recognise these unions in some way. In *Schalk and Kopf*, there was an opening for the possibility that same-sex marriage could fall under the Article 12 right to marry. However, so far, the Court has declined to find a thus-framed right as guaranteed by the Convention.

What I referred to as the contextual conditions that led same-sex couples to have their demands met are completely lacking in the case of non-conjugal families. Non-conjugal couples have not yet attracted much public attention and their legal recognition is at best scattered and insufficient. In conclusion, in light of the current doctrinal developments, non-conjugal families can only aspire to an extension of specific entitlements before the ECtHR.

II. Stage 2: A Comprehensive Approach (Registration)

If the parallel with same-sex couples holds true, at a later stage the framework of the Convention might offer an opportunity to argue that non-conjugal couples merit comprehensive protection. Notably, they might be able to request a 'specific legal framework', along the lines of what same-sex couples did in *Oliari*.[81]

This will be made possible by contracting parties having introduced more legal protections domestically for non-conjugal families. The higher the number of jurisdictions that recognise non-conjugal couples, the higher the likelihood that at some point the Court will consider that these changes have morphed into a European consensus on the issue. How a consensus can be traced is the subject of the next section. Suffice it to say that, once ascertained, a consensus is conducive to compelling those states swimming against the tide to also recognise non-conjugal families.

Now, one could raise the objection that introducing new regimes domestically is easier said than done and that the action of the Court should not be contingent on the states' willingness to act. However, it is worth recalling that the ECtHR is an international court; as such, it must have a subsidiary role and can by no

[81] *Oliari* (n 75).

means act as a full-fledged substitute for domestic courts. Without a traceable consensus, a Court's decision would be perceived as tantamount to a minority of states forcing their views on all Contracting States. And even worst it might be seen as the Court – namely an international body which is not well acquainted with the reality of national systems – forcing its own view on Contracting States. This would arguably result in a political backlash that might not only jeopardise the perceived legitimacy of the Court but also its very existence if it results in the states' withdrawal from the Convention.

Hence, all the Court can do is to compel a minority of states to align with the majority of states – however adventurously 'majority' can be defined – once some enabling conditions are met, which is no small thing, especially compared to other regional human rights systems. The main of these enabling conditions is an identifiable European consensus or trend towards the formation of such a consensus.

4. Legal Arguments before the ECtHR

Venue	The ECtHR
Remedies	Extension of specific familial benefits
Legal arguments	1. Stage 1: protection of family life and ban on discrimination 2. Stage 1: protection of property and ban on discrimination 3. Stage 1: general ban on discrimination 4. Stage 2: *Oliari*-like protection of family life

While liberty-based arguments are not entirely absent, they have less traction if one wishes to extend family benefits. This is why new families tend to prioritise equality-based lines of argument before the ECtHR. An obligation for the state to protect new families could arise under:

(i) Article 8 alone (right to respect for private and family life);
(ii) Article 8 (right to respect for private and family life) in conjunction with Article 14 (ban on discrimination);
(iii) Article 1 of Protocol No 1 (protection of property) in conjunction with Article 14 (ban on discrimination); or
(iv) Article 1 of Protocol No 12 (general ban on discrimination).

The decision as to which argument to employ depends on the remedy sought. If one seeks to challenge narrow eligibility requirements to access a familial benefit, the approaches in options (ii), (iii) and (iv) are suitable, either in combination or alone. By contrast, if one wishes to compel the government to introduce a scheme that comprehensively recognises non-conjugal families, the only available approach at present is approach (i), claiming a violation of the right to respect for one's family life. I will analyse each line of argument in turn.

I. Stage 1: Protection of Family Life and Ban on Discrimination

Article 8 of the Convention enshrines the right to respect for private and family life. The right can suffer from restrictions only if made in accordance with the conditions set out in paragraph 2. This paragraph lists amongst the public interests that can justify a restriction national security, public safety or the economic well-being of the country, the prevention of disorder or crime, the protection of health or morals, or the protection of the rights and freedoms of others.

The notion of private life refers to personal autonomy and choice. At a minimum, it encompasses a right to establish and develop relationships with other human beings,[82] a right to personal development[83] and a right to self-determination.[84] It prevents the state from interfering with the physical and mental health of persons, as well as interfering with their personal data or intimate choices, including those pertaining to sex or gender.

The notion of family life is more specific. It applies to family ties between individuals. As I will illustrate below, the concept is sufficiently large to encompass a variety of situations, including potentially non-conjugal relationships. However, Article 8 alone is of reduced utility to the cause of non-conjugal unions as it only aims at preventing unauthorised intrusions into the personal sphere with limited exceptions.[85] In principle, it cannot be construed as requiring public authorities to confer entitlements attaching to legal recognition.[86] The Court has noted on several occasions that Article 8 does not guarantee unmarried partners a right to receive legal benefits, such as benefits under a social insurance scheme.[87] Therefore, it is necessary to add another conceptual layer, namely discrimination, by reading Article 8 in conjunction with Article 14.

Article 14 sets forth a ban on discrimination. The right to non-discrimination is not a free-standing right and must be linked to another substantive provision of the Convention. This is not to say that another substantive provision must be violated. The Court moves to the anti-discrimination claim even in the absence of a breach of the related substantive provision. It is enough that the matter falls within the 'ambit' of the provision.[88] In order for a matter to fall within the ambit of a right, the facts of the case should merely broadly relate to issues protected under the Convention. The target of an anti-discrimination claim can thus extend well beyond the narrow boundaries of the substantive right. To provide an example, it has been held that the extension of accident and health insurance coverage to

[82] *Niemietz v Germany* (1992) 16 EHRR 97.
[83] *Bensaid v UK* (2001) 33 EHRR 205.
[84] *Pretty v UK* (2002) 35 EHRR 1.
[85] But see s 4.IV below on the positive obligations arising under art 8 ECHR.
[86] *Şerife Yiğit v Turkey* (2011) 53 EHRR 25 [97]–[98] and [102].
[87] *Stec and Others v UK* (2006) 43 EHRR 47 [53].
[88] See, eg, *Abdulaziz, Cabales and Balkandali v UK* (1985) 7 EHRR 471 [71].

unmarried couples falls within the ambit of the right to respect for family life, as it improves the personal and family life of the applicant – a connection that at first sight might seem thin.[89]

Article 14 prohibits both direct and indirect discrimination. In the Convention system, indirect discrimination refers to discrimination which disproportionately affects a group, despite appearing a seemingly neutral classification. As regards the structure of an anti-discrimination claim, the claimant should first point to a difference in treatment compared to a group in an analogous or relevantly similar situation or to identical treatment with respect to a group which is not in an analogous or relevantly similar situation. If an infringement is found, the defendant (state) bears the burden of justifying the measure. The measure is not justified if it lacks an objective and reasonable justification. The condition is met if the measure pursues a legitimate purpose and there is a relationship of proportionality between the means employed and the purpose.[90]

Article 14 has an open-ended list of grounds as it refers to 'other statuses'. In addition to the listed grounds,[91] thus far, many others have been incorporated. These include, inter alia, sexual orientation, age, disability, parenthood and marital status.[92] The most notable developments in the area of family law were achieved by harnessing the prohibition to discriminate based on sex and sexual orientation. There are few cases where the Court has enforced the prohibition to discriminate based on marital status. Amongst these few cases is *Sahin v Germany*,[93] in which the Court found that a denial of a father's visitation rights to a child born out of wedlock violated Article 14, and *Sommerfeld v Germany*,[94] where the Court struck down differences in treatment between married and unmarried fathers. Overall, it is apparent that the Court is reluctant to uphold the prohibition to discriminate based on marital status in situations involving delicate decisions of social policy; its reluctance only increases in cases regarding the extension of marital defaults to new families.

Yet, I argue that there is no special doctrinal hindrance to effecting the prohibition to discriminate based on marital status. The impediment, if any, is of a political nature. It derives from states not welcoming with open arms decisions that interfere with their domestic social policy. However, if the prohibition to discriminate based on marital status is to have any meaning, a braver approach to marital status discrimination must be taken. How this braver approach should be put to work is

[89] *PB and JS* (n 79) [33].

[90] ibid [38].

[91] These grounds are sex, race, colour, language, religion, political or other opinion, national or social origin, association with a national minority, property and birth.

[92] European Union Agency for Fundamental Rights and Council of Europe, *Handbook on European Non-discrimination Law* (Luxembourg, Publications Office of the European Union, 2018) 224.

[93] *Sahin v Germany* (2004) 38 EHRR 736.

[94] *Sommerfeld v Germany* (2004) 38 EHRR 35.

illustrated below, where I investigate whether a non-conjugal family can mobilise a line of argument based on Articles 8 and 14 ECHR.

i. The Substantive Provision

The first step requires assessing whether the matter falls within the 'ambit' of a substantive provision – in this case, Article 8. This inquiry raises two preliminary questions: do non-conjugal families enjoy a right to respect for their family life? And do they enjoy 'family' life in the first place?

Family life is an autonomous concept that hinges upon the existence of close family ties.[95] The adoption of an autonomous definition of family within the ECHR framework is a major difference compared to the EU, where the definition of family status is parasitic of that of Member States. Conversely, while the ECtHR does not ignore national definitions, it never refers to them in order to restrict the scope of Convention rights.[96]

The notion of family life is essentially aimed at enabling a family unit to live together so that a normal family relationship can unfold[97] and that its members can enjoy each other's company.[98] The notion presupposes the existence of family ties. Hence, the Court has always rejected arguments to the effect that Article 8 encompasses a right to form a new family.[99] The 'right to found a family' only exists under another article: Article 12. However, it is unclear whether unmarried families can invoke Article 12: an accredited interpretation is that the right to found a new family forms a pair with the right to marry, and thus that the two cannot be conceptually distinguished under the Convention.[100] This interpretation seems to be buttressed by a comparative analysis between Article 12 and the analogous right in Article 9 of the Charter of Fundamental Rights of the European Union. While the latter carefully sets the two apart and speaks of a right to marry *and* a right to found a family, the Convention does not.[101]

However, the requirement that a family must pre-exist in order to receive protection under Article 8 should not be overstated either. A series of judgments cast doubt on the pure retrospective nature of the right. For instance, even in the absence of an established familial tie, the Court has been willing to protect

[95] *Paradiso and Campanelli v Italy* (2017) 65 EHRR 2 [140].

[96] V Zagrebelsky, 'Famiglia e vita familiare nella Convenzione Europea' in MC Andrini (ed), *Un nuovo diritto di famiglia europeo* (Padua, Cedam, 2007) 117.

[97] *Marckx v Belgium* (1979) 2 EHRR 330.

[98] *Olsson v Sweden* (1989) 11 EHRR 259 [59].

[99] The applicant's request to develop a not-yet-existent 'family life' with her nephew by becoming a legal guardian did not amount to 'family life' in *Lazoriva v Ukraine* App No 6878/14 (ECtHR, 17 April 2018) [65].

[100] Zagrebelsky (n 96) 118. See, contra, G Ferrando, 'Il Contributo della Corte europea dei Diritti dell'Uomo' in Andrini (n 96) 139 (arguing that the right to found a family has a meaning independent of the right to marry and encompasses de facto families).

[101] 'Explanation on Article 9 – Right to marry and right to found a family' in *Explanations Relating to the Charter of Fundamental Rights* [2007] OJ C303, 17–35.

the potential relationship between a biological father and a child born out of wedlock.[102] Especially when the lack of a pre-existing relationship is not attributable to the will of the applicant, the Court resolves to protect the potential relationship.[103]

Crucially, Article 8's family is not necessarily dependent on legal sanction or recognition. As an illustration, the lack of recognition of a religious marriage under national law is no bar to a finding that there is a family life.[104] The notion is inherently functional, interested as it is in the actual rather than the formal attributes of a family unit. This aspect has two relevant consequences. First, while married or registered couples usually fall within the scope of the law for the sole reason of being married or in a registered partnership, the Court is still inclined to conduct a fact-driven inquiry into the actual attributes of their relationship. Second – and by the same token – when a family lacks legal recognition, the Court engages in an inquiry into the existence of de facto family ties. Consistent with this approach, thus far the Court has found that the following formations enjoy a family life:

(i) married couples and registered partnerships, provided that a genuine relationship exists;[105]
(ii) unmarried conjugal couples, as long as they show some functional attributes, such as long-term cohabitation and subsistence of the relationship;[106]
(iii) relatives, such as siblings, uncles/aunts and nephews, and grandparents and children if they can offer evidence that they are in a close relationship.

I shall focus on the third category. The ECtHR has a penchant for protecting relatives when 'close family ties' are at issue. The reason is that close relatives can play an essential role in each other's lives. Thus, within the composite category of non-conjugal unions, there is no special hurdle to finding that close relatives enjoy the institution of family life under Article 8. Surely, siblings do enjoy it. In *Moustaquim v Belgium*,[107] the government of Belgium violated Article 8 by deporting the applicant and separating him from his family, including his seven siblings. Likewise, in *Mustafa and Armağan Akın v Turkey*,[108] the forceful separation of the two siblings amounted to an unjustified violation of the right to respect one's family life.

In *Boyle v UK*, the Court extended the reach of family life to aunts/uncles and nieces/nephews. It thereby found a violation of the mentioned Article in the UK government's refusal to grant visitation rights to an uncle.[109] Subsequent decisions

[102] Research Division, European Court of Human Rights, *Guide on Article 8 of the European Convention of Human Rights* (Strasbourg, Council of Europe, 2018) 45.
[103] *Pini and Others v Romania* (2005) 40 EHRR 13 [143] and [146].
[104] *Abdulaziz et al* (n 88) [63].
[105] Absence of a genuine relationship in marriage has been at times derived by the lack of cohabitation. See Research Division, European Court of Human Rights (n 102) 47–48.
[106] *Şerife Yiğit* (n 86).
[107] *Moustaquim v Belgium* (1991) 13 EHRR 802 [36].
[108] *Mustafa and Armağan Akın v Turkey*, App No 4694/03 (ECtHR, 6 April 2010) [19].
[109] *Boyle v UK* (2008) 47 EHRR 19 [41]–[47].

found Article 8 engaged in the case of grandparents and grandchildren.[110] However, the right usually tends to be framed in terms of a right to maintain a normal relationship through contact.[111] Thus, unsurprisingly, its scope varies depending on the existence of natural parents: if natural parents are not in the picture, the Court applies the provision to permit grandparents and grandchildren to live together; by contrast, in 'normal' circumstances – ie, when natural parents are present – the relationship 'calls for a lesser degree of protection'.[112]

There is a direct corollary from this conceptualisation of the right: Article 8's focus on vertical family relationships as opposed to horizontal, adult–adult relationships. In the cases mentioned above, the person who is severed from a close relative is usually a minor. When the person at stake is an adult rather than a minor, the relationship does not attract protection, unless the Court finds additional elements of dependency. However, problematically, in the case of adult relatives, the threshold of dependency is nearly impossible to meet, with dependency often coinciding with disability. A conspicuous illustration of this is the Court's finding that the threshold is met in the case of paranoid schizophrenia[113] and quadriplegia.[114] This approach has drawn criticism as fails to account for the many families made up of adult relatives beyond families with disabled members.[115] By contrast, a family life is found when adult second-generation migrants are at stake and the government deports one of them. Notably, it is found when second-generation migrants have lawfully resided in the country with their relatives and are 'socially integrated' within the country – with actual ties with such relatives then becoming less relevant.[116]

However, this restrictive approach to protecting adult relatives is extrinsic to the Court seeing family life as always engaged in the case of close family ties. It is also extrinsic to its emphasis on a functional notion of family. The effectiveness of family ties 'among people who mutually support and care for each other from an economic, educational and emotional point of view'[117] has been the linchpin of its case law on family life. It is a matter of consistency to require that the Court follows through with its own case law and expands family life to adult relatives as well. When the relevant elements of family life exist (long-term cohabitation, economic interdependency etc), adult relatives should attract the same degree of protection as relationships with minors.

[110] *Marckx* (n 97) [31] and [45].

[111] Research Division, European Court of Human Rights (n 102) 55.

[112] ibid, citing *Mitovi v Former Yugoslav Republic of Macedonia*, App No 53565/13 (ECtHR, 16 April 2015) [50].

[113] *Anam v UK* (2011) 53 EHRR SE13.

[114] *Emonet v Switzerland*, App No 39051/03 (ECtHR, 13 December 2007).

[115] C Draghici, 'Adult Children and Elderly Parents in Strasburg Proceedings: A Misconstrued Approach to "Family Life"' (2018) 32 *International Journal of Law, Policy and the Family* 42.

[116] ibid 48 (noting that the fact that these migrants are seen as quasi-citizens led the Court to find the private life limb rather than family life limb engaged, as they had developed multiple ties over the years warranting protection regardless of whether they were familiar with one another).

[117] SS Caballero, 'Unmarried Cohabiting Couples before the European Court of Human Rights: Parity with Marriage?' (2004) 11 *Columbia Journal of European Law* 151, 152.

A useful analogy to envision whether the substantive provision – and its family life limb – can apply to non-conjugal adults is that of same-sex couples. Until 1998, the Court declined to hold that same-sex partners enjoy a private life or a family life. Starting with *Karner v Austria*, the Court found that unmarried same-sex couples merit respect for their home, under the private life limb, but not family life.[118] In *Schalk and Kopf*, it finally ruled that same-sex couples enjoy the institution of family life since they were found to be just as capable as opposite-sex couples of forming a committed and stable relationship.[119] However, this consideration alone could not warrant the important conclusion that the Court reached. Their functional equivalence with opposite-sex couples was coupled with an observation that there was a growing European consensus on the acceptance of equal rights for same-sex couples.

In *Pajić v Croatia*, the Court continued its position.[120] In its final decision, it found an incompatibility with the Convention when Croatia denied a residence permit to a same-sex unmarried partner. The conclusion was buttressed by a growing consensus towards the legal recognition of same-sex families as of 2015 and by the parallel system of protection of the EU having dropped any reference to gender in its provision setting forth a right to marry and found a family.[121] The Convention is structurally suited to detect and embrace change when such change is under way. As the oft-quoted mantra of the Court has it, 'the Convention is a living instrument which … must be interpreted in the light of present-day conditions'.[122] It is thanks to this realistic and flexible approach that the Court can account for all sorts of family relationships and can include in the notion of family life de facto families, non-conjugal families made up of relatives, illegitimate families and many more formations.

This analogy induces us to think that in order for the Court to consider family life as engaged, there should be an identifiable 'trend' towards the legal recognition of non-conjugal families. There is no arithmetic calculus behind this observation. As section 1.I has illustrated, legal reforms have already been enacted in Belgium, Slovakia and the Netherlands and debates on the subject have taken place in other states, such as Italy and France. Again, a consensus has at times been found in positive law, at other times in practices and at yet others in debates. Thus, it might be sufficient that the issue of the recognition of non-conjugal couples gains greater traction. However, legal recognition remains a clearer indicator of a potential consensus compared to mere debates. Once a trend is identifiable, under the current case law, the chances are high that it will morph into a legal obligation for reluctant states to amend their laws.

[118] *Karner* (n 78).
[119] *Schalk and Kopf v Austria* (2011) 53 EHRR 20.
[120] *Pajić v Croatia*, App No 68453/13 (ECtHR, 23 February 2016).
[121] Article 9 of the Charter of Fundamental Rights of the European Union.
[122] *Tyrer v UK* (1979–80) 2 EHRR 1.

Continuing the analogy, non-conjugal adults might even encounter lower obstacles in the courtroom compared to same-sex couples. The case law analysis has illustrated how attentive the Court is to protecting close family ties. Further, it has shown how close relatives presumptively engage the institution of family life, although with adult relatives attracting lower levels of protection. The starting point is thus more favourable if one considers the resistance with which the first demands of same-sex couples were met in the Court.

ii. Difference in the Treatment of Relevantly Similar Situations

The first prong of the equality analysis involves a comparison: there must be a differentiation between persons in an analogous or relevantly similar situation.

Finding the right comparison point (a 'comparator') is crucial. However, a case law analysis illuminates how prone this aspect is to manipulation by the Court and the respondent state. In *Ratzenböck and Seydl v Austria*, an opposite-sex couple sought access to the Austrian civil partnership, as it saw the regime as more flexible compared to marriage.[123] The Court laconically dismissed the challenge, in the absence of a relevant comparator: the opposite-sex couple, it argued, was not in a relevantly similar situation with respect to same-sex couples. Unlike same-sex couples, the two claimants could access marriage. This conclusion is conceptually implausible. Since no other group had access to marriage, a cis-sex couple unhappy with marriage can never advance an equality claim because no other group is similarly situated. On the one hand, a more pertinent comparator could have been a same-sex couple that following gender re-assignment finds itself in a registered partnership, despite being ideologically opposed to a conversion of marriage.[124] On the other hand, this also attests to the limits of requiring a search for the right comparator each and every time, despite some situations not easily lending themselves to rigid comparisons. In any case, the conclusion in practice that a cis-sex couple cannot claim equality is untenable because its logical premises in the comparative analysis are flawed.

The *Burden* case is a conspicuous illustration of the shortcomings of the Court's approach to the comparator analysis. Despite the claim being based on the protection of property, the equality analysis is identical and thus is applicable to this context as well, where we take Article 14 in conjunction with Article 8. The case is known in layman's terms as the 'spinster sisters'. It involved two elderly sisters residing in the UK who had been living in a house built on their jointly inherited property for some 40 years. The two alleged that they were discriminated against

[123] *Ratzenböck and Seydl v Austria*, App No 28475/12 (ECtHR, 27 October 2017).

[124] See H Fenwick and A Hayward, 'Equal Civil Partnerships: Implications of Strasbourg's Latest Ruling for Steinfeld and Keidan' *UK Human Rights Blog* (21 November 2017), www.ukhumanrightsblog.com/2017/11/21/equal-civil-partnerships-implications-of-strasbourgs-latest-ruling-for-steinfeld-and-keidan-helen-fenwick-andy-hayward.

because they could not enjoy the same exemption from inheritance tax as married couples and civil partners. The sisters further contended that should one of them die, the tax, which would be payable on the estate passing to the survivor sister, would have forced the latter to sell the house.[125]

In order to prove discrimination, the sisters advanced an argument that they were in a relevantly similar situation compared to married and civil partners. The court of first instance glossed over the question.[126] The Grand Chamber, by contrast, concluded that their relationship differed substantially from that of spouses and civil partners. The reason was that the relationship between the two sisters was founded on consanguinity, and marriage and civil partnerships expressly listed consanguinity as a disqualifying condition that barred access to the status.[127] In its boundary-setting activity, the Court equated marriage and civil partnerships, whose formal and solemnised commitment was deemed sufficient to set these relationships apart from families who had not formalised their commitment.[128]

However, the reasoning of the Court is at best circular when it involves persons who cannot enter into marriage (or a civil union). The two sisters were nothing like civil partners because they could not enter into a civil partnership. This argumentative move is tautological since no one doubts that consanguinity prevented the sisters from formalising their relationship at the time. It also rendered the prohibition to discriminate based on marital status devoid of significance. By declining to move ahead to the question of whether the difference in treatment fell within the acceptable margin of appreciation – as the court of first instance did – the Grand Chamber merely put a rubber stamp on the status quo. Nicola Barker provides a lucid critique of this judgment.[129] She contrasts it with the linear and more logically sound reasoning in *Muñoz Diaz v Spain*. In *Muñoz Diaz*, the Third Chamber censured a refusal to grant a survivor's pension to an applicant who married under Roma customs. On that occasion, the Court firmly dismissed the defendant's attempt to argue that the applicant 'could have married' in order to earn the benefit:

> The prohibition of discrimination enshrined in Article 14 of the Convention is meaningful only if, in each particular case, the applicant's personal situation in relation to the criteria listed in that provision *is taken into account exactly as it stands*. To proceed otherwise in dismissing the victim's claims on the ground that he or she could have avoided the discrimination by altering one of the factors in question – for example, by entering into a civil marriage – would render Article 14 devoid of substance.[130] (Emphasis added)

[125] P Backer, 'Burden v Burden: The Grand Chamber of the ECtHR Adopts a Restrictive Approach on the Question of Discrimination' (2008) 4 *British Tax Review* 329.

[126] *Burden and Burden v UK* (2007) 44 EHRR 51.

[127] *Burden* (n 38) [62].

[128] *Burden* (n 38). For a critique to the Court's approach, see Gross (n 40) 274.

[129] N Barker, 'Rethinking Conjugality as the Basis for Family Recognition' (2016) 6 *Onati Socio-Legal Series* 1249, 1268.

[130] *Muñoz Díaz v Spain* (2010) 50 EHRR 49 [70].

To increase the likelihood of success of litigation before the ECtHR, it is thus necessary to replace this ingrained formalist way of thinking with a functionalist approach to the comparative analysis. Instead of focusing on formal requirements (eg, eligibility to enter a family regime), emphasis should be placed on a more open-ended interdependency relationship model. In other words, a proper inquiry of allegedly similar situations requires focusing on the functional attributes of the two types of relationships rather than formalities, as the Court did in *Burden*. The approach would be consistent, inter alia, with the Court's frequent insistence on actual family ties and with the approach taken by other Western jurisdictions such as Canada, Australia and New Zealand.[131]

A more positive example of comparative analysis comes from the Court's opinion in *Vallianatos*, where Greek registered partnerships were opened up to same-sex couples. The decision rightly homed in on commitment and stability to argue that same-sex couples were similarly situated to opposite-sex couples in stable relationships.[132] In the Court's view, the two types of relationships were equally capable of forming an enduring and stable bond. This reasoning also applies to non-conjugal families. Any line of argument with a discrimination prong could thus employ it and emphasise the capability of non-conjugal couples to enter into an enduring, stable bond.

iii. Legitimate Aim

The next step is to ascertain if an interference with the right is justified. The state must point to the legitimate aim pursued by the measure and must argue that it is proportionate.

Traditionally, there are a number of state objectives that have been put forward to exclude new families from recognition, especially same-sex couples or informal cohabitants. These public interests are often highly contextual. They commonly focus on the purpose of the scheme the eligibility requirements of which are being challenged. As regards state aims of 'general applicability' – ie, that are commonly invoked with the aim of restricting access to familial benefits – the chief one is to strengthen a traditional understanding of family.[133] Other interests focus on children and go something like this: 'allowing parents to raise their biological children'[134] or 'protect[ing] children born to different-sex couples in [informal]

[131] In relation to Canada, see the Adult Interdependent Relationships Act, Statutes of Alberta 2002, c A-4.5. In relation to Australia, see, eg, the 1994 Domestic Partnership Act in the Australian Capital Territory, recognising any two individuals providing 'personal or financial commitment and support of a domestic nature' to the other, regardless of a sexual relationship, and the 1999 amendments in New South Wales introducing the category of 'close personal relationships' across a number of areas, defined as two cohabitants who provide each other with domestic support and personal care. See R Graycar and J Millbank, 'From Functional Family to Spinster Sisters: Australia's Distinctive Path to Relationship Recognition' (2007) 24 *Washington University Journal of Law and Policy* 121, 147–48.

[132] *Vallianatos and Others v Greece* (2014) 59 EHRR 12 [78].

[133] *GAB v Spain*, App No 21173/93 (ECtHR, 30 August 1993); *Karner* (n 78) [35].

[134] *Vallianatos* (n 132) [62].

partnerships'.[135] What lurks behind these interests is a desire to conflate the family with the traditional nuclear family with biological children.

As mentioned above, the most 'popular' interest is the protection of a traditional understanding of family. When confronted with the issue of whether the ban on discrimination prevented states from attaching a special status to marriage, the Court answered no without any hesitation. Indeed, the Court has repeatedly held that it is legitimate for state legislation to attach special benefits to marriage.[136] The legal irrelevance of informal cohabitants was initially upheld by reason of this indisputable interest. The Court affirmed as early as 1979 that 'support and encouragement' of the traditional family was in principle a legitimate state interest.[137] At the time, the Court saw such an interest not only as valid, but also as 'praiseworthy'. In the 1980s, its acknowledgement that de facto couples enjoy an increasing level of social acceptance did not undermine trust in the salience of this interest.[138]

The Court's conviction regarding the weighty nature of this interest wavered a bit in *Karner*.[139] In this case, it described the protection of a traditional understanding of marriage as 'rather abstract'[140] and as able to encompass a wide spectrum of measures. This statement preluded a positive outcome for the claimant: the Court held that the exclusion of same-sex partners from tenancy rights was incompatible with the Convention. In its view, the measure – this exclusion – was unnecessary in order to achieve the proffered interest. In reaching this conclusion, the Court stressed the fact that granting rights to another group 'does not result in the group who already had those rights and benefits losing them'[141] or in diluting such rights.[142] This is a common objection to extending rights to other categories, whose rejection can thus benefit non-conjugal couples as well.

Another critical observation is that while preserving the special status of marriage will realistically continue to be a legitimate and even weighty interest, the Court's case law asserts that it cannot be utilised to justify all unfair outcomes. For instance, it cannot buttress a differentiation between children born out of wedlock and legitimate children.[143] A further instance in which the ECtHR has partially eroded this interest is *Vallianatos*. In this case, the ECtHR continued to acknowledge the significance of protecting marriage and yet included language that had the effect of limiting the incidence of a generalised use of this interest. It urged that the Convention be interpreted dynamically to account for the shifting social

[135] ibid [63].
[136] K Reid, *A Practitioner's Guide to the European Convention on Human Rights*, 4th edn (London, Sweet & Maxwell, 2012) 374.
[137] *Marckx* (n 97) [31].
[138] *Lindsay v UK* (1986) 9 EHRR 513.
[139] *Karner* (n 78)
[140] See also *Vallianatos* (n 132) [83]–[84].
[141] *Karner* (n 78).
[142] JM Scherpe, 'Legal Recognition of Same-Sex Couples in Europe and the Role of the European Court of Human Rights' (2013) 10 *Equal Rights Review* 83, 92.
[143] *Mazurek* (n 77).

developments which legitimise intimate connections that at one time were not endorsed: 'there is not just one way or one choice when it comes to leading one's family or private life', it concluded.[144]

In *Burden*, the above-mentioned 'spinster sisters' case, the Grand Chamber did not even reach the justification stage. The court of first instance, by contrast, had done so. The justifications put forward by the UK government consisted of bolstering stable, committed same-sex and cis-sex relationships. The interest was achieved through a measure of financial security in favour of the surviving partner upon the death of the other partner. This is a composite interest that touches upon distinct aspects in a not entirely coherent way. First, in referring to stable, committed same-sex and cis-sex relationships, it contradicts itself. If stability is the concern, then functional rather than formal attributes are germane to identifying stable couples. As a consequence, the proffered interest actually works to the advantage of stable and interdependent non-conjugal families, and more generally to all stable and interdependent families. Second, in focusing on the economic rationale of the measure, it unveils the cracks of the government's reasoning. The measure was allegedly promoting stable, committed same-sex and cis-sex relationships by offering financial relief to the surviving partner. The question arises as to why sexual orientation is relevant to achieving the objective. Does it add something to the locution 'stable, committed relationships'? Non-conjugal couples are as capable as conjugal couples of entering into stable and committed relationships.[145] Likewise, they are as capable as conjugal couples of enduring the vulnerability ensuing from forming bonds of interdependence. Hence, upon the death of one party, the survivor might experience the same economic fallout, which theoretically justifies the measure. In other words, an inclusion of non-conjugal couples would better effectuate the stated aim of the measure.

A set of other interests refer to children. Some non-conjugal families might want to raise children,[146] while others might not – like any other family. The fact that non-conjugal couples are not necessarily nuclear, while marriage by definition is nuclear – despite many marital families not having children – is amenable to exploitation by the respondent state. A recurring state interest is the need to protect the interests of children. However, the Court in *Vallianatos* rightly noted that the exclusion of same-sex couples from a civil partnership cannot be upheld based on this objective. The challenged Greek law on civil partnerships was aimed at introducing a new non-marital regime for adults; it was not aimed at protecting the best interests of the child. Thereby, the Court severed the vertical dimension

[144] *Vallianatos* (n 132) [84].

[145] See, eg, B Gusmano, 'Subvertir la heteronorma a través de la amistad. Convivencia y redes de cuidado en la precariedad' (2018) 14 *TransVersos* 90; and S Roseneil, 'Why We Should Care about Friends: An Argument for Queering the Care Imaginary in Social Policy' (2004) 3 *Social Policy and Society* 409.

[146] See N Bakht and L Collins, 'Are You My Mother? Co-parenting in a Non-conjugal Family' (2018) 31 *Canadian Journal of Family Law* 105.

of parenting, rightly observing that such a dimension is not engaged by legislation that creates a new recognition mechanism. Likewise, most family benefits have little to do with parenting. To follow through with the previous example, a survivor's pension is conferred upon the surviving partner regardless of whether they had children with the deceased partner. Further, assuming that the child's best interest is engaged, the Court argued that the respondent state had not demonstrated that the exclusion of same-sex partners was 'necessary' to achieve it. This is to say that even in the unlikely event that the Court upholds the interest as valid, the government bears the burden of showing why protecting children effectuates it.

It must be noted that the attitude of the Court tends to be permissive at this stage. The Court will most likely 'concede' that the protection of the family in the traditional sense is, in principle, a legitimate and/or weighty justification for differential treatment. Yet, the 'concession' is made in order to steadfastly move on to the next and more crucial stage – that is, the proportionality stage.

iv. Proportionality and the Margin of Appreciation

The last step of the justification stage is the proportionality assessment. In order to carry out the assessment, the Court proceeds to accord either a narrow or broad margin of appreciation. The Court's deference to national authorities in using discretion when balancing competing interests is variable.[147] However, the margin is not synonymous with non-justiciability as it always entails supervision of the use of discretion by the states. This is to say that the Court will police its use and will avoid it resulting in an interference with the rights enshrined in the Convention.

The margin can be narrow or wide depending on several conditions. This part of the justification stage is highly fact-driven. However, I intend to provide some theoretical background to predict the type of margin that the Court could employ. First, the margin is narrow in cases involving differences based on sex or sexual orientation. Most challenges to restrictions to LGBTQ rights were successful because they could not withstand the higher scrutiny the Court employs in cases involving sex-based or sexual orientation-based discrimination. A narrow margin entails that 'the principle of proportionality does not merely require that the measure chosen is in principle suited for realising the aim sought. It must also be shown that it was necessary in order to achieve that aim to exclude certain categories of people'.[148]

However, non-conjugal couples do not engage the grounds of sex or sexual orientation. Amongst the two, one could push for an expansive and heterodox interpretation of sexual orientation as encompassing a right to be in a relationship of a non-sexual nature. Yet, this move is problematic because it risks conflating the

[147] *Handyside v UK* (1976) 1 EHRR 737.
[148] ibid [41].

category of non-conjugal families with that of asexuals. This conflation would be misplaced as it would erroneously convey the idea that non-conjugal families are asexual. Needless to say that parties to a non-conjugal relationship do have sexual relationships with other persons, despite not attaching the label 'family' to these sexual relationships.

The prediction is thus that the margin will be variable and potentially depend on more than one factor. Amongst such factors, European consensus – in French, 'dénominateur commun aux systèmes juridiques des États contractants' – is likely to play a key role. To a considerable extent, the application of the margin of appreciation doctrine has been inconsistent so far. However, the existence, or lack thereof, of a consensus frequently plays a pivotal role in the decision on the use of the margin. Usually, the broader the consensus, the less room there is for departure. Once a consensus is discernible, the doctrine is indeed the most effective tool to entrench it by outlawing attempts to part from it.[149] A search for consensus is especially warranted when it comes to balancing rights in relation to touchy subjects. This includes matters involving morals,[150] sexuality and equality interests.[151] It is also warranted when it comes to rights at a transitional stage, as could be the case with the rights of non-conjugal families.[152]

I will now return to the same-sex couple analogy. In 2013, the Court had no special trouble in finding that there was an emerging trend towards the legal recognition of same-sex couples.[153] Likewise, in *Oliari*, it noted the existence of a rapid movement towards their legal recognition. In the absence of a full-fledged consensus, an emerging trend or rapid movement was the conceptual referent for finding a breach of the Convention. A variation on the theme is the so-called 'nette tendance'. In *Mazurek*, the Court was content to observe 'une *nette tendance* à la disparition des discriminations à l'égard des enfants adultérins', that is, 'a clear direction towards the disappearance of discrimination against illegitimate children'.[154] However, this intermediate position whereby the Court finds no consensus and yet sees a rapid movement towards something is prone to manipulation. It could be maintained that when the ECtHR wishes to reject the argument, it places stress on the lack of consensus.[155] Conversely, when it intends to make strides in new families' recognition, it puts emphasis on a rapid movement being under way.

I am of the opinion that non-conjugal families are in a comparable situation to same-sex couples in the mid-1990s in terms of their degree of official recognition

[149] JA Sweeney, 'Margins of Appreciation: Cultural Relativity and the European Court of Human Rights in the Post-Cold War Era' (2005) 54 *ICLQ* 459, 469 ('[i]n respect to original states the Court balanced human rights against state sovereignty more warily').

[150] *Handyside* (n 147).

[151] See *Petrov v Bulgaria*, App No 15197/02 (ECtHR, 22 May 2008).

[152] *Frette v France* (2002) 38 EHRR 438.

[153] *Vallianatos* (n 132).

[154] *Mazurek* (n 77).

[155] *Hämäläinen v Finland* (2015) 1 FCR 379; *Chapin and Charpentier v France*, App No 40183/07 (ECtHR, 9 June 2016).

in Europe. Back then, only Denmark (1989), Sweden (1995), Iceland (1996) plus Norway (1993) recognised civil unions for same-sex couples. In a similar manner, nowadays, only a handful of states in Europe officially recognise non-conjugal families. This is to say that, in light of 'present-day conditions', a consensus around the issue can hardly be found. At best, it could be considered 'thin' and insufficient. Therefore, it would lead to a rejection of claims brought by non-conjugal couples along the lines of what occurred in the 1990s in the context of LGBTQ litigation.

I have previously argued that a precondition for a successful claim before the Court is that more European states enact protective measures for non-conjugal unions at the domestic level. Once more measures are in place, non-conjugal couples can argue that a consensus on the issue is traceable. Yet, this is not to say that these couples are powerless until that point is reached. Non-conjugal unions are already in a position to further their cause. As the same-sex couples saga powerfully illustrates, at first claimants referred to a mere 'rapid movement' or 'nette tendence'. These terms are not synonymous with consensus and allow more flexibility in terms of carrying out the proportionality assessment. If one looks at recent evolutions in European family law, an emerging trend pointing to a direction – the recognition of more families beyond the traditional family – is already visible.

Moreover, it is at least open to debate that there is an emerging trend towards the legal recognition of non-conjugal families. As shown above, a handful of states (including Belgium and the Netherlands) have already enacted protections for non-conjugal families. While such examples differ in terms of their personal and material scope, they both translate evolving notions of family into legal reform which is more aligned with modern family structures. A similar evolution is epitomised by a global trend of legalisation of these relationships. In *Oliari*, the ability of the Court to couple the emerging European trend with a concomitant global trend towards the recognition of same-sex couples was critical to the outcome. Likewise, in the case of non-conjugal families, major reforms have taken place in the West in jurisdictions like the Canadian province of Alberta, several states in the US, Australia and New Zealand.[156]

In addition, if no emerging consensus or *tendance* can be discerned, there is a further option available. This option is best typified by the dissenting opinion in *Hämäläinen*, a major decision on trans*[157] rights. In the judgment, Justices Sajo, Keller and Lemmens noted that the consensus-based analysis is inherently flawed. European consensus is but one of the factors that weigh in the decision on the breadth of the margin.[158] I concur with critical views expressing concern that the consensus-based analysis employed by the Court is too conceptually vague

[156] See n 131 above.

[157] Trans* is the umbrella concept used for transsexual and transgender.

[158] E Benvenisti, 'Margin of Appreciation, Consensus, and Universal Standards' (1999) 31 *New York University Journal of International Law & Politics* 483.

and amenable to inconsistent application.[159] Urgent questions to answer include consensus with respect to what (social acceptability or legal recognition and, if so, which kind of recognition) and how this should be demonstrated (national legislation, practices or even debates).[160] And how much consensus is consensus (arithmetic majority or non-majoritarian emerging trend)?[161]

The dissenting judges in *Hämäläinen* rightly took the view that strict scrutiny should be triggered by the issue touching upon a significant aspect of one's private life. This should occur regardless of consensus. The *Goodwin* precedent was but one example that the judges relied upon to buttress this conclusion.[162] The decision in *Goodwin*, acknowledging the possibility for transsexuals to change their sex and gain legal recognition upon gender re-assignment, did not contain a single mention of the word 'consensus'. This eschewed the daunting task of tracing an existing consensus on the legal recognition of transsexualism in Europe. The move was especially beneficial to the extent that national approaches to the issue vary considerably across Europe. The proposed approach in the dissenting opinion in *Hämäläinen* would thus circumvent the need to find a consensus on the subject of non-conjugal families. Besides the insufficient recognition that at present hinders the possibility of finding one is the absence of a principled approach to tracing it. This would work to the disadvantage of non-conjugal families. It would increase the unpredictability on the use of the margin and would render it more amenable to manipulation. Ultimately, the proposed approach is useful as it corroborates the contention that family life and the intimate decisions relating to this are amongst the most significant aspects of one's private life. As such, they deserve heightened scrutiny not because a majority of states see them as worthy of protection, but because they are inherently valuable and prized in European societies.

II. Stage 1: Protection of Property and Ban on Discrimination

A second line of argument alleges a violation of Article 1 of Protocol No 1 ECHR taken in conjunction with Article 14. The first provision protects property, while Article 14 sets forth the ban on discrimination.

The definition of 'property' is broad enough to encompass a variety of legal benefits, including tax or social welfare benefits. However, it must be emphasised

[159] P Martens, 'Perplexity of the National Judge Faced with the Vagaries of European Eonsensus' in European Court of Human Rights, *Dialogues between Judges* (Strasbourg, Council of Europe, 2008) 58.

[160] LR Helfer, 'Consensus, Coherence and the European Convention on Human Rights' (1993) 26 *Cornell International Law Journal* 133, 134.

[161] M Shahid, 'The Right to Same-Sex Marriage: Assessing the European Court of Human Rights' Consensus-Based Analysis in Recent Judgments Concerning Equal Marriage Rights' (2017) 10 *Erasmus Law Review* 184, 194.

[162] *Goodwin* (n 76).

that Article 1 of Protocol No 1 does not grant a right to acquire property. This is not tantamount to saying that the article only protects an existing possession; yet, in order for a claim to succeed, the applicant must argue that they have at least a 'legitimate expectation' to the possession, with such expectation being more substantiated than a 'hope'.

Since it does not consist of a right to acquire property, the policy choices regarding whether to introduce social benefits are usually compatible with the right.[163] While this is true in general, individuals cannot be deprived of property on a discriminatory basis. Undoubtedly, states continue to be better positioned to design their own social programmes. However, if they enact legislation conferring a benefit as of right to certain beneficiaries who meet all the conditions set out in the statute, this creates a proprietary interest which determines the applicability of the Convention.[164]

It is telling that the only case involving a non-conjugal couple, *Burden*, prioritised precisely this line of argument instead of the argument based on Articles 8 (the right to respect for private and family life) and 14 (the ban on discrimination). This should come as no surprise. The concept of family is a double-edged sword. On the one hand, it signals long-term commitment, stability and mutual care, since there is a presumption that these qualities attach to the family, both socially and legally. A number of family benefits are based on a non-rebuttable presumption that the spouses are economically interdependent, despite this not necessarily being the case. For instance, when seeking compensation for the wrongful death of their spouse, the surviving spouse must not demonstrate that they had a joint bank account, pooled assets etc. This is why it seems reasonable to harness the evocative power of 'family'.

On the other hand, family is a highly value-laden concept. It exhibits a strong social and cultural connotation. As such, the decision to conjure it up might prove counterproductive. For instance, the Court might draw a parallel between non-conjugal and same-sex couples, for the latter have taken centre stage in current debates on new family recognition. There is no mobilisation of non-conjugal families comparable to that of same-sex couples. While academic debates on non-conjugal coupledom are becoming increasingly popular, the intensity of public debates is significantly lower compared to those spurred by advocates of the rights of same-sex couples. Legal recognition is also scattered and at an initial stage. The term 'family' might thus impose an additional barrier on claimants, who might need not only to prove that their union is worthy of protection, but also that it deserves protection because it is 'familial'. A similar problem does not arise in the context of the more ideologically neutral notion of property. Focusing on the protection of property shifts attention from the type of relationship to the intrinsic rationality of the public programme that is being challenged.

[163] *Stec* (n 87) [53].

[164] ibid [53]; see also *Gaygusuz v Austria* (1996) 23 EHRR 364 (concerning the availability of emergency assistance for the unemployed from which the applicant was excluded due to her nationality).

i. The Substantive Provision

According to this line of argument, the substantive provision is Article 1 of Protocol No 1. At this stage, the Court will ascertain whether the case falls within the ambit of the right. As argued above, states are free to enact and design social programmes, inheritance laws, tort law and so on. However, if they enact legislation conferring a benefit upon beneficiaries who meet all conditions but one (the one which is the cause of the discrimination), this creates a proprietary interest protected under the Convention.

In order for a right to arise under Article 1 of Protocol No 1, state action must amount to an interference with a 'possession'. The notion of possession is conceptually broad; it encompasses a wide variety of economic interests to which a person can lay claim. A broad interpretation is consistent with the French version of 'possessions', which speaks of 'biens' and relates to all pecuniary rights.[165]

The most telling example is the Court's consideration of claims for compensation for torts as an 'asset' under Article 1 of Protocol No 1. The relevant case involved Belgium, which at the time had changed its tort law, pending litigation of two shipowners who had an accident in Belgian waters. The fact that the claim for compensation (possession) arose at the moment of the accident was deemed sufficient to create a valid proprietary interest.[166]

The Court has also found taxation to fall under this provision. Taxation 'deprives the person concerned of a possession, namely the amount of money which must be paid'.[167] In *Burden*, the two cohabiting sisters argued that an exemption from the succession tax amounted to 'property' under the Convention. The state responded that they were not entitled to the exemption as a matter of law and thus that Article 1 of Protocol No 1 was inapplicable. In other words, the government argued that if one is not included in the list of eligible beneficiaries, one cannot invoke Article 1 of Protocol No 1 by definition. The Court reached the opposite conclusion. It observed that the duty to pay the tax in the event that one sister predeceased the other was highly probable. Therefore, the likely possibility of one of the sisters paying taxes on existing property was sufficient to engage the right to protection of property.

Likewise, welfare and social security benefits can be considered possessions for the purposes of the Convention. They fall under the scope of the provision if they are enjoyed as a result of being a legal rather than a discretionary right. Clearly, the Court is cautious in its approach: the claim that an omitted category of beneficiaries must be included could be deemed an improper request to acquire property, a result that the Convention does not command. The relevant test is whether 'but

[165] A Grgic et al, *The Right to Property under the European Convention on Human Rights – A Guide to the Implementation of the European Convention on Human Rights and its Protocols* (Strasbourg, Council of Europe, 2007).

[166] *Pressos Compania Naviera SA v Belgium* (1996) 21 EHRR 301.

[167] *Burden* (n 38) [59].

for the condition of entitlement about which the applicant complains, he or she would have had a right, enforceable under domestic law, to receive the benefit in question'.[168] In *Müller*, the Court recognised that pensions are possessions for the purposes of the Convention.[169] The payment of compulsory contributions to a pension fund gave rise to a legitimate expectation, which was not met when the applicant received a lower amount due to her nationality. Interestingly, the Court was also open to the possibility that voluntary payments to a pension fund could give rise to a legitimate proprietary interest. Yet, it has never decided whether that is the case.

One last example of possession can be inferred from *Muñoz*. The case was brought by a couple who had married under Roma rites, without entering into a civil marriage. Crucially, the fact that their customary marriage was recognised for some administrative purposes but not for the purpose of conferring the survivor's pension was deemed sufficient to engage Article 1 of Protocol No 1. Hence, it seems that scattered legal recognition might also give rise to a proprietary interest worthy of protection.

ii. Difference in the Treatment of Persons in Relevantly Similar Situations

The Article 14 analysis offered above also applies here. Therefore, in conducting the comparator analysis, non-conjugal claimants can argue that they are similarly situated with respect to married and registered couples in terms of the nature and seriousness of their commitment. However, in order for this argument to be successful, it is necessary to reject the current formalistic approach to line-drawing between deserving and non-deserving families. The issue should not be whether non-conjugal families can marry or enter into civil partnerships, but their actual attributes and ability to form enduring bonds.

iii. Legitimate Aim

Likewise, the analysis conducted above applies here. At this stage, the Court will likely concede that the declared aim is a legitimate one, be it the preservation of traditional marriage or of stable and committed (same-sex and cis-sex) relationships.

iv. Proportionality and Margin of Appreciation

Section 4.I above largely focused on consensus to predict the intensity of the Court's scrutiny. Despite consensus remaining central to the determination of the

[168] *Stec* (n 87) [55].
[169] *Müller and Others v Austria* (1991) 13 EHRR 212.

margin, the breadth of the margin can also be affected by the type of right. The Court is not consistent in its use of the type of right as a relevant factor in relation to this determination. Yet, some aspects can be flagged up. An important distinction concerns weak rights, amongst which is the protection of property and all socio-economic rights, and strong rights, which include the remaining rights. Measures that interfere with weak rights usually attract a broad margin of appreciation. Exceptions in this regard are limited. The margin is broad 'unless they give rise to results which are so anomalous as to render the legislation unacceptable'.[170] As a consequence, if weak rights are engaged, the ECtHR will only cross out anomalous outcomes.

This consideration weighs against employing lines of argument based on protection of property. As a weak right, it likely warrants less intense supervision and a broader margin of appreciation. By contrast, this point suggests that claimants should turn their attention to Article 8 (either alone or taken in conjunction with Article 14), as interferences with family life usually enjoy a stricter scrutiny.

A second aspect can play a role in the determination of the margin: the matter which is the subject of the litigation. In matters concerning taxation and social benefits, the limit of this nearly unfettered margin is that the policy/rule is 'manifestly without reasonable foundation', meaning that it is absurd or completely illogic.[171]

In addition to attracting a broad margin, when the issue raised relates to taxation or social benefits, the problem is usually (re)framed as one of intrinsic rationality of the challenged scheme. This is to say that recourse to Article 1 of Protocol No 1 risks distracting attention from the discrimination limb of the analysis. Intrinsic rationality is only one aspect of the issue. Discriminatory considerations are a further aspect that is often factored into the concrete design of a public programme. The case of the sisters in *Burden* is a powerful illustration of this undue shifting from the impermissibility of the exclusion to the type of programme being targeted and of the dangers that follow.[172]

III. Stage 1: General Ban on Discrimination

There is an additional line of argument, although I consider this to be 'residual'. It relies on Article 1 of Protocol No 12. The provision sets out a general prohibition on discrimination. Unlike Article 14, which is an ancillary right, the ban enshrined in this protocol is a free-standing right to be free from discrimination.

[170] *JA Pye (Oxford) Ltd v UK* (2008) 46 EHRR 45 [83].
[171] See, eg, *James and Others v UK* (1986) 8 EHRR 123 [46].
[172] *Burden* (n 38) 60 ('the central question under the Convention is not whether different criteria could have been chosen for the grant of an inheritance tax exemption, but whether the scheme actually chosen by the legislature … exceeded any acceptable margin of appreciation').

Therefore, it has a broader material scope compared to Article 14.[173] It applies to 'any right set forth by law' rather than only by the Convention, and to discrimination perpetrated 'by any public authority'. Hence, the main difference with respect to Article 14 is the possibility to invoke the general ban whenever there is a legal rather than only a Convention right set forth under domestic law. Notwithstanding the different scope, the meaning of discrimination in this Protocol was meant to be identical to that of Article 14.[174] Likewise, the same equality analysis applies. As a consequence, any interference needs to be justified in terms of the aim pursued and the proportionality of the measure.

A partial overlap with Article 14 is already visible. In the (quite likely) event of an overlap, it is preferable to prioritise lines of argument based on Article 14. The discrimination ban in Article 14 underpins a substantially larger set of precedents compared to Protocol No 12. The latter only entered into force in 2005 and as of October 2020 had been ratified by 20 out of 47 states. Furthermore, all notable advancements regarding family status were achieved under the umbrella and impulse of Article 14.

If the general ban is to have any independent utility, this would only be in very limited circumstances. For instance, it is a resource of last resort in the event that the Court refuses to find that non-conjugal families enjoy a family life. It is worth recalling that Article 14 also applies to cases where the substantive provision is not violated. Yet, the impugned measure must at least fall within the ambit of the provision. Should the measure fall outside the ambit of the Convention, the Protocol offers an additional avenue to argue that the measure is discriminatory.

Perhaps more realistic is the possibility of using this legal basis when tackling discrimination in the distribution of public subsidies. The Explanatory Report of the Protocol clarifies that the prohibition to discriminate covers a host of situations, amongst which is discrimination 'by a public authority in the exercise of discretionary power (for example, granting certain subsidies)'.[175] Its applicability is broader than that of Article 1 of Protocol No 1; in relation to the latter right, welfare and social security benefits qualify as protected possessions only if they are enjoyed as a result of being a legal rather than a discretionary right.

However, so far, there is no precedent that gives the general ban independent consideration. For instance, a recent claim concerned a refusal to allocate some privileges to churches that had not entered into an agreement with the state. The churches complained that they had been discriminated against based on religion under both Article 14 and Protocol No 12, a claim that was possible in light of the fact that discrimination was carried out 'by a public authority in the exercise of

[173] *Sejdić and Finci v Bosnia and Herzegovina* (2013) 57 EHRR 8.

[174] *Pilav v Bosnia and Herzegovina* [2016] ECHR 498 [40].

[175] Explanatory Report to the Protocol No 12 to the Convention for the Protection of Human Rights and Fundamental Freedoms (Rome, 4.XI.2000) ETS 177 [22].

discretionary power'.[176] However, the Court noted that once it was ascertained that the law violated Article 14, it was not necessary to assess the claim under Protocol No 12. Arguably, most claims under Protocol No 12 will be made in parallel to claims under Article 14, and thus will share the same fate.

IV. Stage 2: *Oliari*-Style Protection of Family Life

Stage 2 is a hypothetical future stage where seeking comprehensive legal recognition is an option for non-conjugal families. The relevant legal basis would be the right to respect for family life under Article 8.

At first sight, this might sound surprising. I previously hinted at the fact that Article 8 enshrines a negative liberty. Legal recognition, both sectorial and comprehensive, implicates affirmative entitlements. Hence, if this route is problematic in the context of extending access to single benefits, it should be a fortiori problematic when seeking comprehensive legal recognition. While this is true in principle, at times, the ECtHR has gone beyond non-interference as a conceptual centrepiece of its Article 8 decisions. There is no doubt that, under Article 8, the primary obligation for the state is to prevent arbitrary interference. However, the right also triggers positive obligations. At a minimum, it includes an obligation to ensure the effectiveness of the protection of private and family life,[177] 'even in the sphere of the relations of individuals between themselves'.[178] The intensity of the obligation will hinge on the discrepancy between social reality and administrative/legal practice, and on whether the obligation is narrow and precise or broad and indeterminate.[179]

The principles governing negative and positive obligations are the same. In both cases, the issue remains whether the state has reached a fair balance between the right and the community interest. Article 8, it is worth recalling, is a qualified right. Therefore, an interference can be justified if it falls within the scope of the public interests set forth in paragraph 2. As usual, in striking a balance, the state enjoys a margin of appreciation. The breadth could depend on several factors. First, it can hinge on whether the issue concerns a particularly important facet of one's private life. A second factor is whether consensus can be discerned either as to the importance of the interest at stake or the best measure to implement the obligation.[180] The Court recently added another factor: whether the claim concerns 'core' rights as opposed to 'supplementary' rights which might or might not arise from a union.[181] Crucially, when state action impinges upon core rights and thereby on 'the general need for recognition', the margin accorded is narrow.

[176] *Savez crkava 'Riječ života' and Others v Croatia* (2012) 54 EHRR 36.
[177] See, eg, *X and Y v The Netherlands* (1985) 8 EHRR 235 [23].
[178] *Oliari* (n 75) [159].
[179] *Botta v Italy* (1998) 26 EHRR 241 [35].
[180] ibid [35].
[181] *Oliari* (n 75) [177].

Notwithstanding this significant advancement, the Court never translated it into a positive duty to recognise same-sex marriage. Faced with the issue of whether the Convention mandated the introduction of same-sex marriage, it said no: as a decision of 'general social strategy', it warranted a broad margin of appreciation.[182] Yet, the finding that same-sex couples were in a relevantly similar situation to opposite-sex couples paved the way for the Court to mandate 'some form' of comprehensive legal recognition. *Vallianatos* is the main stepping-stone to this doctrinal development. In 2013, the ECtHR held that by its decision to restrict access to civil unions to opposite-sex couples, Greece violated Articles 8 and 14.[183] On that occasion, it stressed that when a state introduces a new non-marital regime, it cannot do so in a discriminatory manner.

Then, in *Oliari*, the Court went one step further in finding a breach of the aforementioned right in a case where there was no specific legal framework.[184] The Court was of the opinion that the lack of a specific legal framework for same-sex couples violated Article 8 alone. This is a significant development. Not only does the right to non-discrimination command access to existing non-marital regimes from which same-sex couples are excluded, but it might also impose the introduction of a brand-new recognition mechanism, should there be no such mechanism in force in the country.

Now, the received wisdom has it that *Oliari* recognises a right to same-sex registered partnerships as such. However, one cannot easily discern whether the decision only applies to Italy. The Court has missed an opportunity to clarify this crucial aspect in a subsequent case on LGBT rights in Russia.[185] The reason to doubt the existence of a generalised right to same-sex registered partnerships is the strong emphasis that the Court places on the peculiar situation of Italy. This situation was one in which the Italian government deliberately ignored its supreme and constitutional court rulings urging reform in this field. It was also one in which there was a scattered approach to the recognition of same-sex couples.[186]

Nevertheless, *Oliari* contains passages that are valuable to non-conjugal families. The judgment first found a positive obligation for Italy to recognise same-sex unions. This was long overdue, the Court argued, in light of the sharp conflict between the law and the social reality in the country and of the uneven treatment these couples received from the different branches of government. The Court resolved to grant a narrow margin of appreciation. In so doing, it relied on the following factors: the fact that the claim involved core rights as opposed to supplementary rights, and the existence of a European and global trend towards

[182] H Fenwick, 'An ECHR Right to Access a Registered Partnership?' in Scherpe and Hayward (n 17) 478.

[183] *Vallianatos* (n 132).

[184] *Oliari* (n 75).

[185] *Alekseyev and Others v Russia*, App Nos 4916/07, 25924/08 and 14599/09 (ECtHR, 27 November 2018).

[186] Fenwick (n 182) 492–96; *Oliari* (n 75) [172–73]. See also *Taddeucci and McCall v* Italy, App No 51362/09 (ECtHR, 30 June 2016).

the recognition of same-sex unions. It then considered the margin to have been overstepped due to Italy's failure to put forward a valid community interest and a repeated failure to comply with the decisions of its own domestic courts.

The takeaways from the Court's jurisprudence are twofold. The first is the insufficiency of a scattered mode of recognition. The Court explained how a case-by-case approach whereby partners must resort to domestic courts to gain some 'core rights', with the uncertainties this implies – such as exposing an intimate choice to the personal convictions of a judge – is unjust to the group. The second is the importance that couples attach to official recognition. Both decisions rightly focus on the sense of legitimacy this type of recognition conveys. In *Oliari*, the Court reasoned that 'the recognition in law of one's family life and status was crucial for the existence and well-being of an individual and for his or her dignity'.[187] In *Vallianatos*, the Court also stressed the significance of comprehensive official recognition. In Greece, same-sex couples could sign agreements and procure some form of protection under ordinary law by virtue of their status as de facto couples. Despite this, the Court added the principle that access to material resources is not a bar to a finding that the right to respect for family life has been breached; only official recognition confers a sense of legitimacy and equal moral worth.[188]

Ultimately, it is worth emphasising that while the ECtHR has recognised a right to access to civil partnerships, it is not as eager to recognise a right of choice between different regimes. The Court has continuously rejected arguments furthering the value of family legal pluralism. It has done so in the context of both same-sex couples willing to access marriage and cross-sex couples willing to access registered partnerships.

First, in 2006, the Court refused to uphold an argument that a couple, whose marriage was forcibly converted into a civil partnership upon the gender re-assignment of the applicant, has a right to keep the marriage alive.[189] The Court reached this outcome by noting a lack of consensus on the subject of same-sex marriage and some unsurmountable limitations vis-a-vis enforcing positive obligations upon the state.[190] In these cases, proportionality is the stage that the Court focuses on. On closer examination, it seems that *any* form of recognition is likely to satisfy the proportionality test.

In *Chapin and Charpentier v France*, the *pacsés* same-sex couple lamented discrimination because 'heterosexuality' granted access to three family regimes: *concubinage*, Pacs and *mariage*.[191] However, again, the Court was not prepared to issue a decision that somehow implied a right to same-sex marriage. However,

[187] *Oliari* (n 75) [107].

[188] I Trispiotis, 'Discrimination and Civil Partnerships: Taking "Legal" out of Legal Recognition' (2014) 14 *Human Rights Law Review* 343, 355.

[189] *R and F v UK*, App No 35748/05 (ECtHR, 28 November 2006).

[190] Fenwick (n 182) 482.

[191] *Chapin* (n 155).

the same conclusion with respect to opposite-sex partners trying to access a non-marital regime defies any logic. In *Ratzenböck and Seydl v Austria*, an opposite-sex couple sought access to the Austrian civil partnership scheme. In their view, the regime was more flexible compared to marriage: it conferred a more limited package of rights and obligations, and a shorter statutory period in order to obtain a divorce.[192] The Court laconically dismissed the question. In so doing, it reiterated that so long as one formalised status is available, there is no breach of the Convention.

This differs from the approach of the UK Supreme Court in *Steinfeld*.[193] In this decision, the UK's top court found the exclusion of opposite-sex partners from civil partnerships to be incompatible with Articles 8 and 14 ECHR – and Parliament later modified the law accordingly. Presumably, the different result arises out of the peculiar situation in the UK, in which cross-sex couples were allegedly subject to reverse discrimination: while same-sex couples could access both marriage and civil partnerships, cross-sex couples could only marry. Was this an affront to heterosexual privilege?

This small digression shows that legal reforms cannot be invoked on legal pluralist grounds. In the context of the ECHR, this is a no-go argument. By contrast, receiving some form of legal recognition when the state has a policy of blanket non-recognition is an enforceable claim. The greater the consensus on the recognition of non-conjugal couples, the more persuasive the argument will be that Contracting States must provide a legal framework for their recognition.

Conclusion

This chapter has examined the different approaches to recognising non-conjugal families before the ECtHR. It has supplied a theoretical framework and legal analysis to navigate the complex legal landscape in Europe. It has also offered a critical methodology for building legal arguments, based on the state-of-art jurisprudence of the ECtHR.

The chapter has proceeded by imagining two distinct phases. In a first phase, non-conjugal families can realistically pursue three lines of arguments. The two most promising ones are equality-based arguments either based on non-discrimination and respect for family life or non-discrimination and protection of property. The latter option is made possible by the Court offering an expansive interpretation of the notion of property as encompassing a host of private and public law entitlements. The first option is made possible by the Court's emphasis on a functional notion of family under Article 8.

[192] *Ratzenböck* (n 123).

[193] *R (on the Application of Steinfeld and Keidan) v Secretary of State for International Development* [2018] UKSC 32.

After states introduce more family regimes open to non-conjugal families and/or debates on the issue have taken hold domestically, it is possible to move on to claim comprehensive recognition. This is what I call stage 2. At this prospective stage, the landmark decisions in *Oliari* and *Vallianatos* are precious resources for arguing that lack of recognition through status is tantamount to authoritative condemnation and that official recognition is critical to one's sense of legitimacy and moral worth.

6

The European Union

1. The EU and Family Law: A Complex Relationship

This chapter focuses on the European Union ('EU' or 'Union') and its 27 Member States. The subconstitutional and constitutional landscape of such jurisdictions was explored in Chapter 5 on the European Convention of Human Rights (ECHR). This chapter, by contrast, seeks to discern whether the EU is a viable route for enhancing the legal protection of non-conjugal couples in Europe.

The legal framework seems to be richer compared to that of the ECHR, which contains only two provisions explicitly referring to the family in Articles 8 and 12. A first key legal instrument is the Charter of Fundamental Rights and Freedoms of the European Union (hereinafter 'the Charter'). At the time of its enactment, the Charter was not binding upon the Member States. It was then given the same binding force as other treaties from 2009, when the Treaty of Lisbon entered into force.

This legal instrument enshrines numerous provisions directly or obliquely relevant to family regulation. It enshrines a right to equality before the law,[1] which the Court of Justice recognised as a foundational principle of Community law even before its 'codification',[2] and a non-discrimination principle.[3] The Charter also pledges to ensure the respect of private and family life under Article 7, and guarantees a right to marry and to found a family under Article 9.[4] Importantly, the right to marry is laid out in gender-neutral terms and, notwithstanding an authoritative clarification that the content of Article 9 parallels that of Article 12 ECHR, Article 9 is actually broader in its scope. The official explanations offer interpretative guidance in this regard. They clarify that the Convention has been taken as a benchmark but also modernised so as to 'cover cases in which national legislation recognises arrangements other than marriage for founding a family'.[5] At first glance,

[1] Article 20 of the Charter of Fundamental Rights and Freedoms of the European Union.

[2] Judgment of the Court of 13 November 1984, *Firma A Racke v Hauptzollamt Mainz*, C-283/83, EU:C:1984:344; Judgment of the Court of 17 April 1997, *EARL de Kerlast v Union régionale de coopératives agricoles (Unicopa) and Coopérative du Trieux*, C-15/95, EU:C:1997:196; Judgment of the Court of 13 April 2000, *Kjell Karlsson and Others*, C-292/97, EU:C:2000:202.

[3] Article 20 of the Charter.

[4] ibid arts 7 and 9.

[5] 'Explanation on Article 9 – Right to marry and right to found a family' in *Explanations Relating to the Charter of Fundamental Rights* [2007] OJ C303, 17–35.

this explanation is useful to non-conjugal families and all new families. Yet, Article 51 also recalls that the Charter is without prejudice to the allocation of powers set out in the Treaties[6] and, as I will illustrate below, the EU lacks competence over substantive family law. In relation to other potentially relevant provisions, Article 33 of the Charter provides that '[t]he family shall enjoy legal, economic and social protection' and that the reconciliation of familiar and professional life should be encouraged.[7] Ultimately, the Charter guarantees the rights of children, the elderly and the disabled.[8]

The principle of equality, which has implications for how families are treated under the law, has been further substantiated into directives. Directives are legal instruments that bind Member States in terms of the objectives to be achieved, but not the means to use in order to achieve them. Of relevance is the Employment Equality Directive,[9] and sectorial anti-discrimination directives such as the Race Directive[10] and the Gender Directive.[11]

Notwithstanding a legal framework that seems prima facie richer, legal arguments grounded in EU law must come to terms with some structural facets of the European legal order. Amongst the structural limits that might reduce the likelihood of success of these arguments are:

(i) the lack of EU competence over substantive family law;
(ii) the model of judicial review of discriminatory acts; and
(iii) the functionalisation of the EU for the achievement of its institutional goals, which mostly coincide with market freedoms.

EU competence is based on the principle of conferral, and, therefore, the EU can only exercise the competences conferred upon it by the Member States through the Treaties.[12] It is worth recalling that the power to regulate family law is retained by Member States. Such power has never been surrendered to or shared with the EU, with only limited exceptions. The Union is only endowed with the power to harmonise private international law rules applying to families with a cross-border element.[13] This competence has been exercised in the Brussels IIa Regulation,[14]

[6] Article 51 of the Charter; and 'Explanation on Article 51 – Field of application' in *Explanations* (n 5).

[7] Article 33 of the Charter.

[8] Respectively, ibid arts 24, 25 and 26.

[9] Council Directive (EC) 2000/78 of 27 November 2000 establishing a general framework for equal treatment in employment and occupation [2000] OJ L303, 16–22.

[10] Council Directive (EC) 2000/43 of 29 June 2000 implementing the principle of equal treatment between persons irrespective of racial or ethnic origin [2000] OJ L180, 22–26 (hereinafter 'the Race Directive').

[11] Directive (EC) 2006/54 of the European Parliament and of the Council of 5 July 2006 on the implementation of the principle of equal opportunities and equal treatment of men and women in matters of employment and occupation [2006] OJ L204, 23–36 (hereinafter 'the Gender Directive').

[12] Article 5(2) of the Treaty on European Union (TEU).

[13] Article 81(3) of the Treaty on the Functioning of the European Union (TFEU).

[14] Council Regulation (EC) 2201/2003 of 27 November 2003 concerning jurisdiction and the recognition and enforcement of judgments in matrimonial matters and matters of parental responsibility [2003] OJ L338, 1–29.

which sets out jurisdictional rules governing divorce (but not the dissolution of registered partnerships).[15] It has also been exercised in two subsequent regulations implementing enhanced cooperation in the field of property and registered partnerships[16] and in matrimonial property regimes.[17] A lack of institutional competence corresponds to a lack of an institutional actor entrusted with the mission to pursue family law reform. So far, initiatives, such as the important work of the Commission on European Family Law (CEFL),[18] have been limited in their impact, in that they could only elaborate principles which do not bind Member States.

However, a lack of power over substantive family law has not prevented the EU from shaping notions of family.[19] The Union has in fact found its way around the above-mentioned allocation of powers to make its own contribution to the development of family law. Its influence has been exerted indirectly by means of a host of directives, non-binding recommendations and purposive use of the preliminary reference under Article 267 of the Treaty on the Functioning of the European Union (TFEU) by the Court of Justice of the European Union (CJEU or 'the Court').[20] Especially remarkable was the Court's widening of the personal scope of benefits, privileges and rights attached to family status (such as pensions). In regulating these important areas, the EU and the Court have made strides in terms of the moulding of family law definitions beyond the traditional family. The Court's role in expanding definitions in the employment context is especially noteworthy. A second important area of intervention has been that of relationships with a cross-border element and the area of family reunification. However, what is problematic is the Court being adamant in its conviction that when the EU adopts an autonomous definition of 'non-marital partner', the definition does not include non-conjugal couples. I will illustrate this position in section 3 below.

A second structural limit is the model of judicial review of discriminatory acts adopted by the Court. Like the ECHR system, the EU adopts an equality-based

[15] R Lamont, 'Registered Partnerships in European Union Law' in JM Scherpe and A Hayward (eds), *The Future of Registered Partnerships: Family Recognition Beyond Marriage?* (Cambridge, Intersentia, 2017) 501.

[16] Council Regulation (EU) 2016/1104 implementing enhanced cooperation in the area of jurisdiction, applicable law and the recognition and enforcement of decisions in matters of the property consequences of registered partnerships [2016] OJ L183, 30–56. This regulation currently binds 23 of the 27 EU Member States.

[17] Council Regulation (EU) 2016/1103 implementing enhanced cooperation in the area of jurisdiction, applicable law and the recognition and enforcement of decisions in matters of matrimonial property regimes [2016] OJ L 183, 1–29. This regulation currently binds 23 of the 27 EU Member States.

[18] On which see K Boele-Woelki and D Martiny, 'The Commission on European Family Law (CEFL) and its Principles of European Family Law Regarding Parental Responsibilities' (2007) 8 *ERA Forum* 125.

[19] JM Scherpe, *European Family Law Volume IV: The Present and Future of European Family Law* (Cheltenham, Edward Elgar, 2016) 1–2.

[20] See, eg, European Parliament, Resolution of 8 September 2015 on the situation of fundamental rights in the European Union 2013–2014 (2014/2254(INI)) [2015] A8-0230/2015; on this, see S de Vries, H de Waele and M-P Granger (eds), *Civil Rights and EU Citizenship: Challenges at the Crossroads of the European, National and Private Spheres* (Cheltenham, Edward Elgar, 2016) 35–36.

approach to non-traditional family recognition; however, unlike the ECHR system, it adopts a closed model under which there is a fixed list of grounds of discrimination and the equality test is legislatively mandated (ie, the cases in which discrimination is justified are limited to those expressly listed). Marital status is not included within the prohibited grounds of discrimination and, in accordance with the closed model, the Court cannot add it judicially. Furthermore, not only is marital status not protected, but secondary sources often reiterate that matters of marital status are left to the Member States. In the preambles to directives or regulations, it is often asserted that the directive/regulation 'is without prejudice' to the power of the Member States to regulate family status and benefits arising from this. Therefore, the Treaty-based distribution of powers and the entrenchment of this distribution in secondary sources in principle limit attempts to modify family law definitions – despite crucial steps forward being made, as I show in Section 3 below.

Same-sex couples deserve separate discussion. Critical judicial victories were achieved in light of the explicit prohibition to discriminate based on sexual orientation. This explicit prohibition enabled the Court to question a state choice to differentiate between the treatment of same-sex and cis-sex partners. In the EU, the absence of a specific ground which non-conjugal couples can invoke might render the analogy with same-sex couples less solid.

The third point illustrated above is the functionalisation of the system to the achievement of market freedoms. This is another aspect – which is traceable back to the origins of the EU – that weighs against considering the EU as a viable forum for strategic litigation. It is especially linked to the original intuition according to which mitigating economic competition amongst historical rivals, the major driving force behind the two twentieth-century world wars, would have in turn ensured long-lasting peace on the continent.

However, functionalism should be taken at face value. First, it does not entail that the protection of human rights is not on the agenda. It would be grossly misplaced to overlook the increasing expansion of the EU towards new areas that stretch well beyond market freedoms. A case in point is the transmogrification, as it were, of European citizenship, which is no longer the citizenship of economically active individuals. This status has now become the citizenship of Member State nationals as such, independent of whether they are economically active or not.[21] Case law[22] and secondary sources[23] clearly establish that the EU nowadays

[21] K Kaesling, 'Family Life and EU Citizenship: The Discovery of the Substance of the EU Citizens' Rights and its Genuine Enjoyment' in K Boele-Woelki, N Dethloff and W Gephart (eds), *Family Law and Culture in Europe* (Cambridge, Intersentia, 2014) 294.

[22] Judgment of the Court of 20 September 2001, *Rudy Grzelczyk v Centre public d'aide sociale d'Ottignies-Louvain-la-Neuve*, C-184/99, EU:C:2001:458, para 31; Judgment of the Court of 17 September 2002, *Baumbast and R v Secretary of State for the Home Department*, C-413/99, EU:C:2002:493, para 82.

[23] See, eg, Recital 3 of Directive (EC) 2004/38 of the European Parliament and of the Council of 29 April 2004 on the right of citizens of the Union and their family members to move and reside freely within the territory of the Member States [2004] OJ L158, 77–123 (hereinafter 'the Citizens' Rights Directive').

confers what Advocate General Antonio La Pergola came to define as 'a new legal standing'.[24]

Yet, a recent case exemplifies how functionalisation has not been entirely abandoned and offers an example of its consequences in terms of human rights protection. Even in cases where the Court issued pivotal decisions touching upon fundamental rights, functionalisation re-emerges at the argumentative level. *Coman*,[25] a ruling on the free movement of same-sex spouses, exemplifies this point. On that occasion, the Court ruled for the first time that the third-country same-sex partner of the Romanian applicant (Mr Coman), with whom he concluded a valid marriage in another Member State (Belgium), should enjoy residence rights in Romania. The Court reasoned that if no such right were granted, the static citizen would be 'discouraged' from moving to another Member State in the first place. Returning to the home state would then be impractical should they not be able to bring back their partner. The case was therefore grounded in freedom of movement and was decided based on Article 21(1) TFEU, which enshrines the right of residence in another Member State for the EU citizen.[26] By contrast, the discrimination prong of the argument was entirely sidelined in favour of arguments closely related to freedom of movement.

Yet, this approach comes at a cost. In order for the holding to apply, the parties in a same-sex marriage must meet two conditions: having contracted a valid marriage in another EU Member State and having developed and consolidated a family life in that Member State.[27] Unlike a non-discrimination right that is applicable across the board, this holding does not apply to an EU citizen who got married in a third country or to a citizen who has moved to Belgium for the sole purpose of getting married. With market freedoms as the doctrinal centrepiece of its decisions, the CJEU's room for manoeuvre is more reduced. The functionalisation of the system to the achievement of market freedoms calls for a constant effort to justify an intervention based on 'canonical' paths. This could in turn limit the scope of decisions involving fundamental rights, as *Coman* attests to.

Hence, point (iii) above is not to imply that the EU is not interested in human rights protection or that human rights protection is not pursued in practice. The reason why I include it as part of the list of structural limits is that such functionalisation could in principle limit the outreach to areas which are not either directly or collaterally linked to the market as well as the scope of the decisions involving fundamental rights.

In light of these structural limits, at present I am sceptical in considering the EU a viable forum for enhancing the legal recognition of non-conjugal families. In order to justify this scepticism, this chapter will ferret out the only remedy that

[24] Advocate General La Pergola's Opinion delivered on 1 July 1997, *María Martínez Sala v Freistaat Bayern*, C-85/96, EU:C:1997:335 [20].

[25] Judgment of the Court (GC) of 5 June 2018, *Relu Adrian Coman and Others v Inspectoratul General pentru Imigrări and Ministerul Afacerilor Interne*, C-673/16, EU:C:2018:385.

[26] Article 21(1) TFEU.

[27] *Coman* (n 25) [56].

could be pursued (which is an area-specific remedy) in view of the current allocation of powers. In addition, it will examine the case law of the Court in three key areas where family definitions 'matter' – employment, the legal treatment of the EU staff, and free movement under the Citizens' Rights Directive – without endeavouring to build legal arguments. My contention is that legal arguments aimed at recognising non-conjugal families would not stand a chance doctrinally, at least at present.

2. Remedy

I. An Area-Specific Approach

The EU is not the forum for achieving far-reaching family law reform. Most assuredly, it is not the appropriate forum for introducing new regimes, such as civil partnerships. The principal reason for this is the oft-repeated lack of EU competence over substantive family law. In principle, this rigid allocation of powers prevents EU institutions from interfering in the design of what Duncan Kennedy calls FL1 and FL2 rules, ie, the rules governing entrance to and exit from family regimes, and rules on the defaults attendant to family regimes, respectively.[28]

However, in practice, the CJEU has not fallen short of shaping FL2 rules in a host of areas. The relevant areas especially include employment and immigration. Thus, I contend that an area-specific approach, whereby claimants seek to expand the eligibility requirements of single benefits, is more suitable. The domains in which the CJEU has been more active in disentangling inequalities for same-sex couples were related to the application of the Citizens' Rights Directive on free movement and to the employment context. Its intervention was not obvious. Both the Treaties and the applicable secondary sources of law were firm in demarcating the field by stressing that marital status is a matter reserved to the discretion of Member States. As such, the Court had to proffer principled reasons in order to justify an intervention. In paying lip service to the distribution of powers enshrined in the Treaties,[29] it argued that the Member States continue to retain competence over family regimes and the benefits arising from these. However, it continued, they cannot hide behind this competence to violate EU law and notably its well-established principle of non-discrimination.

[28] D Kennedy, 'Savigny's Family/Patrimony Distinction and its Place in the Global Genealogy of Classical Legal Thought' (2010) 58 *American Journal of Comparative Law* 811.

[29] Judgment of the Court (GC) of 1 April 2008, *Tadao Maruko v Versorgungsanstalt der deutschen Bühnen*, C-267/06, EU:C:2008:179 [58]–[60]; Judgment of the Court (GC) of 10 May 2011, *Jürgen Römer v Freie und Hansestadt Hamburg*, C-147/08, EU:C:2011:286 [38]; Judgment of the Court of 12 December 2013, *Frédéric Hay v Crédit agricole mutuel de Charente-Maritime et des Deux-Sèvres*, C-267/12, EU:C:2013:823 [26].

The EU enshrines a principle of non-discrimination in the Treaties, which can be found in Article 19 TFEU[30] and Article 21 of the Charter.[31] This principle binds both the EU institutions and the Member States in their capacity to implement EU law and it is often re-stated in regulations and directives themselves. This is to say that in light of the principle of non-discrimination, the Court managed to carve out room to scrutinise national family laws (and EU laws) to ensure that they were not discriminating against certain categories.

To further buttress my contention that an area-specific approach is more suitable than a comprehensive approach, I will highlight some passages in the *Coman* decision the landmark decision in terms of LGBTQ equality rights. A first noteworthy aspect is the Court's avoidance of arguments pivoting on dignity, which had been referenced in the Advocate General's Opinion.[32] A reluctance to employ dignity-based arguments sits well with an area-specific approach. When applying such an approach, the focus is attached to functional considerations – the purpose that the family benefit at hand is seeking to effect in practice. This is not to say that a survivor's pension benefit will not confer dignity or a sense of legitimacy upon the claimant; it is merely to say that it is much easier to disentangle dignity from claims concerning material benefits than it is to disentangle it from claims concerning status-based regimes. The majority of status-based schemes, marriage and civil unions amongst them, were notably opened up in light of their capacity to convey the symbolic or expressive benefits of recognition, amongst which undoubtedly is dignity. Dignity-based lines of argument are not alien to claims aimed at extending specific benefits; yet, they are more extricable from such claims should it be 'necessary' to overcome states' resistances.

Second, there is an important passage in the *Coman* decision regarding the objection that imposing a derivative right of residence for same-sex partners on Romania runs counter to the country's national identity.[33] The objection was only raised by an intervener during a hearing, but the Court took pains to clarify that 'an obligation to recognize such marriages for the sole purpose of granting a derived right of residence to a third-country national does not undermine the national identity'.[34] It also stressed that the recognition of the derivative right of residence (the single protection) cannot be equated with imposing same-sex marriage on the Member State. The implication of this line of reasoning is that while granting a legal benefit does not run counter to the national identity of the Member

[30] Article 19 TFEU refers to the grounds of 'sex, racial or ethnic origin, religion or belief, disability, age or sexual orientation'.

[31] Article 21 of the Charter refers to the grounds of 'sex, race, colour, ethnic or social origin, genetic features, language, religion or belief, political or any other opinion, membership of a national minority, property, birth, disability, age or sexual orientation'.

[32] Advocate General Wathelet's Opinion delivered on 11 January 2018, *Relu Adrian Coman and Others v Inspectoratul General pentru Imigrări and Ministerul Afacerilor Interne*, C-673/16, EU:C:2018:2 [2].

[33] *Coman* (n 25) [43].

[34] ibid [46].

State in question, the imposition of status might (and of marriage certainly does, according to the Court).

This elucidation is critical to the analysis as Article 4(2) TFEU sets forth a duty to respect the national identity of Member States. The notion of national identity gives special weight to objections based on the Member States' fundamental political structures, most notably their constitutions.[35] Chapter 5 attests to marriage and family being a matter that has a constitutional underpinnings nearly everywhere. Not only can we find a host of provisions on marriage and family, but a certain conception of family is also entrenched as a foundational element of the fabric of the nation. Therefore, it is unlikely that the EU could impose a uniform definition of family and marriage across all Member States without impinging on the core identity of the Member States. In the end, the clarification that imposing single legal protections does not run counter to Article 4(2) TFEU can be read as an implicit opening for further litigation aimed at obtaining specific family benefits.

There are additional reasons militating against the adoption of a comprehensive status-based approach. In the employment context, where the Court has been more active in extending legal protections in favour of same-sex couples, this notable achievement was only possible in light of some Member States having 'voluntarily adopted' a recognition mechanism open to such couples.[36] Therefore, thus far, the Court has never attempted to impose the introduction of new family regimes, such as civil partnerships, to countries (especially those in located in Central and Eastern Europe) that do not have them in place. This approach differs from that adopted by its other European counterpart, the European Court of Human Rights (ECtHR), which has been as bold as to compel Italy to introduce a 'specific legal framework' (ie, a family regime) for the recognition of same-sex couples.[37]

3. The Relevant Jurisprudence of the Court of Justice

There are three main areas where 'EU' family definitions come into play: employment; free movement of persons; and the treatment of the personnel of the EU. Each area is governed by its own set of secondary sources (especially regulations or directives). I shall analyse each area in turn below.

I. The Employment Equality Directive

The Employment Equality Directive prohibits discrimination on several bases in the domain of employment: sexual orientation, religion or belief, age and

[35] E Cloots, 'National Identity, Constitutional Identity, and Sovereignty in the EU' (2016) 2 *Netherlands Journal of Legal Philosophy* 82.

[36] *Maruko* (n 29).

[37] *Oliari and Others v Italy* [2015] 65 EHRR 26.

disability.[38] Unlike the Race Directive,[39] this directive only applies to the domain of employment and does not extend to social and welfare benefits, education and healthcare. A proposal to further extend its reach to these subject areas was rejected.[40] Notwithstanding their formal exclusion, social benefits can fall within the reach of the directive if they are found to be equivalent to 'pay'. Starting in the 1970s, a progressive interpretation of the term 'pay' led to pensions being encompassed within the notion under two conditions: that they are a general scheme under the law and that they are obligatory for a category of workers.[41]

Before the Employment Equality Directive[42] and the ECtHR's *Karner* decision in 2003, the Court of Justice fell short of extending both specific and comprehensive protections to same-sex couples. For instance, in *Grant*,[43] it held that differential treatment of a worker's same-sex partner in relation to travel benefits did not amount to sex discrimination. A few years later, it re-affirmed this position when it found that the differential treatment between (same-sex) civil unions and (cis-sex) marriage in Sweden did not amount to discrimination on the basis of sex or sexual orientation.[44]

In *Karner*,[45] the ECtHR found that unmarried same-sex partners enjoy the institution of family life as much as unmarried cross-sex partners. After the decision, the Court seemed eager to align itself to the more progressive stance of the ECtHR. In the famous *Maruko* case, the Court of Justice applied Article 2 of the Employment Equality Directive, prohibiting sexual orientation discrimination, to protect two claimants in a same-sex relationship. To this effect, it held that if same-sex registered partners are found to be in a comparable situation to opposite-sex spouses as regards the professional pension scheme, this would be direct discrimination for which no justification would be acceptable.[46]

This is the first of a string of cases arguing that Member States cannot invoke their competence over marital status as a pretext to violating binding EU laws and principles, amongst which is the principle of non-discrimination. In particular, the CJEU carved out some room for intervention in cases where same-sex couples were already recognised under national law, but were not considered to be fully equivalent to opposite-sex couples. This is to say that the Court was especially determined to further push the recognition of same-sex couples in Member

[38] Article 1 of Directive (EC) 2000/78 (n 9).

[39] Race Directive (n 10).

[40] European Commission, 'Proposal for a Council Directive on implementing the principle of equal treatment between persons irrespective of religion or belief, disability, age or sexual orientation' COM (2008) 426 final.

[41] Judgment of the Court of 25 May 1971, *Gabrielle Defrenne v Belgian State*, C-80/70, EU:C:1971:1:55.

[42] Directive (EC) 2000/78 (n 9).

[43] Judgment of the Court of 17 February 1998, *Lisa Jacqueline Grant v South-West Trains Ltd*, C-249/96, EU:C:1998:63.

[44] Judgment of the Court of 31 May 2001, *D and Kingdom of Sweden v Council of the European Union*, C-122/99 P and C-125/99 P, EU:C:2001:304.

[45] *Karner v Austria* (2003) 38 EHRR 528.

[46] *Maruko* (n 29).

States that were already receptive of their demands, despite this not resulting in full protection.

In *Maruko*, the conclusion favourable to same-sex couples was reached after considering that:

(i) Germany voluntary adopted life partnerships[47]; and
(ii) the regime placed partners of the same sex in a situation comparable to that of spouses as regards the survivor's benefit.[48]

The latter conclusion did not result from an autonomous assessment, but rather was reached after considering the position of the German referring court. The domestic court saw claimants as being in a comparable situation in light of recent amendments to life partnerships, attesting to a gradual but steadfast process of harmonisation of life partnerships and marriage.

There are two aspects of the decision that are worth mentioning here. First, the voluntariness of the adoption of the regime entails that the judgment cannot apply to Member States that lack a general legal framework: currently, Bulgaria, Latvia, Lithuania, Poland, Romania and Slovakia. The second point regards the comparability assessment. Point (ii) above calls for an inquiry into the comparability of registered same-sex couples and opposite-sex spouses. In both *Maruko* and *Romer*,[49] the Court refrained from engaging in the comparability assessment and left the issue to the domestic courts. However, it clarified that courts must not conduct the assessment in the abstract (looking at marriage and the non-marital regime as such), but in relation to the specific benefit under examination.[50] In any event, the two situations should not be identical but merely comparable.

In subsequent case law, the CJEU autonomously conducted the comparability assessment. In a case regarding the Pacte Civil de Solidarité (Pacs) regime in France, the CJEU held that a marriage bonus and paid leave granted under a national collective agreement are 'pay' for purposes of the Employment Equality Directive[51] and provided guidance regarding the comparability assessment. As such, it reiterated that for the purposes of the comparability analysis, the differences between marriage and the non-marital regime are irrelevant.[52] Such analysis only concerns the specific benefits at issue, namely the bonus and the paid leave. Regardless, it argued that same-sex *pacsés* couples were comparable because at the time Pacs was the only recognition mechanism. Therefore, the fact that they had taken steps to formalise their relationship and had publicly committed to support each other materially and emotionally amounted to evidence that their commitment was comparable to that of cis-sex spouses. This guidance is valuable

[47] *Gesetz über die Eingetragene Lebenspartnerschaft* (registered life partnerships) of 16 February 2001 (BGBl 2001 I, 266).
[48] *Maruko* (n 29) [80].
[49] *Römer* (n 29).
[50] ibid [42]; *Maruko* (n 29) [67]–[69].
[51] *Hay* (n 29).
[52] ibid [39].

in that Pacs doubtlessly provides a much narrower cluster of rights and obligations compared to marriage, especially regarding property and parenthood. Based on this judgment, the Court is likely to make a finding of discrimination whenever the couple in question is legally prevented from marrying yet has otherwise formalised the union.

Continuing the position taken in *Maruko* and *Römer*, the CJEU concluded in *Hay* that a distinction that is 'neutral' on its face, as allegedly based on marital status, cannot pass muster if it is contrary to the principle of non-discrimination. Thus-framed distinctions must be considered as direct discrimination based on sexual orientation, though there is no mention of the ground of sexual orientation in the impugned provision.[53]

However, the utility of this passage for non-conjugal families is reduced. The Court was able make this doctrinal move due to the existence of the prohibited ground of sexual orientation in both the Treaties and the applicable Employment Equality Directive. In other words, marital status discrimination was only remedied in cases where there was a compound violation involving both marital status and another listed ground of discrimination. This second ground mainly coincided with sexual orientation, although at other times it was sex. For instance, in *Teuling*, the Court found that:

> [A] system of benefits in which, as in this case, supplements are provided for which are not directly based on the sex of the beneficiaries but take account of their marital status or family situation *and in respect of which it emerges that a considerably smaller proportion of women than of men are entitled to such supplements* is contrary to article 4(1) of the directive.[54] (Emphasis added)

The adverse impact of the measure on women was crucial to upholding a finding of discrimination. However, in the absence of proof of an impact on women, there could have been no autonomous marital status discrimination claim. Not only is marital status absent from the list of prohibited grounds of discrimination, but measures relating to marital status are expressly left to the discretion of the Member States. Therefore, absent a compound violation, the protection of marital status can hardly be achieved in the courtroom.

Overall, the reviewed case law is of reduced utility for non-conjugal families, as they are unable at present to link their discrimination to any of the listed grounds. I find it unpersuasive to frame non-conjugal coupledom as a form of sexual orientation or sex. I have explored the reasons for this in Chapter 3.[55] As applied to

[53] ibid [44] ('The difference in treatment based on the employees' marital status and not expressly on their sexual orientation is still direct discrimination because only persons of different sexes may marry and homosexual employees are therefore unable to meet the condition required for obtaining the benefit claimed').

[54] Judgment of the Court of 11 June 1987, *JW Teuling v Bestuur van de Bedrijfsvereniging voor de Chemische Industrie*, C-30/85, EU:C:1987:271 [13].

[55] See ch 3, s 4.I.

Europe, they boil down to sexual orientation conveying the misplaced idea that non-conjugal couples are asexual and to the sex of the parties no longer being a disqualifying condition to enter into a family regime in the majority of European states.

II. Staff Regulations

The series of decisions regarding EU staff are the most 'progressive'. In this domain, the Court adopts the broader and most inclusive definition of 'family'. A progressive stance was possible in view of the EU adopting an autonomous definition of 'family' in this area, and logically so since the matter covered by EU law is the personnel of the EU. Therefore, in this area, there is no need to resort to the usual self-restraint adopted when intruding in matters of domestic family law.[56]

Remarkably, starting in 2004, the so-called Staff Regulations[57] included within their scope the 'non-marital partner', ie, the partner outside of wedlock.[58] Yet, in a similar fashion to the employment context, the Regulations do not mention the prohibition of marital status discrimination, except as regards two relatively marginal categories of workers: hiring contract or temporary staff.[59] Nevertheless, it seems that in this area, the EU often adopts concepts and lines of reasoning that are typical of marital status discrimination.[60]

Before the 2004 amendments equating non-marital partners and spouses, the Civil Service Tribunal, which was set to handle cases relating to the EU officials as the court of first instance until its dissolution in 2016, resolved to protect non-marital families. The decision in *C v Commission* merits consideration as it went so far as to protect an individual in a de facto relationship. Notably, the Court offered legal protection to a mother in a de facto relationship who was denied an orphan's pension. The result was reached by framing the case as involving

[56] Judgment of the General Court (Appeal Chamber) of 5 October 2009, *European Commission v Anton Pieter Roodhuijzen*, T-58/08, EU:T:2009:385 [87] ('In so far as the definition given relates to a term used in the Staff Regulations, its scope is necessarily circumscribed by the framework of the Staff Regulations. It governs solely the award of certain social benefits granted by the Staff Regulations to officials or other servants of the European Communities, and has no effects in the Member States, which are free to introduce statutory arrangements granting legal recognition to forms of union other than marriage, in accordance with established case-law').

[57] Regulation No 31 (EEC), 11 (EAEC), laying down the Staff Regulations of officials and the conditions of employment of other servants of the European Economic Community and the European Atomic Energy Community [1962] OJ P045, 1385 (hereinafter 'Staff Regulations').

[58] ibid art 1(2) of Annex VII.

[59] Articles 82 and 12 of the 'Conditions of employment of other servants of the European Union' Part in the Staff Regulations.

[60] N Palazzo, 'The EU Family: Is Marital Status Emerging as a Prohibited Ground of Discrimination?' in E Bernard, M Cresp and M Ho-Dac (eds), *La famille dans l'ordre juridique de l'Union européenne* (Brussels, Larcier/Bruylant, 2020).

discrimination based on personal conviction:[61] The decision not to marry was based on personal convictions which, in principle, cannot factor into the subsequent state's decision to grant legal protections, especially having regard to contemporary social developments.[62] Further, the Court availed itself of a typical functional line of reasoning to argue that the deceased partner had recognised and supported the child materially while he was alive. Therefore, the distinction drawn between married and unmarried couples was under-inclusive: the decision failed to include partners who had legally recognised the child and who acted as parents in practice.

A non-formalist line of reasoning was also employed in *W v Commission*.[63] On that occasion, the Tribunal granted a housing allowance to a claimant with dual (Belgian and Moroccan) citizenship. The claimant could allegedly not marry without incurring the risk of prosecution in Morocco, where homosexual acts were criminally prohibited. The Court found in his favour and ruled that measures excluding unmarried partners from family benefits are over-inclusive whenever they do not carve out an exception for those who cannot marry in practice.

The case of highest relevance to non-conjugal families is *Roodhuijzen*,[64] which dealt with a worker at the Eurostat who had entered a cohabitation agreement under Dutch law with his same-sex partner. The worker wished to have his partner recognised under the Joint Sickness Insurance scheme applicable to EU personnel. The cohabitation agreement, as noted previously,[65] is a contractual agreement entered before a notary which confers a pared-down list of rights and obligations compared to marriage and registered partnerships.[66] Through this contractual recognition mechanism, any two persons can formalise their relationship.

The Commission attempted to defend the scheme by arguing that the agreement was essentially private in nature and did not bind third parties. It further considered that the term 'non-marital partnership' under the Regulations should be construed as meaning a partnership 'which, under national law, is designed to have effects *similar* to those of a marriage' (emphasis added).[67] The lack of equivalence of the agreement was then derived from the scheme being open to all sorts of family networks including partnerships that are 'not … intended exclusively for persons wishing to form a "couple"'.[68] Hence, the very fact that the scheme was open to non-conjugal families was proffered as evidence that the legislator did not intend to create a truly alternative union to marriage.

[61] Judgment of the General Court of 30 January 2003, *C v Commission of the European Communities*, T-307/00, EU:T:2003:21.
[62] ibid [51].
[63] Judgment of the Civil Service Tribunal of 14 October 2010, *W v European Commission*, F-86/09, EU:F:2010:125.
[64] *Roodhuijzen* (n 56).
[65] See ch 5, s 1.I.
[66] Lamont (n 15) 515.
[67] *Roodhuijzen* (n 56) [51].
[68] ibid [52].

The Court of Justice upheld Mr Roodhuijzen's claim. It reasoned that there is no need to find an equivalence between the alternative regime and marriage in terms of the types of eligible relationships or the list of subject matters covered therein. The relevant definition of 'non-marital partner' is an autonomous one, the Court argued. It can be 'inferred' from the Staff Regulations, and notably Annex VII to the Regulations, which now enshrines a definition of 'non-marital partner'. In order for the relationship to be eligible, two conditions must be met: first, the agreement must be entered into by two unrelated people; and, second, evidence of formalities shall be provided. Therefore, whether the regime in question allows other persons to enter it is irrelevant; it is the relationship at stake which must be scrutinised. Likewise, the material scope of the non-marital regime is irrelevant.

While the two conditions identified by the Court are in principle applicable to a subset of non-conjugal families – that is, those relationships in which the parties are unrelated – the Court itself anticipates and rejects this prospect. The autonomous definition of non-marital partnership was intended to be akin to that of marriage as far as conjugality is concerned. The Court was adamant in stressing that the autonomous definition of non-marital partners does not include non-conjugal couples or non-dyadic families, a stance that the Court considered to be aligned with that taken by the ECtHR in *Burden*:

> That requirement of a union between two persons means that, in the same way as the spouse, the 'unmarried partner' of an official … is clearly distinct from his dependants, that is to say, children of the official concerned *and other persons dependent on him* … That requirement leads more generally to the exclusion from the concept of 'non-marital partnership' … of all situations which, although no union exists between two persons, are … likely to be covered by a partnership recognised under the relevant national law, such as a 'samenlevingsovereenkomst'. On this point, the concept of 'non-marital partnership' contained in the Staff Regulations thus converges with the definition adopted by the European Court of Human Rights in *Burden v the United Kingdom*, relied on by the Commission.[69] (Emphasis added)

The explicit assertion that conjugality is at the core of EU family definitions at present hinders the further expansion of such definitions to include non-conjugal claimants. This exclusion occurring in an area where the EU courts have been more active in protecting non-traditional families, in light of the adoption of autonomous definitions, carries special weight in terms of predicting future doctrinal developments.

III. The Citizens' Rights Directive

The EU is especially committed to regulating situations with a cross-border element. The theoretical justification is their touching upon one of the core

[69] ibid [84].

freedoms: the free movement of persons. Families come into play as free movement is only ensured when people have the possibility of keeping their family ties intact. Family ties doubtlessly constitute an important facet of one's life and might have a bearing on people's personal decisions, including decisions to move across countries.

The protection attaching to persons moving across the EU varies. It depends on whether the person in question is a third-country national or a European citizen, on whether the person is a worker or otherwise and ultimately on whether the person wishes to move to another Member State or live in their own country. The latter scenario involves so-called static or non-mobile citizens, whose legal status is equated to that of citizens who wish to return to their home country. Family reunification regards third-country nationals residing lawfully in a Member State (so-called sponsors).[70] Their legal status is governed by a separate regime set forth under Council Directive 2003/86,[71] which provides the host state with the discretion to decide of whether to allow the entrance of the dependent ascendants and registered partners, as well as that of the unmarried partner and their children. It only places a positive obligation upon Member States to grant family reunification when this involves the worker's spouse (and minor children). By contrast, when the family member in question is an unmarried partner, a registered partner or a first-degree ascendant, family reunification is only optional.

As far as the EU citizen is concerned, 'in the beginning, it was the worker'. The right to freely move and install oneself in another Member State was conferred upon workers and entailed a possibility for them to bring family members with them. Under the original regulation on migrant workers (hereinafter 'the Regulation'),[72] those who could accompany the worker were predominantly members of the nuclear family. The definition of 'family' for the purposes of the Directive included:

(i) the spouse, and qualified descendants;[73] and
(ii) qualified ascendants of the worker or the spouse.[74]

'Other' family members, whose access only needed to be 'facilitated', included members 'who might also be dependent on the worker or were living under the same roof in the country from where the worker came'.[75]

[70] Pursuant to the European Migration Network Glossary, a 'third-country national' is any person who is not a citizen of the EU or of a country within the Schengen Area; see European Commission, Migration and Home Affairs, 'Third-Country National' in *EMN Glossary*, available at www.ec.europa.eu/home-affairs/content/third-country-national_en.

[71] Council Directive (EC) 2003/86 of 22 September 2003 on the right to family reunification [2003] OJ L251, 12–18.

[72] Council Regulation (EEC) 1612/68 on freedom of movement for workers within the Community, OJ L257, 19.10.1968, 2–12 (Regulation No 1612/68).

[73] Council Regulation 1612/68 applied to '[d]escendants under the age of 21 years or dependants over that age'.

[74] Council Regulation 1612/68 applied to '[d]ependent ascendants of the worker or his spouse'.

[75] E Buttigieg, 'The Definition of "Family" under EU Law' in PG Xuereb (ed), *The Family, Law, Religion and Society in the European Union and Malta* (Msida, European Documentation and Research Centre, University of Malta, 2006) 99.

From the start, the term 'spouse' was interpreted in a robustly traditional way. The notion of 'spouse' only encompassed the marital heterosexual partner,[76] including the separated (but not divorced) spouse.[77] While the struggle over same-sex marriage came about much later, de facto couples were the first to challenge the traditional construction of the term 'spouse'. Faced with the issue in *Reed*,[78] the Court of Justice rejected the application of an unmarried woman seeking to join her lifelong unmarried partner who had moved to the Netherlands for job-related reasons. At the time, the Court was not persuaded that the Regulation applied to de facto couples. Subsequently, it even refused to find that same-sex cohabitants could qualify as cohabitants under EU law, whose access only needed to be 'facilitated'.[79]

The construction of family resulting from the Court of Justice's case law drew criticism. Charges were levelled at its intensely formal approach. This narrow construction not only acted to the detriment of unmarried families, but also to the detriment of divorced families and, in more general terms, of all 'atypical' families, including single-parent families.[80] This clearly had implications for how people exercised their freedom of movement. Yet, at the time, the European Parliament seemed to be the only institution to embrace the concern that a formalistic approach could undermine the free movement of citizens.

In 2004, a new directive amending the Regulation was passed.[81] The relevant provision kept a definition of family member which encompassed the spouse and qualified descendants and ascendants (descendants under the age of 21 or dependants, and ascendants if they were dependent on the citizen). The definition was not extended to include de facto couples, although it did include the new category of 'the partner with whom the Union citizen has contracted a registered partnership'. However, the derivative right of residence of this newly introduced category was made contingent on the principle of home state regulation.[82] Hence, the addition can only benefit registered partners if the host state has enacted a registered partnership and treats it as equivalent to marriage under national law.

Moving on to the category of 'other family members', whose entrance needs only be facilitated, the definition includes:

(i) dependants – either financially or physically – of the EU citizen or members of the household of the citizen;
(ii) the partner with whom the citizen 'has a durable relationship, duly attested'.[83]

[76] *D and Sweden* (n 44).
[77] Judgment of the Court of 13 February 1985, *Aissatou Diatta v Land Berlin*, C-267/83, EU:C:1985:67.
[78] Judgment of the Court of 17 April 1986, *State of the Netherlands v Ann Florence Reed*, C-59/85, EU:C:1986:157.
[79] Judgment of the Court of 17 February 1998, *Lisa Jacqueline Grant v South-West Trains Ltd*, C-249/96, EU:C:1998:63.
[80] T Hervey, 'Migrant Workers and Their Families in the European Union: The Pervasive Market Ideology of Community Law' in J Shaw and G More (eds), *New Legal Dynamics of European Union* (Oxford, Clarendon Press, 1996) 91, 106.
[81] Citizens' Rights Directive (n 27).
[82] ibid art 2(b).
[83] ibid art 3.

The entrance of these individuals need only be facilitated in the sense that the decision to grant the derivative right of residence should be made following an extensive examination of the circumstances in the case in question. Further, the rejection of an application should be thoroughly justified.[84] Besides these procedural requirements, entrance is optional and the decision concerning their admission is left entirely to the appreciation of Member States.

The interpretation of the notion of 'spouse' recently underwent a significant evolution. The *Coman* decision marks a watershed moment where the Court adopted an autonomous definition of spouse applicable to the cross-border regulation of marriage.[85] The extension of the autonomous definition to cases involving free movement is notable. It is hardly conceivable that, at the time of the drafting of the Directive, the Member States intended to include same-sex spouses in the definition of 'spouse'. In 2004, only the Netherlands had introduced same-sex marriage, and the notion had a robust traditional understanding in the Member States, as witnessed by their domestic family laws.

While the decision is a pivotal stepping-stone to furthering equality for same-sex marital couples, it leaves the question of whether the two claimants constituted 'dependants on members of the household'[86] or the partner in a durable relationship under Article 3 of the Directive unanswered. The Court indeed declined to answer questions 3 and 4 in the preliminary reference, whereby the applicants asked whether they fell within the scope of the category. Hence, the judgment is of reduced utility for non-conjugal couples. It falls short of clarifying the contours of the two categories that could have a bearing on their legal identity – dependants/members of the household or partners in a durable relationship. More generally, so far the Court has not provided guidance regarding the meaning of Article 3 of the Directive. The only clarification concerned the term 'facilitation', which, in the Court's view, at a minimum encompasses a need to examine applications thoroughly and offer a justification in the event that the permit is denied. From this scant clarification, Mark Bell rightly inferred that 'facilitate' means at a minimum that a process whereby non-marital couples can apply must be in place and that a blanket ban on non-marital couples would surely run counter to the Directive.[87] Besides this, we don't know much else, let alone whether non-conjugal couples qualify.

A further option for non-conjugal claimants is to qualify as registered partners. Yet, the prospects for them to do so are significantly reduced. This hinges on the state having put in place a regime that is open to non-conjugal families (at present only Belgium has such a regime). There is an additional reason why the category of

[84] Judgment of the Court (GC) of 5 September 2012, *Secretary of State for the Home Department v Muhammad Sazzadur Rahman and Others*, C-83/11, EU:C:2012:519 [21].

[85] *Coman* (n 25).

[86] See also Recital 6 of the Citizens' Rights Directive speaking of family 'in the broadest sense'.

[87] M Bell, 'EU Directive on Free Movement and Same-Sex Families: Guidelines on the Implementation Process' (Report ILGA-Europe, October 2005) 8.

registered partnership is of reduced utility. So far, the Court has granted substantial deference to national immigration laws, even when restrictive immigration laws resulted in situations of manifest discrimination for same-sex couples. This is consistent with the principle of home state regulation. The principle essentially entails that the decision whether to equate married and registered couples is left to the discretion of the Member States: not only does the rule entail that these states must have enacted registered partnerships, but also that they should have set out the criteria under which they will consider the regime to be equivalent to marriage. This is where the 'trick' lies. For instance, Ireland requires that the relationship under scrutiny be: same-sex, formally registered, dissolvable only by a court order and exclusive. In view of these strict requirements, many registered partners do not qualify for entrance and residence, and have their movement freedoms routinely violated. This is why for instance, partners in a French Pacs or an Italian civil union are not granted residence rights under Irish law (since the relationship is not dissolvable only by court order).

This persistent reluctance to protect mobile same-sex couples leaves little if any room for hope that the Court could push for an interpretation of registered partners which encompasses non-conjugal couples even in the unlikely circumstance that they can access a registration scheme.

Concluding Remarks

The EU is not the proper venue to pursue legal change. At present, there seem to be both institutional and doctrinal limits that stand in the way of considering it as a viable path for non-conjugal families.

The picture is variegated. The three areas analysed above show that in some cases, the Court has been willing to make strides in the advancement of recognition of same-sex families. The most activist approach has been taken in the area of the legal treatment of EU staff. This is understandable and perhaps predictable in light of the reduced impact of these decisions on domestic family laws. Highly interesting are also the cases decided under the Employment Equality Directive. The relevant decisions were notable in that they managed to extend a set of legal benefits to same-sex couples in spite of the prohibition against interfering with family statuses and benefits, which were built into primary and secondary EU law.

The 'employment saga' demonstrates that the allocation of powers enshrined in the Treaties is not a complete hindrance to improving the situation of new families. However, such a holding could only be reached in light of the prohibition to discriminate based on sexual orientation, which can be found in both the Treaties and the applicable directives. Since there is no comparable ground on which non-conjugal families can rely in order to challenge discriminatory laws, the conclusion is that they could hardly replicate the litigation strategy of same-sex couples. Ultimately, the decisions in the area of freedom of movement rights are of no use. There, the Court has been wearier to act even in favour of same-sex couples, except for its recent decision in which it expanded the notion of 'spouse' – a category that has no bearing on the status of non-conjugal families.

However, it is worth emphasising that the EU offers greater protection when it comes to material benefits compared to the ECHR. The litigation involving same-sex couples is a fruitful example in this regard. Same-sex couples obtained landmark victories giving access to various employment and immigration law benefits. By contrast, the ECtHR is less willing to act in situations involving matters of social engineering, as exemplified by the broad margin of appreciation it grants when such matters are at stake.

Further, it should be recalled that the EU is not an international but a supranational legal system. So far, it is indeed the most developed model of regional integration. What is illustrative in this regard is the fact that EU law is binding on the Member States and in some circumstances is even directly applicable. In the event of a Member State's non-compliance, the enforcement mechanism is stronger compared to the ECHR system and might lead to an infringement procedure against such a state. These are but two aspects attesting to the EU being a powerful 'ally' should (several) changes at the doctrinal and/or institutional level occur. If the current allocation of competences (what I refer to as institutional limits) cannot be circumvented judicially, the only way left is going true the cumbersome process of treaty revision: easier said than done. Doctrinally, an extension of the autonomous conception of family to a larger number of families is indispensable. This would mitigate, inter alia, the limits associated with the current allocation of powers between the EU and the Member States. Moreover, a bolder approach to using lines of arguments based on marital status discrimination, even in the absence of a compound violation, is needed.

Conclusion

With 'new' family values and 'new' families taking hold everywhere in the West, the question revolved around understanding why the state does not make them visible in law. A state's desire to promote a singular, often defined as 'traditional' conception of family was noted. The philosophical foundations of this attachment to a singular conception mapped onto states' repulsion for all that is disruptive knowledge, which we defined 'queer'. Queer knowledge flows from the array of personal experiences which deviate from proscribed steps. In its unravelling of the contingent, constructed, only seemingly neutral state-sponsored understanding of family, this kind of knowledge poses a direct threat to the legal-political order. As a consequence, concealment rather than acknowledgement and facilitation has been the state's response to the reality of new families.

Western jurisdictions have nonetheless made an effort to articulate the reasons for tacking the traditional family as the target of state support. However, what I referred to as verbalised functions tell only half the story. Part II of this volume focused on non-conjugal couples. The chapters therein have gathered the state interests that have been proffered to preserve the traditional family in the Euro-American context. Its preservation has been justified on several grounds. Western jurisdictions have, for instance, pointed to an allegedly self-evident interest in protecting the best interests of the child. As a result, they have deliberately conflated vertical and horizontal relationships so as to exploit fears associated with the corruption of children, despite new families not necessarily being interested in having children. At other times, new families were described as a fraud. Entering into such arrangements, governments argued, poses a threat to scarce financial resources: the individuals concerned do not intend to create a 'family', but just play the system to steal public resources. However, this interest is conceptually indistinguishable from that of protecting the traditional family; it just seems an animus-driven variant whereby new families are depicted as unworthy, deceptive and suspicious, being situated outside the boundaries of normalcy. At other times, these jurisdictions have referred to a generalised state interest in protecting the public purse (because expanding the definition of family would be too costly for the state). Interestingly, this interest can profit new families in one respect: it opens the door for the legal recognition of obligations when private law benefits are at stake, such as maintenance obligations, because private parties bear the costs of recognition. By contrast, it is adverse to the extension of entitlements which are costly for the state, such as social benefits. Ultimately, sometimes it is argued that preserving a traditional understanding of marriage or family is per se a legitimate and weighty interest.

Yet, the reality is more complex. Unspeakable state interests lie at the core of the promotion of the traditional family. Amongst these is a biopolitical desire to cover lives and bodies through top-down regulation as a key strategy for the governance and steering of society. While biopolitical aims explain the strategy behind this approach, critical legal pluralism has explained how the law played a central role in achieving it. The supposedly inevitable top-down and prescriptivist conception of law, with its ability to facilitate the expulsion of legal actors from the creation of legal rules has been particularly 'helpful' in this respect.

This bifurcated theoretical framework helps unravel all that is behind this government strategy, its objectives and tools. The contingency of this strategy has been exposed by outlining what a different recognition mechanism that is more respectful of self-authorship would look like. This was the task undertaken in Chapter 2. Yet, I was also aware of the limits of policy-based arguments in terms of tackling the invisibility of new families. Western legal systems are caught up with long-standing ideas on notions of 'family', such as their being sexual 'by definition'; thus, disentangling similar ideas one by one seemed wiser. Further, several advantages flow from a decision to pursue legal strategies in the courtroom. These were listed in Chapter 1. Amongst them is the need to 'motivate' law-makers through legal precedents. Further, the insulation that courts enjoy in conducting their intellectual tasks and the reduced impact of short-term self-interests are also an asset. Taken together, these aspects suggest that focusing on legal strategies as opposed to political avenues would be a more productive way forward.

Part II thus provided an articulated legal analysis of the ways in which Western countries approach the problem of the legal recognition of new families. In outlining the 'legal shape' the problem would take in each jurisdiction, Part II offered the required conceptual tools to tackle it. Likewise, it also supplied tools to predict the hindrances to be overcome. Yet, conducting a comparative legal analysis is not without its difficulties. It requires being deeply cognisant of the peculiarities and differences of each legal system under examination. The decision to focus on the Euro-American context, comprising two relatively homogeneous North American jurisdictions and the two meta-national European systems, was aimed at enhancing the scientific rigour of the research. The decision to focus on a specific subset of new family, the non-conjugal (dyadic) family, was also conducive to building tighter arguments and avoid generalised assumptions relating to situations that warrant separate analysis.

Based on the inquiry contained in Part II, a few inferences can be drawn. It is likely that Canada is the jurisdiction which has the greatest potential to introduce legal protections for non-conjugal families. In Canada, there is a robust equality framework. At the constitutional level, despite the non-linearity and unpredictability of the equality test, cohabiting couples and same-sex families have gained nearly all marital defaults in common law provinces well before other countries. This outcome derives from adopting an approach to new family recognition which relies on function rather than formalities. Despite the government having discarded the issue of non-conjugal couples' recognition in 2002, such an approach holds special promise for the further expansion of family definitions. The focus on actual attributes and the ability to achieve the purpose of a given benefit/law are compelling lines of argument to overcome stereotypes around family. With their avoidance of value-laden evaluations as to what family is and their focus on actual attributes, functional lines of argument are hard to rebut. This optimistic prediction (in terms of Canada being a receptive place for the expansion of notions of family) is further buttressed by the dynamic interplay between the equality jurisprudence and human rights fora. Human rights commissions have been powerful allies of same-sex couples. They have carried out intense lobbying activity both inside the courtroom and before the general public well before same-sex couples gained social acceptance. Tellingly, in so doing, the federal human rights commission (the Canadian Human Rights Commission) has advocated in its annual reports a notion of family which, at first glance, already covers non-conjugal families.

For all these reasons, Canada in the future might be a receptive place for non-conjugal couples' demands. Yet, this jurisdiction has also its limits. The most visible of these is not unique to Canada, but is shared to an extent with the US. I refer here to the doctrine reluctant to upholding affirmative entitlements, especially via constitutional litigation. This aspect is nested within larger conceptions of both the constitution and constitutionalism which the two countries adopt. Liberal constitutionalism – to which the Canadian and US experiences can be ascribed – were born out of a concern that the people should be protected from excessive state intrusion into their intimate and private sphere. According to this view, liberty is the fundamental value of the legal culture. The liberty-centred doctrine has morphed into a conspicuous mistrust towards claims that aim at obtaining affirmative entitlements. While this mistrust is more sharply manifested in the US, its legacy is also visible in Canada, where the Supreme Court routinely rejects arguments which endeavour to introduce entitlements that are costly for the state (eg, a pension or means-tested welfare benefits). Likewise, the doctrine has informed the concept of equality, which is seen as an expression of liberty and thus 'freedom from' discrimination. Therefore, even though litigants must pursue equality-based lines of reasoning in Canada, they must recall that conceptions of equality are strongly influenced by the liberal (instead of socio-democratic) roots of the Canadian Constitution.[1]

By contrast, the subsequent phase of constitutionalism to which continental European jurisdictions belong is less adverse to introducing costly entitlements as a matter of constitutional law. European constitutions include socio-democratic rights and take on a host of positive duties toward citizens that go well beyond the protection of liberty. In this sense, such jurisdictions would pose a less insurmountable wall to arguments the acceptance of which implies an increase in public expenditures. However, this book has only obliquely focused on domestic jurisdictions. Its two objects of analysis were the EU and the ECHR framework. These systems are also cautious when it comes to extending costly benefits, although

[1] This conclusion is consistent with the analysis in JQ Whitman, 'The Two Western Cultures of Privacy: Dignity versus Liberty' (2004) 113 *Yale Law Journal* 1151.

to a different degree and for distinct reasons. The principal reason for this is that they are not full-fledged domestic jurisdictions, but only derivative meta-national projects. As to the different degree of self-restraint each of the two systems displays, the ECHR system is extremely wary in terms of intruding into matters of social engineering, such as what a pension system should look like. By contrast, the EU, as an advanced supranational project and model of regional integration, is more incisive when it comes to applying EU law to matters involving financial interests. Hence, detecting the European organisation which is better suited to widening the coverage of benefits involving financial interests is straightforward: it is the EU.

In addition to the protection of public resources, a ground on which Western jurisdictions have opposed the recognition of new families, especially same-sex couples, is morals and tradition. It is worth noting that such interests have less and less purchase in the West, especially the variation involving morals. The case of the US is emblematic in this regard. Starting from the *Lawrence* decision, the US Supreme Court has stressed that when state action is animated by a desire to force the state's own moral views on the people, this interest would be rejected as unconstitutional. This contention was embraced in *Obergefell*, which was a landmark decision leading to the legalisation of same-sex marriage. The ECtHR has displayed a more cautious and deferential approach to the issue – and understandably so, as it is an international court. It has routinely upheld the interest in the preservation of the special status of marriage. Yet, tellingly, it has also clarified that such an interest cannot be utilised to justify all unfair outcomes, such as drawing distinctions between legitimate children and those born out of wedlock. In other words, while it 'concedes' that such an interest is legitimate, the key 'battlefield' where it will decide whether the distinction passes muster is the proportionality stage. At this subsequent stage, it checks whether there is a rational connection between means and purpose, and whether the less restrictive means has been employed to achieve the purpose. By contrast, a thus-framed interest is hardly traceable in the Canadian context. The more robust equality framework, as applied by courts, might have discouraged federal and provincial governments from pursuing the protection of morals or a traditional understanding of family as a state objective. Popular interests were instead the aforementioned protection of the public purse, the respect of choice (of those who wish not to marry) and the modulation of different legal regimes (eg, marital and non-marital regimes).

In all jurisdictions, a grounds-based anti-discrimination approach is adopted. The issue thus revolves around understanding whether non-conjugal families could benefit from this approach or fall through its cracks. Non-conjugal families can benefit from the constitutionally protected marital status ground in Canada, while a subset should seek to introduce a new 'analogous' ground – that of family status. The inclusion of the marital status ground at the constitutional level amongst the list of prohibited grounds is one reason for the pervasiveness of the Supreme Court's scrutiny over government decisions on family policy. No such ground is present in the US or in the EU, while its incidence in the context of the ECHR is only marginal. In the latter context, while the Court has sparingly referred to a prohibition to discriminate based on marital status to protect children born out of wedlock or unmarried fathers, its application to non-marital families, including non-conjugal families (like the two Burden sisters), has not yet occurred. So far, the Court has taken a formalistic approach to the issue, drawing a circular distinction between those who can enter into family status (marriage or civil partnerships) and those who cannot. By contrast, the case of Canada demonstrates how taking marital status discrimination seriously is key in terms of advancing the recognition of new families. In Canada, functional lines of reasoning have informed the application of the prohibition to discriminate based on marital status, thereby greatly enhancing the legal status of both unmarried couples and same-sex couples.

The most suitable ground for discrimination in Europe is marital status. This requires claimants to make an effort to overcome the aforementioned formalist approach to the construction of the ground before the ECtHR. In the EU, the required effort is even greater. Structural limits prevent the Court of Justice from more incisively employing lines of arguments typically associated with marital status discrimination, the main one being a lack of competence of the EU over substantive family law matters. A case law analysis does not offer an optimistic picture. Not even in the context of the EU staff was the Court ready to make an opening regarding the possibility of protecting non-conjugal families. Its approach in this area could have been more courageous since the treatment of EU staff does not affect domestic family laws. Truth is that the Court has not adjudicated a case involving a non-conjugal couple. Yet, what it has done is emphasizing that same-sex couples merit protection because they are not *non-conjugal*'.

The second problem is that the Court of Justice's case law requires linking marital status to another prohibited ground in order to enjoy its protection (eg, sex or sexual orientation). Same-sex couples, for instance, only managed to obtain increased protection in light of the prohibition to discriminate based on sexual orientation. No comparable ground is available for non-conjugal couples. In all jurisdictions, I have made the argument that non-conjugal couples should not invoke sex or sexual orientation.[2] Sexual orientation would convey the misplaced idea that non-conjugal couples are asexual. Sex – a ground that same-sex couples successfully invoked at the beginning of their equality litigation – is not engaged; it is no longer a disqualifying condition to enter into a family regime in the US, Canada and most European jurisdictions. This aspect is also relevant to constitutional litigation in the US, where in the absence of marital status, the fact that they cannot invoke sex or sexual orientation entails that a deferential rational basis standard is triggered in the context of equality-based arguments.

In relation to the strategy that non-conjugal families can follow in practice, all systems under examination warrant adopting what we called an area-specific approach. Through this approach, the parties seek access to the benefits of a

[2] See esp ch 3, s 4.I.

specific legal protection (eg, a pension, employment benefit). Only at a later stage could they inductively move from the specific to the general, as same-sex couples have in Canada and in Europe. Especially notable is the possibility within the ECHR framework to apply *Oliari*-like lines of reasoning to argue at a later time – once more area-specific legal protections have been obtained – that non-conjugal couples deserve recognition through a 'specific legal framework', such as a registered partnership.

The issue of the venue is also highly context-specific. The situation in Canada and the US attests to this. In the US, it seems that family law litigation is more promising. Unmarried couples gained legal recognition through this avenue. Especially suitable are the functional lines of reasoning courts employ when it comes to redressing severe emotional distress, compensating parties for the wrongful death of a family member or more generally in the context of common law torts. The case law analysis reveals how non-conjugal couples are already covered by the family definitions as shaped therein. Thus, despite scholarship paying most of its attention to constitutional litigation as the key avenue for the recognition of new families, the analysis suggests that its gaze should be redirected to (the overlooked potential of) family law litigation. The analysis also suggests that only in very limited circumstances would constitutional litigation be a suitable path in the US, namely when the case in question involves close relatives. Close relatives could profit from their bond falling under the protection of the due process clause, especially if they qualify as an 'extended family household'. The US Supreme Court has indeed defined extended families as 'equally venerable and equally deserving of constitutional recognition' as the nuclear family. A second option is the equality tack. Here, however, the 'hope' is that the rational basis standard which applies to non-conjugal families is not applied in an excessively deferential manner.[3]

By contrast, in Canada, a twofold strategy working at the level of human rights and constitutional litigation is likely to have more success. The court decisions grappling with the concept of conjugality demonstrate that family law litigation was also potentially suitable.[4] However, past cases of litigation involving same-sex couples suggest that the focus should be on constitutional arguments and arguments grounded in human rights codes. On the one hand, human rights commissions are well positioned to mould public sentiments and persuade both courts and legislators to expand definitions of family. They have also led to expand major employment-related benefits and 'services', such as pensions on a case-by-case basis. On the other hand, constitutional litigation has proven especially effective in terms of enlarging notions of family in the relevant statutes conferring legal benefits, first by including within their scope common law spouses and then same-sex couples.

[3] *Moore v City of East Cleveland*, 431 US 494, 504 (1977).
[4] See ch 4, s 4.I.ii.

Europe deserves an analysis of its own. As was argued in Chapter 6, in matters involving financial interests, the EU seems to be at better positioned to tackle the invisibility of non-conjugal families. However, several constraints exist, amongst which are the absence of a suitable doctrine of marital status for non-conjugal families and the absence of EU competence over substantive family law matters. In light of the current allocation of competences, the EU adopts family definitions that are parasitic on those of Member States. Recently, however, the EU has extended an autonomous definition of 'spouse' to the area of freedom of movement. Does this open the door to the possibility of a further extension of the autonomous conception of family to a larger set of families? Only future developments will tell.

The ECHR system is particularly advanced as an international system, especially in light of the strong enforcement mechanism it adopts, which includes an individual complaint mechanism. It is also a system that is specialised in the protection of human rights and has built up an increasingly solid reputation over the last few decades. However, at the same time, judgments based on the ECHR are mostly symbolic and in, the face of persistent violations, the Council of Europe has not managed to tackle them with any effectiveness; ultimately, the Court always grants a certain 'margin of appreciation' to the states. On balance, yet, it seems that the Court has had a positive impact on the innovation of domestic family regimes in fields as varied as the recognition of same-sex and the rights of illegitimate children. Thus, despite the potential limits outlined above, the ECHR remains the privileged site in Europe in terms of achieving legal precedents in favour of non-conjugal couples.

Tying together the various chapters in this volume it is possible to conclude that Western states have devoted quite an obsessive level of attention to the family. The rich content analysis of judicial opinions, doctrinal advancements, and constitutional and subconstitutional rules illuminates how the family is the key referent for a host of economic and social policies. Further, it shows how the family is loaded with social expectations and is a repository of values and (sometimes radically different) views of society. Individuals' own aspirations and objectives got somewhat lost in the process as states made inroads into family life. However, this book casts doubt on the inevitability and irreversibility of this process. It helps us to navigate our way through a narrative where the state's control over our most intimate decisions is taken for granted. A different story can be told and the lawyer can be the storyteller. Contrary to common credence depicting law as inherently unsuitable, law can fruitfully accommodate the stunning diversity of modern families. The route is uphill, of course, as the need in Part II to focus only on a subset of new family, non-conjugal families, and on carefully tailored legal strategies attests to. But it is nonetheless worth the effort: in the end, people's lives and decisions around the way they should unfold are at stake.

REFERENCES

Aloni, E, 'Registering Relationships' (2013) 87 *Tulane Law Review* 573

——. 'Deprivative Recognition' (2014) 61 *UCLA Law Review* 1276

——. 'The Puzzle of Family Law Pluralism' (2016) 39 *Harvard Journal of Law and Gender* 317

Alpa, G, *Status e capacità. La costruzione giuridica delle differenze individuali* (Rome/Bari, Laterza, 1993)

Aviram, H and GM Leachman, 'The Future of Polyamorous Marriage: Lessons from the Marriage Equality Struggle' (2015) 38 *Harvard Journal of Gender and Law* 269

Backer, P, '*Burden v Burden*: The Grand Chamber of the ECtHR Adopts a Restrictive Approach on the Question of Discrimination' (2008) 4 *British Tax Review* 329

Baines, B, 'Using the Canadian Charter of Rights and Freedoms to Constitute Women' in B Baines and R Rubio-Marin (eds), *The Gender of Constitutional Jurisprudence* (Cambridge, Cambridge University Press, 2005)

Bakht, N and L Collins, 'Are You My Mother? Co-parenting in a Non-conjugal Family' (2018) 31 *Canadian Journal of Family Law* 105

Barberis, M, 'Eguaglianza, ragionevolezza e diritti' (2013) *Rivista di filosofia del diritto 191*

Barcellona, P, 'Famiglia (dir. civ.)' in *Enciclopedia del diritto*, vol XVI (Milan, Giuffrè, 1967)

Barker, N, 'Sex and the Civil Partnership Act: The Future of (Non)Conjugality?' (2006) 14 *Feminist Legal Studies* 241

——. 'After the Wedding, What Next? Conservatism and Conjugality' in N Barker and D Monk (eds), *From Civil Partnership to Same-Sex Marriage: Interdisciplinary Reflections* (Abingdon, Routledge, 2015)

——. 'Rethinking Conjugality as the Basis for Family Recognition' (2016) 6 *Onati Socio-Legal Series* 1249

Bawin-Legros, B, 'Intimacy and the New Sentimental Order' (2004) 52 *Current Sociology* 241

Beck, U and E Beck-Gernsheim, *Individualization: Institutionalized Individualism and its Social and Political Consequences* (London, Sage, 2002)

Benvenisti, E, 'Margin of Appreciation, Consensus, and Universal Standards' (1999) 31 *New York University Journal of International Law & Politics* 483

Berlant, L and M Warner, 'Sex in Public' (1998) 24 *Critical Theory* 457

Bernstein Sycamore, M, *That's Revolting!: Queer Strategies for Resisting Assimilation*, revised edn (New York, Soft Skull Press, 2008)

Blackstone, W, *Commentaries on the Law of England* (Chicago, University of Chicago Press, 1979 [1725])

Blichner, LC and A Molander, 'Mapping Juridification' (2008) 14 *European Law Journal* 36

Blocher, J, 'What State Constitutional Law Can Tell Us about the Federal Constitution' (2011) 115 *Penn State Law Review* 1035

Boele-Woelki, K and D Martiny, 'The Commission on European Family Law (CEFL) and its Principles of European Family Law Regarding Parental Responsibilities' (2007) 8 *ERA Forum* 125

Bonini Baraldi, M and M Oderkerk, 'Olanda' in F Brunetta D'Usseaux (ed), *Il Diritto di Famiglia nell'Unione Europea* (Padua, Cedam, 2005)

Borrillo, D, 'The "Pacte Civil de Solidarité"' in France: Midway between Marriage and Cohabitation' in R Wintemute and M Andenas (eds), *The Legal Recognition of Same-Sex Partnerships: A Study of National, European and International Law* (Oxford, Hart Publishing, 2001)

Boulouis, J, 'Famille et droit constitutionnel' in *Études offertes à Pierre Kaiser*, vol 1 (Aix-en-Provence, Presses Universitaires d'Aix-Marseille, 1979)
Bradley Kar, R, 'Transformational Marriage' in R Fretwell Wilson (ed), *The Contested Place of Religion in Family Life* (Cambridge, Cambridge University Press, 2018)
Brennan Jr, WJ, 'State Constitutions and the Protection of Individual Rights' (1977) 90 *Harvard Law Review* 489
Brook, K, 'Cameos from the Margins of Conjugality' in R Leckey (ed), *After Legal Equality: Family, Sex, Kinship* (Abingdon, Routledge, 2015)
Budgeon, S and S Roseneil, 'Editors' Introduction: Beyond the Conventional Family' (2004) 52 *Current Sociology* 127
Butler, J, *Gender Trouble: Feminism and the Subversion of Identity* (London, Routledge, 1990)
Buttigieg, E, 'The Definition of "Family" under EU Law' in PG Xuereb (ed), *The Family, Law, Religion and Society in the European Union and Malta* (Msida, European Documentation and Research Centre, University of Malta, 2006)
Caballero, SS, 'Unmarried Cohabiting Couples before the European Court of Human Rights: Parity with Marriage?' (2004) 11 *Columbia Journal of European Law* 151
Caggia F and A Zoppini, 'Art 29' in R Bifulco, A Celotto and M Olivetti (eds), *Commentario alla Costituzione*, vol I (Turin, Giappichelli, 2006)
Cain, PA, 'Legal Guidance for Same-Sex Couples Considering Marriage' (2016) 35 *ABA Tax Times* 1
Cesarini Sforza, W, *Il diritto dei privati* (Milan, Giuffrè, 1963 [1929])
Challborn. R and L Harder, 'Sex and the genuine marriage:consummation and conjugality in Canadian citizenship', (2019) 23 Citizenship Studies 407
Chambers, D, *A Sociology of Family Life: Change and Diversity in Intimate Relations* (Cambridge, Polity Press, 2012)
Chemerinsky, E, 'Substantive Due Process' (1999) 15 *Touro Law Review* 1501
Cloots, E, 'National Identity, Constitutional Identity, and Sovereignty in the EU' (2016) 2 *Netherlands Journal of Legal Philosophy* 82
Constant, B, 'De la liberté des Anciens comparée à celle des Modernes' in *Collection complète des ouvrages*, vol IV, pt 7 (Paris, Béchet Libraire, 1820)
Cossman, B and B Ryder, 'What is Marriage-Like Like? The Irrelevance of Conjugality' (2001) 18 *Canadian Journal of Family Law* 269
Cover, R, 'Nomos and Narrative' (1983) 97 *Harvard Law Review* 4
Croce, M, *The Politics of Juridification* (London, Routledge, 2018)
Curry-Sumner, I, 'All's Well That Ends Registered?' in *The Substantive and Private International Law Aspects of Non-marital Registered Relationships in Europe* (Antwerp, Intersentia, 2003)
D'Onorio, JB, 'La protection constitutionnelle du mariage et de la famille en Europe' (1988) *Revue trimestrielle de droit civil* 1
De Vries, S, H de Waele and M-P Granger (eds), *Civil Rights and EU Citizenship: Challenges at the Crossroads of the European, National and Private Spheres* (Cheltenham, Edward Elgar, 2016)
Den Otter, RC (ed), *Beyond Same-Sex Marriage: Perspectives on Marital Possibilities* (Lanham, MD, Lexington Books, 2016)
Di Rosa, G, 'Famiglia e matrimonio: consolidate tradizioni giuridiche, innovative discipline interne e attuale sistema comunitario' in B Montanari (ed), *La costruzione dell'identità europea: sicurezza collettiva, libertà individuali e modelli di regolazione sociale* (Turin, Giappichelli, 2013)
Diduck, A, *Law's Families* (London, Butterworths, 2003)
——. 'Introduction' in A Diduck (ed), *Marriage and Cohabitation: Regulating Intimacy, Affection and Care* (Aldershot, Ashgate, 2008)
——. 'Autonomy and Vulnerability in Family Law: The Missing Link' in J Wallbank and J Herring (eds), *Vulnerabilities, Care and Family Law* (London, Routledge, 2013)
Dienes, CT, 'To Feed the Hungry: Judicial Retrenchment in Welfare Adjudication' (1970) 58 *California Law Review* 555
Draghici, C, 'Adult Children and Elderly Parents in Strasburg Proceedings: A Misconstrued Approach to "Family Life"' (2018) 32 *International Journal of Law, Policy, and the Family* 42
Eekelaar, J, *Family Law and Social Policy* (London, Weidenfeld & Nicholson, 1984)

Eggermont, S, *De juridische bescherming van private relaties* (Antwerp, Intersentia, 2016)
Eichner, M, 'Principles of the Law of Relationships among Adults' (2007) 41 *Family Law Quarterly* 433
Ertman, MM, 'Marital Contracting in the Post-Windsor World' (2015) 42 *Florida State University Law Review* 479
Eskridge, WN, 'Family Law Pluralism: The Guided-Choice Regime of Menus, Default Rules, and Override Rules' (2012) 100 *Georgetown Law Journal* 1884
Eskridge, WN and ND Hunter, *Sexuality, Gender, and the Law*, 2nd edn (New York, Foundation Press, 2006)
European Union Agency for Fundamental Rights and Council of Europe, *Handbook on European Non-discrimination Law* (Luxembourg, Publications Office of the European Union, 2018)
Fallon, RH, The Dynamic Constitution: An Introduction to American Constitutional Law and Practice (Cambridge, Cambridge University Press, 2004)
Faraday, F, 'One Step Forward, Two Steps Back? Substantive Equality, Systemic Discrimination and Pay Equity at the Supreme Court of Canada' (2020) 94 *Supreme Court Law Review* (forthcoming)
Feinberg, JR, 'Avoiding Marriage Tunnel Vision' (2013) 88 *Tulane Law Review* 259
Fenwick, H, 'An ECHR Right to Access a Registered Partnership?' in JM Scherpe and A Hayward (eds), *The Future of Registered Partnerships: Family Recognition Beyond Marriage?* (Cambridge, Intersentia, 2017)
Ferrando, G, 'Il Contributo della Corte europea dei Diritti dell'Uomo' in MC Andrini (ed), *Un nuovo diritto di famiglia europeo* (Padua, Cedam, 2007)
Ferreres Comella, V, 'The European Model of Constitutional Review of Legislation: Toward Decentralization' (2004) 2 *International Journal of Constitutional Law* 461
——. *Constitutional Courts and Democratic Values: A European Perspective* (New Haven, Yale University Press, 2009)
Ferreri, S, Falsi amici nelle corti. Leggere le sentenze di Common Law evitando le trappole linguistiche (Turin, Giappichelli, 2019)
Fineman, MA, 'Masking Dependency: The Political Role of Family Rhetoric' (1995) 81 *Virginia Law Review* 2181
——. *The Neutered Mother, The Sexual Family and Other Twentieth Century Tragedies* (New York, Routledge, 1995)
——. 'The Vulnerable Subject and the Responsive State' (2010) 60 *Emory Law Journal* 251
——. 'Feminism, Masculinities and Multiple Identities' (2013) 13 *Nevada Law Review* 619
Foucault, M, 'The Birth of Biopolitics' in P Rabinow (ed), *Michel Foucault: Ethics, Subjectivity, and Truth*, vol 1 (New York, The New Press, 1997)
——. *The Will to Knowledge: The History of Sexuality*, vol 1, trans R Hurley (New York, Pantheon Books, 1998)
Friedman, WG, 'Some Reflections on Status and Freedom' in RA Newman (ed), *Essays in Jurisprudence in Honour of Roscoe Pound* (Indianapolis, New York, Bobbs-Merrill Co Inc, 1962)
Fundamentals of Human Rights Law in Canada (Toronto, Carswell, 2017)
Garrison, M, 'Reviving Marriage: Could We? Should We?' (2008) 10 *Journal of Law and Family Studies* 279
Giacomelli, L, *Ripensare l'eguaglianza. Gli effetti collaterali della tutela antidiscriminatoria* (Turin, Giappichelli, 2018)
Giddens, A, *The Transformation of Intimacy: Sexuality, Love and Eroticism in Modern Societies* (Cambridge, Polity Press, 1992)
Goldberg, SB, 'Why Marriage?' in M Garrison and ES Scott (eds), *Marriage at the Crossroads: The Brave New World of Twenty-First Century Families* (Cambridge, Cambridge University Press, 2012)
Grande, E and L Pes, Più cuori e una capanna: Il poliamore come istituzione (Turin, Giappichelli, 2018)
Grammond, S, *Identity Captured by Law: Membership in Canada's Indigenous Peoples and Linguistic Minorities* (Montreal, McGill-Queen's University Press, 2009)
Graycar, R and J Millbank, 'From Functional Family to Spinster Sisters: Australia's Distinctive Path to Relationship Recognition' (2007) 24 *Washington University Journal of Law & Policy* 121

Greer, S, 'What's Wrong with the European Convention on Human Rights?' (2008) 30 *Human Rights Quarterly* 680

Grgic, A et al, *The Right to Property under the European Convention on Human Rights: A Guide to the Implementation of the European Convention on Human Rights and its Protocols* (Strasbourg, Council of Europe, 2007)

Grillo, R, *The Family in Question: Immigrant and Ethnic Minorities in Multicultural Europe* (Amsterdam, Amsterdam University Press, 2008)

Gross, A, 'The *Burden* of Conjugality' in E Brems (ed), *Diversity and European Human Rights: Rewriting Judgments of the ECHR* (Cambridge, Cambridge University Press, 2003)

Grossi, P, *Società, Diritto, Stato. Un recupero per il diritto* (Milan, Giuffrè, 2006)

Gusmano, B, 'Subvertir la heteronorma a través de la amistad. Convivencia y redes de cuidado en la precariedad' (2018) 14 *TransVersos* 90

Halley, J, 'Recognition, Rights, Regulation, Normalization: Rhetorics of Justification of the Same-Sex Marriage Debate' in R Wintemute and M Andenas (eds), *The Legal Recognition of Same-Sex Partnerships: A Study of National, European and International Law* (Oxford, Hart Publishing, 2001)

——. 'Behind the Law of Marriage (I): From Status/Contract to the Marriage System' (2010) 6 *Unbound* 1

Halley, J and K Rittich, 'Critical Directions in Comparative Family Law' (2010) 58 *American Journal of Comparative Law* 753

Halley, J et al, 'From the International to the Local in Feminist Legal Responses to Rape, Prostitution/Sex Work and Sex Trafficking: Four Studies in Contemporary Governance Feminism' (2006) 29 *Harvard Journal of Law and Gender* 335

Halsaa, B, S Roseneil and S Sümer (eds), *Remaking Citizenship in Multicultural Europe, Women's Movement, Gender and Diversity* (Basingstoke, Palgrave Macmillan, 2012)

Hayek, FA, *Law, Legislation and Liberty*, vol 1 (London, Routledge, 1998 [1973])

Heath, S, 'Peer-Shared Households, Quasi-communes and Neo-tribes' (2004) 52 *Current Sociology* 161

Helfer, LR, 'Consensus, Coherence and the European Convention on Human Rights' (1993) 26 *Cornell International Law Journal* 133

Herring, J, *Caring and the Law* (Oxford, Hart Publishing, 2013)

——. *Vulnerable Adults and the Law* (Oxford, Oxford University Press, 2016)

Hervey, T, 'Migrant Workers and Their Families in the European Union: The Pervasive Market Ideology of Community Law' in J Shaw and G More (eds), *New Legal Dynamics of European Union* (Oxford, Clarendon Press, 1996)

Hirschl, R, 'The Judicialization of Politics' in RE Goodin, *The Oxford Handbook of Political Science* (Oxford, Oxford University Press, 2011)

Hogg, PW, *Constitutional Law of Canada*, 5th edn (Toronto, Carswell, 2007)

Holland, W, 'Intimate Relationships in the New Millennium: The Assimilation of Marriage and Cohabitation?' (2000) 17 *Canadian Journal of Family Law* 114

Holmes Jr, OW, 'The Path of the Law' (1897) 10 *Harvard Law Review* 457

Infanti, AC, 'Decentralizing Family: An Inclusive Proposal for Individual Tax Filing in the United States' (2010) *Utah Law Review* 605

Kaesling, K, 'Family Life and EU Citizenship: The Discovery of the Substance of the EU Citizens' Rights and its Genuine Enjoyment' in K Boele-Woelki, N Dethloff and W Gephart (eds), *Family Law and Culture in Europe* (Cambridge, Intersentia, 2014)

Kahng, L, 'The Not-So-Merry Wives of Windsor: The Taxation of Women in Same-Sex Marriages' (2016) 101 *Cornell Law Review* 325

Kavanagh, A, 'Participation and Judicial Review: A Reply to Jeremy Waldron' (2003) 22 *Law and Philosophy* 451

Kennedy, D, 'Savigny's Family/Patrimony Distinction and its Place in the Global Genealogy of Kennedy, D, 'The Political Stakes in the "Merely Technical" Issues of Contract Law' (2001) 1 *European Review of Private Law* 7

Classical Legal Thought' (2010) 58 *American Journal of Comparative Law* 811

——. 'Three Globalizations of Law and Legal Thought: 1850–2000' in DM Trubek and A Santos (eds), *The New Law and Economic Development: A Critical Appraisal* (Cambridge, Cambridge University Press, 2006)

Kornhauser, ME, 'Love, Money and the IRS: Family, Income Sharing and the Joint Return' (1993) 45 *Hastings Law Journal* 63

Krause, HD, 'Comparative Family Law: Past Traditions Battle Future Trends and Vice Versa' in M Reimann and R Zimmermann (eds), *The Oxford Handbook Of Comparative Law* (Oxford, Oxford University Press, 2008)

Kumm, M, 'Who is Afraid of the Total Constitution? Constitutional Rights as Principles and the Constitutionalization of Private Law' (2016) 7 *German Law Journal* 341

Lamont, R, 'Registered Partnerships in European Union Law' in JM Scherpe and A Hayward (eds), *The Future of Registered Partnerships: Family Recognition Beyond Marriage?* (Cambridge, Intersentia, 2017)

Laslett, P (ed), *Household and Family in Past Time* (Cambridge, Cambridge University Press, 1972)

Leckey, R, 'Chosen Discrimination' (2002) 18 *Supreme Court Law Review* 445

——. 'Families in the Eyes of the Law: Contemporary Challenges and the Grip of the Past' (2009) 15 *IRPP Choices* 1

——. 'L'enrichissement injustifié, l'union de fait et l'emprunt à la common law dans le droit mixte du Québec' (2018) 59 *Les Cahiers de droit* 585

Lee Badgett, MV, 'Predicting Partnership Rights: Applying the European Experience in the United States' (2005) 17 *Yale Journal of Law and Feminism* 71

Lessard, H, 'Charter Gridlock: Equality Formalism and Marriage Fundamentalism' in S Rodgers and S McIntyre (eds), *Diminishing Returns: Inequality and the Canadian Charter of Rights and Freedoms* (Markham, LexisNexis Canada, 2006)

Lévi-Strauss, C, *The Elementary Structures of Kinship* (Boston, MA, Beacon Press, 1969)

Levin, I, 'Living Apart Together: A New Family Form' (2004) 52 *Current Sociology* 223

Levy, S, 'The Relational Self and the Right to Give Care' (2006) 28 *New Political Science* 547

Llewellyn, KN, 'Behind the Law of Divorce: I' (1932) 32 *Columbia Law Review* 1281

Macdonald, RA, 'Here, There … and Everywhere – Theorizing Legal Pluralism; Theorizing Jacques Vanderlinden' in N Kasirer (ed), *Étudier et enseigner le droit: hier, aujourd'hui et demain – Études offertes à Jacques Vanderlinden* (Montreal, Éditions Yvon Blais, 2006)

Macdonald, RA and T McMorrow, 'Wedding a Critical Legal Pluralism to the Laws of Close Adult Relationships' (2007) 1 *EJLS* 319

Magnussen, A-M and A Banasiak, 'Juridification: Disrupting the Relationship between Law and Politics?' (2013) 19 *European Law Journal* 325

Marella, MR, 'Critical Family Law' (2011) 19 *American University Journal of Gender, Social Policy and the Law* 721

Martens, P, 'Perplexity of the National Judge Faced with the Vagaries of European Consensus' in European Court of Human Rights, *Dialogues between Judges* (Strasbourg, Council of Europe, 2008)

McAllister, DM, 'Charter Remedies and Jurisdiction to Grant Them: The Evolution of Section 24(1) and Section 52(1)' (2005) 25 *Supreme Court Law Review* 62

Metz, T, *Untying the Knot: Marriage, the State, and the Case for their Divorce* (Princeton, Princeton University Press, 2010)

Michaels, R, 'The Functional Method of Comparative Law' in M Reimann and R Zimmermann (eds), *The Oxford Handbook Of Comparative Law* (Oxford, Oxford University Press, 2008)

Miles, J, 'Unmarried Cohabitation in a European Perspective' in JM Scherpe (ed), *European Family Law Volume III: Family Law in a European Perspective* (Cheltenham, Edward Elgar, 2016)

Mummé, C, 'At the Crossroads in Discrimination Law: How the Human Rights Codes Overtook the Charter in Canadian Government Services Cases' (2012) 9 *Journal of Law and Equality*

Nader, L, 'A User Theory of Law' (1984) 38 *Southwestern Law Journal* 951

Nicola, F, 'Family Law Exceptionalism in Comparative Law' (2010) 58 *American Journal of Comparative Law* 777

Nierobisz, A, M Searl and C Théroux, 'Human Rights Commissions and Public Policy: The Role of the Canadian Human Rights Commission in Advancing Sexual Orientation Equality Rights in Canada' (2008) 51 *Canadian Journal of Public Administration* 239
Nijhawan, A, 'Alberta's New Adult Interdependent Relationships Act' (2003) 22 *Estates, Trusts and Pensions Journal* 57
Nussbaum, M, 'A Right to Marry?' (2010) 98 *California Law Review* 667
Oliphant, BJ, 'Bobbitt's Paradise: Canadian Constitutional Interpretation and Public Meaning Originalism' (2017) 31 *DPCE Online* 617
Oliver, P, P Macklem and N Des Rosiers, 'Introduction' in P Oliver, P Macklem and N Des Rosiers, The Oxford Handbook of the Canadian Constitution (Oxford, Oxford University Press, 2017)
Örücü, E, 'Developing Comparative Law' in E Örücü and D Nelken (eds), *Comparative Law: A Handbook* (Oxford, Hart Publishing, 2007)
Palazzo, N, 'The Strange Pairing: Building Alliances between Queer Activists and Conservative Groups to Recognize New Families' (2018) 25 *Michigan Journal of Gender and Law* 161
——. 'Equality in Canada: A Tale of Non-normative Groups Struggling with Grounds of Discrimination' (2020) 10 *Oñati Socio-Legal Series* 88
——. 'The EU Family: Is Marital Status Emerging as a Prohibited Ground of Discrimination?' in E Bernard, M Cresp and M Ho-Dac (eds), *Connaissez-vous la famille européenne ?* (Brussels, Larcier/Bruylant, 2020)
Payne, JD and MA Payne, *Canadian Family Law*, 6th edn (Toronto, Irwin Law, 2015)
Perlin, AS, '*United States Department of Agriculture v Moreno*: The "Red Herring" of Social Welfare' (1974) 23 *DePaul Law Review* 1485
Pinelli, C, 'The Combination of Negative with Positive Constitutionalism in Europe' (2011) 13 *European Journal of Law Reform* 31
Plummer, K, 'Intimate Citizenship in an Unjust World' in M Romero and E Margolis (eds), *The Blackwell Companion to Social Inequalities* (Malden, MA, Blackwell Publishing, 2005)
Polikoff, ND, *Beyond (Straight and Gay) Marriage: Valuing All Families under the Law* (Boston, Beacon Press, 2009)
Probert, R, *The Changing Legal Regulation of Cohabitation* (Cambridge, Cambridge University Press, 2012)
Randall Kelso, R, 'Standards of Review under the Equal Protection Clause and Related Constitutional Doctrines Protecting Individual Rights: The "Base Plus Six" Model and Modern Supreme Court Practice' (2002) 4 *Journal of Constitutional Law* 225
Rault, W, 'Is the Civil Solidarity Pact the Future of Marriage? The Several Meanings of the French Civil Union' (2019) 33 *International Journal of Law, Policy and the Family* 139
Reece, H, 'Leaping without Looking' in R Leckey (ed), *After Legal Equality: Family, Sex, Kinship* (London, Routledge, 2015)
Reid, K, *A Practitioner's Guide to the European Convention on Human Rights*, 4th edn (London, Sweet & Maxwell, 2012)
Rescigno, P, 'Situazione e status nell'esperienza del diritto' (1973) *Rivista di Diritto Civile* 211
Research Division, European Court of Human Rights, *Guide on Article 8 of the European Convention of Human Rights* (Strasbourg, Council of Europe, 2018)
Romano, S, L'ordinamento giuridico (Firenze, Nuova Biblioteca, 1977 [1918])
Rosenberg, GN, *The Hollow Hope: Can Courts Bring about Social Change?*, 2nd edn (Chicago, University of Chicago Press, 2008)
Rosenbury, LA, 'Friends with Benefits' (2007) 106 *Michigan Law Review* 189
Roseneil, S, 'Why We Should Care about Friends: An Argument for Queering the Care Imaginary in Social Policy' (2004) 3 *Social Policy and Society* 409
Rosenfeld, M, 'Constitutional Adjudication in Europe and the United States: Paradoxes and Contrasts' (2004) 2 *International Journal of Constitutional Law* 655
Ryan, KA, 'EITC As Income (In)Stability?' (2014) 15 *Florida Tax Review* 583

Ryder, B, 'The Strange Double Life of Canadian Equality Rights' (2013) 62 *Supreme Court Law Review* 261

Šarćević, P, 'Cohabitation without Marriage: The Yugoslavian Experience' (1981) 29 *American Journal of Comparative Law* 315

Scherpe, JM, 'Legal Recognition of Same-Sex Couples in Europe and the Role of the European Court of Human Rights' (2013) 10 *Equal Rights Review* 83

——. *European Family Law Volume IV: The Present and Future of European Family Law* (Cheltenham, Edward Elgar, 2016)

Scherpe, JM and A Hayward (eds), *The Future of Registered Partnerships: Family Recognition Beyond Marriage?* (Cambridge, Intersentia, 2017)

Schmitt, C, *Political Theology: Four Chapters on the Concept of Sovereignty*, trans George Schwab (Chicago, University of Chicago Press, 1985)

Schneider, CE, 'The Channeling Function in Family Law' (1992) 20 *Hofstra Law Review* 495

Schrama, W, 'Marriage and Alternative Status Relationships in the Netherlands' in J Eekelaar and R George (eds), *Routledge Handbook of Family Law and Policy* (New York, Routledge, 2014)

——. 'National Report: The Netherlands' in K Boele-Woelki, C Mol and E van Gelder (eds), *European Family Law in Action Volume V: Informal Relationships* (Cambridge, Intersentia, 2015)

Scott, E and R Scott, 'From Contract to Status: Collaboration and the Evolution of Novel Family Relationships' (2015) 115 *Columbia Law Review* 293

Seidman, S, *Queer Theory/Sociology* (Oxford, Blackwell, 1996)

Shahid, M, 'The Right to Same-Sex Marriage: Assessing the European Court of Human Rights' Consensus-Based Analysis in Recent Judgments Concerning Equal Marriage Rights' (2017) 10 *Erasmus Law Review* 184

Sheppard, C, 'Bread and Roses: Economic Justice and Constitutional Rights' (2015) 5 *Oñati Socio-Legal Series* 225

Siegel, SA, 'The Origin of the Compelling State Interest Test and Strict Scrutiny' (2006) 48 *American Journal of Legal History* 355

Simma, B, 'The Sources of International Human Rights Law: Human Rights Treaties' in S Besson and J d'Aspremont (eds), *The Oxford Handbook of the Sources of International Law* (Oxford, Oxford University Press, 2017)

Sörgjerd, C, *Reconstructing Marriage: The Legal Status of Relationships in a Changing Society* (Cambridge, Intersentia, 2012)

Squillace, SE, *Whether to Wed: A Legal and Tax Guide for Gay and Lesbian Couples* (Boston, Squillace & Associates, 2014)

St-Hilaire, M and L Bich-Carrière, 'La constitution juridique et politique du Canada: notions, sources et principes' in *Droit constitutionnel* (Montréal, LexisNexis Canada, 2011)

Stark, B, 'Marriage Proposals: From One-Size-Fits-All to Postmodern Marriage Law' (2001) 89 *California Law Review* 1479

Strathern, M, *Kinship, Law and the Unexpected: Relatives are Always a Surprise* (Cambridge, Cambridge University Press, 2005)

Strauss, PL, 'The Rulemaking Continuum' (1992) 41 Duke Law Journal 1463

Sunstein, C, 'The Right to Marry' (2004) 26 *Cardozo Law Review* 2081

Sweeney, JA, 'Margins of Appreciation: Cultural Relativity and the European Court of Human Rights in the Post-Cold War Era' (2005) 54 *ICLQ* 459

Swennen, F, *Het personen-en familierecht* (Antwerp, Intersentia, 2014)

——. 'Un-coupling Family Law: The Legal Recognition and Protection of Adult Unions outside of Conjugal Coupledom' (2020) 28 *Feminist Legal Studies* 39

Swennen, F and M Croce, 'Family (Law) Assemblages: New Modes of Being (Legal)' (2017) 44 *Journal of Law and Society* 532

——. 'Cont(r)actualisation: A Politics of Transformative Legal Recognition of Adult Unions' (2020) *Social and Legal Studies* (forthcoming)

Tebbe, N, and DA Widiss, 'Equal Access and the Right to Marry' (2010) 158 *University of Pennsylvania Law Review* 1375

Thomas, CA, 'The Roles of Registered Partnerships and Conjugality in Canadian Family Law' (2006) 22 *Canadian Journal of Family Law* 223

Thornton, M, 'Embodying the citizen' in M Thornton (ed), *Public and Private: Feminist Legal Debates* (Oxford, Oxford University Press, 1995)

Tribe, LH, American Constitutional Law, 3rd edn (New York, Foundation Press, 2002)

Trispiotis, I, 'Discrimination and Civil Partnerships: Taking "Legal" out of Legal Recognition' (2014) 14 *Human Rights Law Review* 343

Venditti, V, 'Exponential Rerritorialization: Reduce, Refuse, Reuse? An Exploration of the Territories of Inclusive Legal Norms and Gender Binary' in P Agha (ed), *Law, Politics and the Gender Binary* (Abingdon, Routledge, 2018)

Von Savigny, FK, *System of the Modern Roman Law*, trans W Holloway (Madras, J Higginbotham, 1867)

Warner, M, *The Trouble with Normal: Sex, Politics, and the Ethics of Queer Life* (Cambridge, MA, Harvard University Press, 1999)

Weeks, J, B Heaphy and C Donovan, *Same Sex Intimacies: Families of Choice and Other Life Experiments* (New York, Routledge, 2001)

Wigmore, JH, EJ Imwinkelried and RD Friedman, *The New Wigmore: A Treatise on Evidence*, 2nd edn (New York, Aspen Publishers, 2010)

Wilkinson, E, 'What's Queer about Non-monogamy Now?' in M Barker and D Langdridge (eds), *Understanding Non-monogamies* (New York, Routledge, 2010)

Wiseman, N, 'Clarifying Provincial Constitutions' (1996) 6 *National Journal of Constitutional Law* 270

Wright, CA and KW Graham, Jr, *Federal Practice and Procedure: Evidence § 5572* (St Paul, West Publishing Co, 1989)

Zagrebelsky, V, 'Famiglia e vita familiare nella Convenzione Europea' in MC Andrini (ed), *Un nuovo diritto di famiglia europeo* (Padua, Cedam, 2007)

——. 'Corte cost. n. 49/2015, giurisprudenza della Corte europea dei diritti umani, art. 117 Cost., obblighi derivanti dalla ratifica della Convenzione' (2015) *Osservatorio dell' Associazione italiana dei costituzionalisti (AIC)* 1

INDEX

NB–page locators in **bold** indicate information in tables and those in *italics* indicate information in figures

www.ingramcontent.com/pod-product-compliance
Ingram Content Group UK Ltd.
Pitfield, Milton Keynes, MK11 3LW, UK
UKHW020808290926
15470UKWH00003B/1021

9 781509 9399